The Journey of an "Invisible" Woman

The Journey of an "Invisible" Woman

How I defied society's mandate that one day I would become
an invisible woman and how you can too

Sandy Camillo

Dear Paula,

Hope you enjoy the Journey.

Best,

Sandy Camillo

The Journey of An Invisible Woman
Copyright © 2021 Sandy Camillo

ISBN-13: 979-8-9855298-2-1(Paperback)
ISBN-13: 979-8-9855298-3-8(e-book)

BISAC Subject Headings:
BIO022000 BIOGRAPHY & AUTOBIOGRAPHY / Women
SOC028000 SOCIAL SCIENCE / Women's Studies
OCC019000 BODY, MIND & SPIRIT / Inspiration & Personal
    Growth

The Book Cover Whisperer:
ProfessionalBookCoverDesign.com

Address all correspondence to:

Penmore Press LLC
920 N Javelina Pl
Tucson AZ 85748

DEDICATION

To My Family,

Throughout the many years that I have searched for fame, fortune, and power, the one certainty I had was that, in your eyes, I was never invisible. Our family lives by the slogan, "One for all and all for one," and we know that we always have each other regardless of what the world throws at us.

Whenever I feel blocked by obstacles that impede my climb to self-actualization, I only need to think about one of you to give me a burst of adrenaline to keep going forward.

My hope for each of you is that you never give up your dreams because, as my mother said to me, "you can do anything!"

"The question isn't who is going to let me; it's who is going to stop me."
This is the summation of statements made by
a character in Ayn Rand's novel, *The Fountainhead.*

"Make the most of yourself by fanning the tiny, inner sparks of possibility into flames of achievement."
— Golda Meir

ACKNOWLEDGEMENTS

My greatest gratitude goes to my mother and father for standing by me during the craziest times in my life and for always letting me know that I was special in their eyes. I only wish that they could be here with me today to share in the fulfillment of one of my greatest dreams of writing a book.

My husband has been the unofficial editor of this book. He's had to put up with my tears, anger, and general bitchiness whenever I became frustrated with my progress on the book or when I lashed out at him for his gentle criticisms. There is no way that I could have written this book without his support. I'll always remember our ridiculous arguments over the proper use of commas or how adamant he was in his rejection of the word, "so". Now I can let him know that, although I let him think I took his advice, many times I would, passive aggressively, not make some of his suggested changes.

My children may not have always understood why I would cut our phone conversations short because I had to write. However, they always made sure that I knew how proud of me they were, although I'm sure that many times they might have preferred a more *Leave it to Beaver* type mom. If I could turn back time, and were given the choice of having children or becoming the CEO of a Fortune 500 company, I'd still pick having my children.

Christopher Bayer is a great friend, who showed enthusiasm for my writing and my passion for women's rights, and encouraged me to sit down and write about my experiences battling injustices against women. Chris is a brilliant psychologist who was always there to listen to my complaints and was invaluable in keeping my spirits up, all without my paying him a nickel. He's one of those good souls who make helping people a priority in his life, not just because it's a responsibility of his profession, but because he truly cares.

Anestine Hector-Mason at The Conscious Press is my editor, but so much more than that. Our relationship started out with her meticulously pointing out my grammatical errors, and graduated to being a real friendship. I never fully understood the frustration that could come from laboring to put an inspiration into words and then realizing that you couldn't quite capture the idea. Anestine was always there to strengthen my resolve to move forward. She wasn't here just to fix my formatting. She was a shoulder for me to lean on.

Finding a publisher is almost as difficult as finding a pot of gold at the end of the rainbow, but I found my pot of gold very quickly. After holding my breath for many months to hear back from publishers whose response time could be one to two years after author submission, I was in shock when I received a positive response regarding my book proposal only a few hours after submitting it to Penmore Press. Publisher Michael James is a man of action. He not only asked for the entire manuscript, but also sounded genuinely excited about the prospect of reading my book. I want to express my gratitude to Michael James, and all of the people at Penmore Press for making my lifelong dream a reality.

I also want to thank my brother, sister, cousins, nieces, nephews, grandchildren and friends for the many hours that they spent listening to my endless recitations of stories in my book. I've existed in a little bubble, because of my obsession with this book. I'm grateful that all of you have been in that bubble with me.

Finally, I want to thank everyone who listened to my stories. I also want to thank you in advance for promising me that you'll never let yourself become an "Invisible Woman."

INTRODUCTION
LOOK AT US; WE'RE STILL HERE

The "free swinging" 60s and "me decade" 70s was a great time to grow up. Social consciousness and self-fulfillment were the focus of those years. Prior generations had done the hard work of establishing economic prosperity for the children of the 60s and 70s, so those children took it for granted that there would always be a roof over their heads, food on the table, and money in their pockets.

The Great Depression of 1929 was something that they read about in their textbooks, and it held no more reality for them than the latest episode of the "I Love Lucy" shows.

It was, indeed, time to play. People were no longer insulated in their family units, but were following the advice of the Beatles to "Come Together" and be free. Protests were the accepted form of social intercourse, as everyone demanded their voices be heard.

Women thought about burning their bras in an expression of independence but never actually got around to doing it. The music was loud, and dancing was a form of exhibitionism that oozed sexuality and flaunted a blatant disregard for the social constraints of past generations.

This was my generation; the generation known as "Baby Boomers." There were 76 million of us born between 1946 and 1964, and our sheer size in numbers had a significant impact on the economic and cultural climate of the world for many years. From the time that I was a young girl, every newspaper, magazine and book that I read, and television program that I watched, portrayed the Baby Boomers as a unique phenomenon characterized by rebellious tendencies and a determination to change the course of the world. The media promoted these ideas until they were widely believed to be the accepted ideology of this generation.

This ideology emphasized that Baby Boomers thought differently than the generations before them, and they felt a personal commitment to redefining the social norms set by the "establishment." They were on the forefront of social change and didn't hesitate to break the rules to achieve their goals. They questioned government authority, and were particularly vocal about their opposition to the war in Vietnam.

They didn't hesitate to boycott companies whose products were environmentally damaging and considered it their mission to address injustices affecting civil and women's rights. Even their music was a tool of countercultural political expression. Joan Baez was known for her protest songs that demanded change. Her song," What Have They Done to the Rain," begged for the termination of nuclear testing. The Boomers took to heart the words of Eldridge Cleaver, writer and one of the leaders of the controversial Black Panthers, who said, "There is no more neutrality in the world. You either have to be part of the solution, or you're going to be part of the problem."

Beginning in the 1950s the U.S economy had entered a stage of economic prosperity unmatched by any previous era. The national income doubled in the 1950s and nearly doubled again in the 1960s. Anyone growing up during these times would naturally assume that there would always be a fortune at the end of the rainbow. I was one of these lucky Boomers and was also growing up in an affluent family.

The combination of these two demographics engendered in me a sense of entitlement and the belief that I was an important person in the world. My teachers, in the rarified atmosphere of the all-girls' prep high school and college that I attended, reinforced this conceit. There was never a doubt that we, girls, were going to stand out in the world, because of our education, social status and appearance. The Boomer's ambition and drive to recreate the world in their image wasn't confined to just society's elite.

My friends who were struggling because of economic limitations, societal prejudices or personal insecurities were still exhorted to reach for the stars, as anything was possible during these years. Although my friends and I came from different backgrounds, we were all united in a common cause and that cause was to claim our autonomy in our personal and professional lives.

It wasn't just my friends and I who were making our marks on the world, women everywhere were opening doors that were shut to them in the past and the world was looking and listening to them. As I got older, reality intruded into this dream world of individual freedoms and change. I started to realize that my friends and I were no longer the center of the universe, and the changes that we were seeing were only skin deep. Women were getting jobs, but men were getting higher salaries and the promotions. I knew that I still turned men's heads; but for each year that passed, it became more difficult to attract much attention, as there were younger and "sexier" women competing for these accolades.

Although my generation of women was told to reach for the sky and not to limit our aspirations, sometimes we felt that we were the rope in a tug of war, and that we were being pulled back and forth between prioritizing the importance of raising a family and achieving success at our jobs. A little voice in our heads whispered to us that, perhaps, we weren't doing so great at either endeavor, but we continued burning the candle at both ends, because the alternative was too grim to contemplate.

We loved our mothers, who sacrificed their own ambitions to nurture us, but we didn't want to emulate them. Getting together with our friends to share recipes seemed as dated as watching television in black and white. It was more our style to network with our friends to learn about exciting job opportunities or the latest new restaurants. Every step we took was deliberate and designed to enhance our visibility in the world.

I had spent countless years asserting my identity, from the time that I was a small child shouting to be heard over my siblings' voices at the kitchen table, to running as a candidate for election to a women's advocacy national nonprofit board. I was determined to have my uniqueness acknowledged by the world. I could do anything! I was Wonder Woman and so was each of my friends. We knew that we could raise children, become CEO's, be glamorous, and if we had doubts and insecurities, we kept them to ourselves.

As the years went by, I wondered if my friends were also noticing that the world wasn't fully cooperating with our grand plan to attain fame and glory. It was getting harder and harder to hold on to my conviction that I would achieve my goals. The applause was getting softer. Younger super women were pushing me to the back of the stage, and I was in danger of getting lost in the crowd. I questioned whether these feelings were mine alone or if other women were experiencing these sentiments. As it turned out, many women felt the same uneasiness about their diminishing importance in the world.

One day, I found out that our mothers, grandmothers, teachers, sisters and friends all shared a secret. That secret was that one-day, we would all become invisible women. From the moment I heard this mandate, I became determined to deny the fulfillment of this prophecy.

This book is my effort to share the many struggles that I, and other women in the past and present day, have experienced because of discriminatory social norms that curtail a woman's empowerment. Although you might declare that you've never experienced my fear of becoming invisible to the world, you might discover a little tingling in your head as you read some of my stories. Perhaps, you'll discover that you can identify with a small snippet of truth in one of these narratives and accompany me on my journey. Hopefully, if you see yourself in my story, then together we can stand up and shout, "LOOK AT US, WE'RE STILL HERE."

CHAPTER 1
AN INVISIBLE WOMAN

I confidently made my way to the bar and said in a loud voice, "I'd like a Grey Goose Martini, straight up in a martini glass, shaken and chilled with no vermouth." During the next five minutes, I repeated my request several times, and I still didn't get my drink. However, I noticed that some men that came in after me all had their drinks.

Something was definitely not right about this scene. I thought about swallowing my pride and asking my husband, Blue Eyes, who was engaged in conversation with friends in another part of the bar, to come and save me. Before admitting defeat, I decided to first peek into the mirror behind the bar to check that I didn't have mascara running from my eyes, or anything caught between my teeth that would make me look repulsive enough for the bartender to avoid serving me. Everything looked all right and I felt better knowing that I didn't look like a bag lady, but as I was getting my nerve up to ask for my drink again, a young attractive blonde approached the bar and immediately received the attention of the bartender.

Apparently, this bar followed a hierarchical order in providing service to its customers. Men were served first, and then you had it made if you were a young, sexy, flirtatious woman. To prove my point, I asked my daughter to participate in a test to validate my hypothesis.

The Journey of an "Invisible" Woman

The next night, my daughter accompanied me to the bar where the night before I had been ghosted by the bartender. We separated ourselves at the bar and both of us requested service. Unsurprisingly my daughter, a young, sexy, flirty blonde received her drink, while I, again, walked away with egg on my face. Obviously, my test didn't take into consideration the wisdom contained in the fitting words, "Insanity is doing the same thing over and over again and expecting different results" (Calaprice, 2010, p.474). I guess that if I had waited long enough, I would have eventually been served, but why did I have to endure this type of treatment? When did I suddenly become the "Invisible Woman?"

As women age, they often blend into the crowd and go unnoticed unless they do something bizarre like walking down the street screaming or tossing out large sums of money. Being an older woman is apparently a guarantee of anonymity. Is a woman's worth based only on her looks, social status, or sexual allure? Women, regardless of their age, sometimes feel insecure, because of imagined inadequacies, while men are confident about their intrinsic value, even if they are overweight, hairless, toothless, illiterate eunuchs.

A significant part of the problem is that society portrays older women negatively, if they portray them at all. On the other hand, many older men often have inflated self-images as they become more respected with age. Their facial lines are considered "distinguished." Magazines are filled with photos of vigorous looking older men actively participating in interesting activities, while older women are highlighted in before-and-after photos for products to correct their imperfections.

Women are continuously bombarded with this type of gender-specific brainwashing until they are convinced that their only path to relevancy in life is to make drastic changes to their appearance. They begin to worship at the altars of L'Oréal, Estee Lauder and Clinique, beseeching these gods to grant them the miracle of instant beauty. If these gods fail to give them the result they've craved, it still won't end their search for a magic pill to add meaning to their lives.

Instead, they'll take it up a notch and appeal to the higher-level deities, who for a small fortune, promise to cut, sew, fill and mold them into the image of the woman they think defines what the world wants them to be. Even if these women alter their appearances in the hopes of becoming visible to others, they still can't escape having gender discrimination negatively affect their professional lives. Sadly, this bias also directly influences a woman's paycheck.

The economic disparity between men and women is apparent in several situations. Men are recruited as highly paid consultants because of their years of experience in their field, while women are encouraged to volunteer in charitable organizations with no compensation. Surprisingly, women accept this financial inequality early in their careers as the natural order of things.

This is evidenced by the raw gender pay gap data that shows that, as of 2020, women earn 82 cents for every dollar men make (PayScale, 2020). In *Experimental Age Discrimination Evidence and the Heckman Critique*, a study of 40,000 job applications, Newmark, Burn, and Button (2016), find "robust evidence of age discrimination in hiring against older women, but considerably less evidence of age discrimination against older men" (p. 303).

Although men support gender equality on an intellectual level, stereotypes still pose a major problem in practice. According to new research by Unilever, women are as guilty as men in adhering to outdated gender stereotypes. Unilever backed up their claim by interviewing more than 9,000 men and women regarding work assignments and found that, "an overwhelming 77% of men and a majority (55%) of women believe that men are the best choice for high stakes projects" (Roderick, 2017, p. 1).

These women might appear to support gender equality but have swallowed society's poison pill that convinces them they aren't truly equal to men. On the other hand, the men in the survey might be worried that, as women's status rises at work, men will be forced to assume their subservient roles. So, should women simply give up and become quiet recluses, or is there something we can do to have others acknowledge our identities and abilities?

The baby boomer generation has always believed the world was there just for them and is shocked to think that they are no longer the center of attention. Our voices, that once demanded more fun, more excitement, more things, are now overshadowed by the voices of our families telling us to give up our dreams. We need to ignore those voices and live our days as if we still had our whole life in front of us. No one knows their expiration date, or if that truck barreling down the road will hit him or her at age 28 or 60.

Don't be afraid to challenge outdated stereotypes about what you should and shouldn't do. If you always dreamed of prosecuting a drug lord, then bite the bullet and apply to Law School, even though you think that you might be too old. When you graduate you still might be older than most students, but now you'll be an older person with a law degree. It's up to you to make a transformative commitment to be your own heroine in the story of your life.

Now, let's think back to that moment in the bar when I first tried to get the bartender's attention. Did he see a self-assured and dynamic person who expected excellent service or did I project a less compelling image? Let's you and I do a little experiment together and make believe that you were the person asking for a drink in the bar. I'll give you some instructions and maybe at the end of our exercise you'll see what the bartender might see when he looked at you.

Look in a mirror and gaze into your own eyes. Think about who you are as you remember the young girl who once looked back at you. Are you now the person who you thought you would become? At what age did you change—was it twenty-five or fifty? What is it about you that changed? What did you see?

Now that you've followed my first directive, I'll follow my inclination as a know-it-all Baby Boomer and offer you some tips on making sure that you're acknowledged in all circumstances. People love to be around others who have knowledgeable, provocative viewpoints. A stimulating conversation rarely begins, "I don't think the flowers on my Louis Vuitton bag reflect the real me." Speak with a confident voice instead of using one that is so soft that people strain to hear you. Only vampires need to hide in the shadows, women need to toot their own horns and make sure that they are seen and heard.

You might be called a bitch for asserting yourself, but that's better than not being acknowledged at all. I just had a funny thought. If a man is called a bitch, it means that he is weak or cowardly. Apparently, gender inequality even extends itself to the ambiguous use of pejorative slang words. Always remember that women have brains and wisdom; don't be afraid to show them!

We care about our bodies, because we care about ourselves. Our perception of who we are affects the image we project to the world. Clothes may not make a woman, but they definitely help improve the way she feels about herself. My suggestion to all women is that you don't become too comfortable in your personal style. Try on those hot pink shoes, as they may give you just the edge you need to feel revitalized. It's okay if you love who you are in an old sweatshirt, as long as you're not afraid to mix it up and explore new possibilities.

Just don't become too set in your ways as you age, because if you do, you're substantiating the stereotypical misconception that older people are narrow-minded and change averse. On the other hand, you shouldn't be too hard on yourself and embarrassed if you feel unsettled by change as this fear is so prevalent that there's even a phobia about it called metathesiophobia.

Even positive change can cause stress and it only becomes problematic if this fear results in inertia, because then our ability to grow is impaired. We need to recognize that most people won't care if your shoes are pink or blue, so loosen up and take some chances just for fun.

There's no better measure of change than our bathroom scales. If you're like me the numbers randomly go up and down but it's important that we acknowledge that there is no magic number on the scale that makes someone attractive. Exercise to remain strong, firm, and healthy, not to emulate the body of an airbrushed beauty in a fashion magazine.

Regardless of size, a beautiful woman is groomed, well dressed, and walks with her head held high. Remember the words "self-esteem" start with the word *self* and its development shouldn't depend on the opinion of others. "The term self-esteem describes a person's overall subjective sense of personal worth or value" (Cherry, 2021), and this personal valuation is a crucial component contributing to a person's professional and personal success.

When sexism and ageism partner together, they land a devastating knockout punch on a woman's ability to unlock her full potential and engage economically, socially and politically. For example, some women fall into the trap of using certain words or phrases that can denigrate their mental abilities.

We have all, laughingly, used or heard our friends use the term, "senior moment." However, there is nothing written in the stars that says we reach a specific birthday and get stupid. We may become lonely, sick, or tired, but not stupid. We never hear the words "ditzy blonde" used to describe a man. Hair color is not gender-specific and has nothing to do with a woman's IQ; grey hair doesn't automatically transform a woman into a frail, little old lady.

Unfortunately, despite the fallacy of these sexist and ageist concepts, the media perpetuates these false female gender norms to exert a major influence on perceptions of desired female roles in society. The 1950s show "Leave it to Beaver" captured the family life of a generation in which women kept the home fires burning and men were usually the sole breadwinners.

Today we might laugh at that description of an ideal family life. Although television reality shows like Bravo's successful Housewives franchise reflect a very different image of the 21st century woman, this modern take on a woman's place in the world also doesn't truly reflect reality.

The Housewives franchise epitomizes the idolization of a certain type of woman, whose days are spent maintaining her "perfect" surgically enhanced appearance and nights guzzling martinis, while partying with her empty-headed friends. These gossipy, back-stabbing gold diggers are never seen scrubbing the bathroom floor or shopping in a discount clothing store. The patriarchal roles of their husbands are emphasized in the men's indulgent attitudes towards their wives' outrageous spending habits. These men are defined by their careers and praised for their achievements and yet, contrarily, allusions are frequently made to the disruptive influence of a housewife's professional success on her love life and parenting skills.

There is constant reference to acceptable gendered behavior as certain housewives are labeled as "too aggressive" and not feminine if they are enthusiastically pursuing their careers. It's clear that the housewives have the traditional responsibility for the home and children, although this usually just consists of overseeing the work of a maid and nanny. If the husbands become involved, it's just to "help." If this is reality, it's a reality that most women don't experience, as few of us are as privileged or as dysfunctional as these housewives. Bravo had to be aware that the term housewife implies domesticity and thus it can't be denied that the Housewives franchise promotes false female gender roles and behaviors.

My guilty admission is that I watch many of the Housewives shows, to vicariously engage in some questionable behavior, but I don't kid myself that the behavior that I'm watching is good, or something I should emulate. These housewives are definitely visible but a woman doesn't have to be beautiful, ultra-thin, wealthy or young, in order to be seen.

The flip side to being a superficial airhead like our television housewives isn't to become so stoic that our faces freeze from the lack of expressing emotions. Learn to giggle again and don't be afraid to act a bit silly, because you won't look "mature." The word, "mature" infers complete ripeness and growth. We only stop growing when we cease to exist and that shouldn't be any woman's aspiration.

At some point in our lives the world might look at us and only see the superficial changes etched on our bodies from sickness, age or heartbreak. These changes may be inevitable but they don't touch the basic essence that makes each of us who we are, even if this essence remains hidden from the world. Up until the day that my mom died at the age of ninety-six, she still entertained the same dreams and desires that she had as a young girl, because these aspirations were an intrinsic part of who she was, even though she never attained them. Some of our dreams and desires may never be fulfilled, but that doesn't mean that we should stop striving to achieve them just because society has decided that we are past our prime. Remember that aged wine is considered the most desirable.

Now that we've gone over some of the ways to make sure that we stand out in a crowd, let's put these ideas into practice and recreate that bar scene one last time, and try to imagine a different outcome. What can you do to guarantee that the bartender will treat you respectfully? Instead of patiently waiting in that bar, you should move in closer and point out to the bartender that other patrons who just came in had been served and you still had not.

This might involve elbowing some linebacker-type blocking your path to the bar and raising your voice a bit. Your actions show that you are confident and aren't afraid of how you look to the other patrons. Now, I bet you get that drink. Remember that patience may be a virtue but, unfortunately, others might not respond the way we hope when we practice this virtue.

Even Scarlet O'Hara, in the movie, "Gone with the Wind," came to the realization that she couldn't save Tara by just batting her eyelashes and behaving like a "lady," so she toughened up.

A big part of toughening up comes from believing in yourself and your value in the world. We can't be afraid to spotlight ourselves. I don't remember any course in school labeled, "How to Blend Into the Background in Any Situation." Just because we have lines etched into our skin or don't spend the days doing complex scientific research doesn't mean that our hearts and brains have stopped functioning. Each of us has had unique experiences that make us who we are. We must draw on these experiences to recapture the enthusiasm for life we had when we were younger. In other words, although cultural biases pressure us to acquiesce to a subservient status to men at home, work, and in the public sector, we must never accept being an "Invisible Woman."

CHAPTER 2
STICKS AND STONES

A woman has to worry about many obstacles that hinder her search for autonomy, but today, she rarely has to be concerned that one deterrent to disobeying society's dictates is being beaten into submission. Although, in modern times, physical abuse is off the table as a tool of coercion, women know that there are other equally effective methods used to keep them in their place.

Most of us have heard the old adage, "sticks and stones may break my bones, but words will never hurt me," (Titelman, 1996, p. 320), but the reality is that sometime words can be as damaging as the pain resulting from a physical attack, and many of us have personally had our self-esteem damaged from a well-aimed insult.

The average person can probably recount many examples of when he or she was the target of verbal abuse unless, of course, they were born to royalty and never were insulted, because an insult to a royal could result in jail time. Nonetheless, it is conceivable that you grew up hearing nothing but praise from everyone around you, but this isn't the case for a typical child.

For example, you might have the opportunity to observe a group of children playing together and decide to move close to them to eavesdrop on their conversation. What you hear

The Journey of an "Invisible" Woman

might convince you that children, often, can exhibit a cruel streak towards one another. Some children seem to possess a special intuitiveness that enables them to pinpoint other children's weaknesses.

They, innately, know whom to target for nasty zingers like; "there's Johnny four eyes," "where's your feed bag, fatso" and "here comes the moron." The name caller may feel powerful calling others derogatory names. Perhaps he or she was never taught not to bully or the bullies themselves were once the target of a bully. His or her actions reveal a deep-seated insensitivity to the feelings of other people.

Children can gradually be taught to feel empathy for others; but once those children become adults and are no longer under parental controls, they may revert to reasserting their power over others through use of words, as tools of intimidation and ridicule. Presenting seemingly innocuous words in a humorous manner can obscure their pernicious intent.

I've been the target of passive aggressive joking many times in my life, especially since I always talked a lot. I think that part of the reason was that I was told constantly by my parents to "shut up;" although, I like to believe my constant jabbering is because I have so much going on in my head that I just have to get it out. Early on, my love of talking got me into a lot of trouble in school, as the teachers didn't love my brilliant musings as much as I did, but I'd gladly sit in detention if it meant that others would hear, and pay attention to my thoughts.

I wasn't really stung by negative allusions to my never-ending chatter until my first serious boyfriend referenced my constant talking by telling me that I had diarrhea of the mouth. At the time, I was crushed by his words and swore to myself that he'd never hear me speak again or have to kiss my vile mouth.

Breaking up with him seemed to be the solution, or so I thought. The truth was that I soon became hesitant to express myself around people, because I feared that they, too, might associate my loquaciousness with this repulsive intestinal condition. My ex-boyfriend had successfully used negative labeling to harm my self-esteem.

Luckily, I soon realized that other people liked to talk as much as I did, so I made a point of associating with other wordy people, never forgetting the power of words. Soon, I started to realize that even seemingly complimentary words could be construed to have dark meanings, depending on their context. I also began to understand that women are particularly vulnerable to word attacks that demean them and minimize their strength.

Even though we shouldn't think that men don't also suffer when words are used as tools against them, it is easy for us to see that their response to such a verbal attack is usually quite different from a woman's response. On the one hand, men are taught to confront adversity by standing up to it and calling it out and possibly throwing a quick punch.

On the other hand, women, particularly of my generation, are encouraged to act as peacemakers, to suffer silently and graciously and above all, to never act pugnaciously.

Although by disengaging with my boyfriend I had successfully ended the pain of being verbally insulted, I knew that there would be many circumstances in life in which I couldn't react by running away. If I wanted to play with the big boys in my professional life, I had to devise a plan to use when nuanced sexist remarks were hurled at me.

All the women in my family possess dramatic, emotional Italian natures that might cause the average person to label us as women with volatile personalities. In addition, we are fast talking and loud. People who don't know us well will often consider us thick skinned and impervious to hurt.

The Journey of an "Invisible" Woman

Unfortunately, our skin is paper-thin, but a woman with a goal to achieve great things in life has to learn to cover that thin skin with an invisible coat of armor, and many women throughout history had to wear this shield full time.

For example, the fictional character Holly Golightly, in "Breakfast at Tiffany's," projected an image of herself as an independent woman who refused to let others interfere with her individuality. Although she was always dressed and spoke as if she were born to the manor, her upbringing was far from privileged.

Holly knew that her survival depended on her adhering to the parameters of female desirability set by the men whose generosity she enjoyed. She picked the men she wanted to date and she charged them for "conversation." Truman Capote, the author, described Holly as an American Geisha, because of her relationships with men.

A perfect example of the double standard judging male and female sexual behavior is apparent in the reaction to Holly's romantic and sexual interactions with men. Movie critics and moviegoers both usually agreed that Holly manipulated her sexuality and charm to attract men, and magazine articles unabashedly declared that she lived off men in exchange for acting as a cypher for men's desires. She didn't promise or always give sexual favors to these men and yet critiques of the film casually label Holly as a "call girl"

The language describing Holly's actions were definitely not complimentary. Yet, apparently the men who shower Holly with presents are pure souls who are simply negotiating a deal to get some loving. Holly however, isn't judged so generously, as condemnatory words frequently paint a negative image of women in this type of relationship. In real life, few women find themselves in relationships that mimic Holly's situation, and yet vile language is often used to describe their character and morality.

If a woman chooses to express her sexuality by engaging in a sexual relationship with a man, the relationship better be long lasting, otherwise the words, whore, slut, tart, hooker, tramp, promiscuous, floozy, etc. might soon be attached to her name. Yet, no one would blink an eye if the man's intent in such a relationship were sexual fulfillment. Words used to describe such a man are decidedly lacking in the negative connotations attributed to the woman.

Conversely, the words womanizer, stud, playboy, player, ladies' man and lady-killer denote someone dashing, who is sexy and attractive to women. Even a search for slang words that indicate promiscuity in men often uncover words such as stud that, glowingly, emphasize that these promiscuous men are just doing what boys do. On the other hand, the moral integrity of women seeking sexual fulfillment is damaged by words that are intentionally used to indicate depravity.

If a woman has a low sex drive or for whatever reason prefers to limit her sexual encounters, she still can't escape being characterized by having critical words hurled at her. One of the less offensive words is the word "frigid." It's obvious that it's not meant to be used as a compliment, but rather to indicate a woman's imperfection. Another favorite word of mine that is commonly used to describe a woman whose manner is slightly aggressive is the word, "bitch." There are numerous opportunities illustrating situations when a woman gets to experience the joy of being called this word. Although I'm sure you can imagine many of them, I'll note of few of my own reflections.

Imagine a conference table in a law office with three men and one woman seated around it. There is a spirited discussion going on among the four attorneys gathered together to negotiate a major commercial real estate deal. Everyone takes a short break and the woman attorney steps into the bathroom before re-entering the conference room. As she opens the door into the hallway, she hears the three male attorneys chatting with each other. She's stunned to hear the two attorneys representing the other investor saying to her partner, "How do you work with her?"

She's such a bitch. She won't bend on anything. We'll never get this deal done if she doesn't shut her mouth." And just when she thinks it can't get any worse, she hears her partner laugh and remark, "Don't get her angry or you'll be sorry, then she really gets bitchier." If we look at this same situation but replace the woman with a male, we would be certain to hear a different conversation. It would probably be something like, "Man, that partner of yours is tough. I bet he's worth his weight in gold when it comes to getting what his client wants. The deal is so much easier to put together when it's clear where everyone stands." Isn't it strange when identical traits are interpreted differently depending on gender?

Words such as "excitable," "emotional" and "high strung" have the ability to trigger in me an intense desire to put on a pair of boxing gloves, and go a few rounds in the ring with the person who uttered such words about me. Being told to stay calm elicits in me a similar fantasy, and results in my blood pressure ratcheting up several points. Strangely enough, I've never heard a man described as excitable, emotional or high strung. Does this indicate that men are all on a daily dose of Zoloft, Xanax or Valium or have they been permanently lobotomized to ensure an even-tempered reaction to life's travails?

A commonly held misconception is that a woman exhibiting an energetic attitude when engaged in conversation is actually experiencing extreme anxiety or hysterics, (another word carelessly attributed to a woman's emotions). However, such a woman might simply be feeling enthusiasm and exuberance.

A man might be greeted with a high five if he just solved a difficult problem at work and is asked to convey the information to fellow workmates. It's understandable if he relates his news in a boisterous, passionate fashion and even refuses to surrender the floor to others until he expands on the significance of his success.

On the other hand, a woman is looked at askew if during a team meeting, she is dominating the conversation while sharing her work product. There will probably also be mutterings that she is a bit hysterical if her delivery is spoken quickly and with a loud voice. Both the man and woman are justifiably excited about what they are doing but they are perceived quite differently because of society's preconceived notions of the ideal behavior of each gender.

Aging also plays a role in the manipulation of language to diminish a woman's presence in the workplace. There is an assumption that the appearance of wrinkles on a woman's face indicates a decrease in energy level. If she is job hunting, she might see in a job advertisement the words, "high energy required." Unless the job requires that she is able to run a full marathon, use of these words is damaging to a women's professional future and yet, human resource departments continue to categorize woman by using such ageist language. You might correctly surmise that both men and women are hurt by ageist connotations of certain words but, as I've noted in previous chapters, a woman's physical appearance as she ages is, generally, judged more harshly than a man's.

Although the degree of injury resulting from using words as weapons might be less for a man than a woman, the injury is still unacceptable. We all have heard the words, "The pen is mightier that the sword" by English author Edward Bulwer-Lytton, written in 1839. Those words indicate that

The Journey of an "Invisible" Woman

communication is a more effective tool than direct violence (Gee, 2015, p.1). This adage is as true today as the day it was written, and reminds us that words can influence and inspire people for both good and bad. However, for many women, words alone may become an insurmountable barrier, preventing their success.

CHAPTER 3
THE THREE FACES OF EVE

Now that we've all acknowledged the power language has to negatively influence our self-image, we can move on to confronting inequitable gender roles, which are the greatest impediment in a woman's journey to achieve equity in her personal and professional life. The social construction of standards setting appropriate societal gender roles is fluctuating and depends on each generation's values and beliefs about gender; but one constant has always been that a woman's role is defined as being subordinate to a man's role.

Before we can make the claim that we will never descend into obscurity, we need to challenge the false assumption of society regarding a woman's place in the world. For those of you who love films, *All About Eve*, starring Bette Davis, was one of the great ones. It explored the life of a woman with dissociative identity disorder.

Although most of us, thankfully, don't suffer from this frightening disorder, all women can acknowledge the multifaceted nature of their identities. Women may be daughters, mothers, wives, grand- and great grandmothers, aunts, partners, career women, housewives and friends. In addition, distinct characteristics are attributed to women as they transition from childhood through old age.

The Journey of an "Invisible" Woman

Now, let's look at societal expectations for women during the 1950s, 1960s and 1970s. Thankfully, much has changed for women's equity in the 21st century because women have become activists on their own behalf.

The Fifties was an era of a booming economy, booming suburbs, and the baby boomers. When I was a young child in the late fifties, a women's place was clearly defined. The *Home Economics High School Text Book* of 1954 taught young women that the duties of a wife were to "have dinner ready, prepare yourself, prepare the children, minimize all noise, be happy to see him, listen to him, and make the evening his." (Lamb, 2011) Wow! Obviously, things have changed, but imagine my thoughts back then about what I had to look forward to when I got married. The thought of what married life had in store for me made me want to forget the whole thing. Apparently, getting married was only advantageous for a man.

The nuns at my elementary school in a suburban New York neighborhood reminded their girl students that they should modulate their voices so that they would appear more feminine. This emphasis on developing "proper" traits in young girls began in kindergarten. The kindergarten classrooms were designed for separation by gender, so there was no misunderstanding about where you should play if you were a girl.

The girls were confined to the kitchen area which was equipped with pots, pans, and little aprons, while in the boys' section exuberant voices could be heard as they competed against each other to, excitedly, demonstrate their engineering prowess in the block corner. Shame, shame, shame on the girl who wanted to play with the trucks in the play corner instead of putting on an apron to pretend to cook something in the Easy Bake oven. I didn't mind the pretend baking, but I also wanted to make buildings in the blocks corner; Sister Mary Joseph quickly discouraged that.

Sister Mary Joseph would have recoiled in horror if she were told that in the near future more and more women would be working in scientific fields, and that the young girls who she taught might not be prepared because she didn't encourage them to develop skills to pursue careers in STEM (Science, Technology, Engineering and Math). It might have made her feel better to be reminded that in the middle ages education was reserved for privileged young men and religious devotees, and this meant that the earliest female intellectuals were nuns. They studied arithmetic, geometry and astronomy. "Among the earliest nun scholars was Juliana Morell, a 17th century Dominican nun who is believed to be the first woman in the Western world to earn a university degree" (Pak, 2019, p.3). Sister Mary Joseph should be proud to know that she would be carrying on the work that God ordained if she did her best to inspire her girl students to pursue a career in STEM.

Thankfully, the Sixties brought about much change for women, but nonetheless some vestiges of Fifties thinking still persisted. This was especially true in my Catholic girls' high school. A young girl's "purity" had to be protected at all costs to make her desirable for marriage, so the "Guard Nuns" closely monitored our school dances. The girls would all sit, primly, in rows—waiting to be asked to dance. But, the reality of these dances was far removed from the fictional dance scenes depicted in the film, "Dirty Dancing."

I've watched this film numerous times, and I still get some impure thoughts when I remember Johnny and Baby dancing to the song, "Hungry Eyes." Their movements were sultry and sensuous, and they held each other as if they were embracing. And then, the sight of Johnny's hand slowly grazing the outline of baby's silhouette—I think you get the point.

There would be no dirty dancing at our school. Catholic school nuns were more vigilant about protecting their girls' honor than prison guards were in securing their prison's inmates. These nuns would walk around the room looking for couples that were dancing too close to each other. The nun would use a ruler to measure the appropriate distance to make sure that we would "leave room for the Holy Ghost." We were so afraid of the nuns that we left room for the entire Holy Family. Needless to say, our high school dances weren't very popular with the boys.

Although I liked Math and Science, the curriculum designers at my high school were still stuck in the 50s mindset about the appropriate academic focus for women, and believed that girls should limit themselves to studying the humanities. Women engineers, scientists and mathematicians were rarely portrayed as role models for my classmates and me, and whatever images we saw of these women, depicted them as frumpy old maids. We were exhorted to do well in our academic studies, but we were also never supposed to forget that our primary goal was to become a wife and mother.

Like all teenage girls with raging hormones, I relished the thought of having some ravishing young man adore me. That was a given, but I couldn't understand why a boy could fall in love and have an exciting career, while a girl had to be content with the love part, but not the exciting career. Now don't get me wrong, a woman could pursue a career in the Sixties, but most women were encouraged to pursue teaching, nursing, and secretarial work. These were all careers that a woman could return to after she spent about twenty years at home raising a family. Job satisfaction for women was not the goal; practicality was.

Sandy Camillo

Even though Betty Friedan wrote *The Feminine Mystique* in 1963 to espouse a rebuttal of the rigid social roles existing for women, the reality was that women were still treated as not equal to men. A woman couldn't take out a loan without someone co-signing for her, and credit cards were under her husband's name. Today, as many women are the breadwinners, it would be unthinkable for a woman to be required to have her husband co-sign for her.

Yet, it is still common for a salesperson in a car showroom to discuss the car's mechanical components with the husband, assuming that women are ignorant of such things. Whenever I purchase a car, I make a point of learning as much as I can about the car's engineering just so I can see the incredulous look on the salesperson's face when I start reciting intricate points about the car's engine.

Although Ms. Friedan didn't hesitate to talk down and dirty about sex in her book, in real life, a women's sexuality was still something to only talk about in whispers, and women were viewed as either saints or as the stars of sexist fantasies. Accounts of bra burning during the 1968 Miss America pageant were inaccurate as no bras were actually burned, although women did bring them and other personal items to throw in a "freedom trashcan" to protest the sexism of the era (See Campbell, 2010; Gay, 2018; Greenfield Boyse, 2008; & Heller, 2018).

The media jumped on the bra burning bandwagon because it was provocative and made for a good read, but eyewitnesses refute those reports as myths. There were no bras burning in the street, instead the protest featured the "freedom trash can" to be used in a ceremonial, symbolic burning of things that represented women's oppression. This concession by the protestors satisfied the wishes of the mayor of Atlantic City, who was disturbed by the thought of actually burning anything, as fourteen stores on the boardwalk had been destroyed by fire just the week before the pageant.

This was a time of much confusion for young girls as they sought to define their identities. I didn't aspire to sainthood, but I didn't want to get a reputation as a bad girl either, so I became an expert in perfecting the alternating persona of a modest catholic schoolgirl during the school day and teenage siren on the weekends.

I remember getting off the school bus at the end of the school day and whipping out my makeup case to apply makeup. Then, I would skillfully roll the waistband of my skirt several times until my prim uniform skirt became a stylish mini skirt. Now I was ready to drop into my local ice cream parlor to mingle with the boys. Sometimes, the pressures of balancing these two aspects of my personality made my head spin, like the girl in the movie, *Exorcist*. My brain, heart, and body were warring with each other, and I never knew who would wind up as the victor in the battle.

I didn't realize that these high school years were just the beginning of my confusion over who I was expected to be and who I really was. In the blink of an eye, my high school days were over, and I was heading off to an all-girls' private college. I thought that, as we were now almost in the Seventies, I'd finally start to see the changes effected by the fledgling feminist movement. I should have gotten a hint that this wasn't the case at my college when I received my invitation to the freshman orientation tea.

The invitation stated that all young ladies must wear appropriate attire, including formal tea length gloves. I was able to quiet the voices in my head telling me to run away by repeating the words, "tradition is good." It wasn't until I registered for my first class and saw the subject, "Hostess Problems," that I knew that I was on a sinking ship without a raft. It was difficult to stifle a laugh as I listened to Sister

Anne explain "how to instruct your maid on the use of fish forks." Clearly, my college still believed that its goal was to educate young ladies to take their places in society as proper wives and mothers. So, I ran away from school and home, and, ironically, fulfilled the school's goal by getting married.

Now, I no longer had to live by my parent's rules, but little did I know that marriage would also require conformance to certain requirements. My first husband was amazingly good-looking, but he was a simple man. He was artistic, but wasn't particularly intellectual.

During my college days, I spent hours in philosophical discussions with fellow students, so it wasn't too long before I realized that there was a disparity between my husband's intellect and mine. I still had aspirations for establishing myself as an important person and knew that I needed to continue educating myself. In the time between getting my Bachelors and Masters degrees, I had a baby son. He took my heart away with the indescribable love I felt for him. It would never again be just about me.

The first five years of my marriage flew by, because I was so busy working towards a Master's degree and raising my child. Although I had already decided that my first husband and I were on divergent intellectual pathways, during the early years of our marriage I still became excited when I looked at his handsome face and he held me in his arms. After five years, this sexual tension wasn't enough to hold the marriage together and we became total strangers to one another.

My husband had no interest in job advancement and was content coming home from his job to watch television, while enjoying a glass of wine. There was nothing wrong with his life's perspective on happiness but I had ambitions that went beyond his vision. We no longer shared the dreams that we

The Journey of an "Invisible" Woman

had when we took our wedding vows. After six years of marriage, we agreed to file for divorce.

Now the direction in my life took a new turn. In the past, I had seen my identity in terms of how it affected me, but now I realized that everything I was and would become, would, more importantly, also affect my son.

It was still the 70s, and I was determined to make up for the forced monogamy of my married years by dating as many men as I could and even going so far as to move to another state to be with a new love. I have to admit that in a corner of my heart, I still felt Sister Mary Joseph's disapproval whenever I would entertain thoughts of participating in some slightly risqué behavior with a new boyfriend. Before too long, I met someone who I'll call Blue Eyes, who I knew would support me in my quest to show the world what I was capable of achieving.

We married and had three more children and each one of them contributed something to my self-awareness. Perhaps the duties of motherhood impeded the speed of my career advancement, but it was a situation that I chose for myself. When the school called to say that one of my children had been injured, I could have asked Blue Eyes to rush to be with our child, but I never wanted to give up that privilege. I always chose to be there for each of them, not because I had to but, because as corny as it sounds, they made me complete.

Although I had to adapt myself to the different demands of each of these roles, my essence as a person remained unchanged. A woman's fundamental being never changes; however, the requirements of each of her markedly disparate roles dramatically changes as societies and economies change over time. The shifting pendulum of moral dynamics regarding women's rights is evident in the birth of equity movements such as the "Me Too" movement.

Proponents of this movement raised the consciousness of society by demanding that the criteria regarding acceptable male behavior towards women be changed. They closely scrutinized male-female interactions to ensure that gender discrimination was no longer tolerated.

Today, there are many positive things influencing gender norm changes. Many of these changes in gender norms "can be driven by broad processes such as economic development, or the spread of communication technology, or by government-led action, such as legal or policy reform or expansion of education and other key services" (Marcus & Harper, 2015). These changes will someday ensure a fair playing field for women.

I had become the master of my own destiny, or so I thought. I confronted the many hurdles thrown my way and managed to maintain my forward progress in my march toward establishing my place in the world. The years quickly passed and as we all do, I got older, and with my aging came the realization that, although I had overcome many injustices because of gender discrimination, I would now have to combat new prejudices that specifically affected only *older* women. I was still me, but in the eyes of the world, I was fading.

CHAPTER 4
BARBIE WAS NO HAG

When I was a little girl, I couldn't envision a future "me" as a wrinkled, grey haired older woman whose relevance in life was vanishing. If unpleasant thoughts about a less than ideal future entered my mind, I repeated to myself my favorite line spoken by Scarlett O' Hara in the movie, *Gone with the Wind*. Tomorrow I'll think of some way, after all, tomorrow is another day." Tomorrow came sooner than I thought, but as a child I really believed that getting older was something other people, did, not I.

During my childhood, subtle manifestations of sexism were everywhere, but I was enjoying my childhood, oblivious to how these attitudes affected my social development. Like most young girls, I had a collection of dolls, but Barbie was the most popular doll to own. Barbie personified the promise of eternal youth and beauty and its manufacturer had designed a doll that captured the then-existing perception of the physical attributes of the perfect woman: blonde, white, anorexic, with a disproportionately ample bust and, most importantly, she was a bit of an airhead.

Naturally, many little girls aspired to be like their favorite doll, so they could snag their very own Ken. It wasn't until 1992 that the manufacturer announced that their Teen Talk

Barbie would no longer say the phrase, "Math class is tough," as it sustained Barbie's empty-headed image.

Unfortunately, by 1992, the women of my generation had already been influenced by the Barbie culture that associated a woman's identity with her attractiveness. The thought was that if you weren't attractive, you weren't visible, and attractiveness and sensuality were attributes reserved for the lucky or the very young.

My mother grew up in the generation that considered marriage as a necessary evil, with one of its requirements taking place at night in the marital bed. She made it clear to me that this sexual union was a part of marriage that a woman must endure, because no nice girl could possibly enjoy it. She, sadly, advised me that I needed to grin and bear my husband's sexual urges until the day came that his desires diminished. She told me not to be disheartened, because that day wasn't far away.

Then, she gave me the really sad news that, although now I was a young wife, adored by her husband, his admiration would dim once I became an older woman. I was outraged by her assumption that his love for me would change once I was no longer young. She wasn't trying to be mean, but she felt it was her duty to let me know that I wouldn't always be the belle of the ball. Her life experiences had revealed to her the diminishing value of women as they age.

Although she never held an executive-level job, she made the most of what life handed her, and did everything in her power to make sure that her daughters were equipped with the tools needed to successfully advance themselves in the world. She instilled in us the belief that neither age, nor looks defined who we were, and that there wasn't any obstacle that we couldn't surmount, regardless of where life took us.

The Journey of an "Invisible" Woman

She taught all of her children to face adversity with resilience, but she reminded each of her daughters that her first priority was to become a wife and mother. She was setting an extremely high bar for me to reach. I would have to jump through some major hoops in order to juggle my future responsibilities as a super wife, mom and high-ranking professional in the workplace. I knew that I had no choice but to accept the challenge.

The world didn't always make it easy for me to live up to my mother's expectations. Many women with less ambitious mothers decided to just lockstep, to stay in line with established 20th century role models for women. These stilted female stereotypes were even used as a basis for gender designs in toy manufacturing, as glaringly evidenced in the design of the Barbie doll. Mattel had their hand on the pulse of the consumer. They knew that this meant that an important part of Barbie's identity depended on her attractiveness to men. Her eternal youth was an important part of her desirability, so there would certainly be no mature Barbie.

My girlfriends and I spent many hours playing with Barbie and marveling over her perfection. We never realized that this admiration for the doll led girls to engage in body objectification by having them associate attractiveness with having a sexualized, hyper thin, forever youthful body; even Doctor Barbie wore skintight jeans. A 2014 study of four to seven-year-old girls found that playing with Barbie actually limited girls' perceptions about what they could be in the future.

Society today continues to perpetuate stereotypical myths about universal characteristics of women at different life stages. Typically, a young woman is portrayed as vibrant, energetic, and sexually alluring, while an older woman is seen as dowdy and undesirable, unless she is performing her role as a saintly, self-sacrificing mother.

The 1950s idealization of the perfect older woman was best conveyed in the television show, *Leave it to Beaver*. The mom, June Cleaver personified a woman who knew her purpose in life, and that was to serve her family.

June epitomized the asexual woman who always wore modest clothing, knew how to do a formal curtsey, had ladylike pastimes, and slept in a twin bed—only near, not with, her husband. Good girls got married; "loose" girls were destined to lurk in the shadows, shunned by polite society. June's style was to appear tasteful, rather than alluring. This characterization seems to be the antithesis of everything that Barbie epitomized, but remember, Barbie was never an older woman; she definitely wasn't created to fit the description of a hag.

The cultural institutionalization of women as socially inferior to men was intrinsic to the theme of another award winning 1950s show, *Father Knows Best*. The show again captured perfectly the common sentiment of the decade that a woman's place was in the kitchen, and men belonged in a professional environment. Although a woman might be queen of her home, men were still in charge of all major decision-making.

I spent many hours, enthusiastically, watching this show as a young girl and yet something kept tickling my brain about its message. Jim Anderson was a great dad, but was this idyllic presentation of family life that promoted a patriarchal power hierarchy something that I wanted for myself? Jim was the man who had answers to complex issues of life, while his wife, Margaret, was confined to ruling the domestic sphere. They seemed content in these roles, but would I be?

The Journey of an "Invisible" Woman

For many girls of my generation, movies also reinforced misconceptions about what should constitute a desirable self-image for a woman. Numerous films such as *Butch Cassidy and the Sundance Kid*, *Goldfinger* and *The Dirty Dozen* focused on the independent, macho man fighting for the greater good, while on the other hand, a woman's purpose in other popular films centered solely on her marriageability. Eliza was nothing until Henry Higgins cleaned her up in *My Fair Lady*.

She was a poor, innocent waif who, after her metamorphosis, would become a beautiful lady with a secure future—as long as she always remembered what she had been taught. In Marriage *Italian Style*, Filumena had to use her looks to enhance her station in life with the fickle Domenico, but once she became older, she lost much of that desirability. Filumena was a sexy prostitute, who flaunted her sexuality and could never seriously be considered as Domenico's wife, especially as she grew older, until she resorted to tricks to hook Domenico.

The movie industry sets what they believe is a high moral standard for women in their films and there is a clear distinction between "bad" and "good" girls. Good girls would find happiness, because they deserved it, while bad girls also got what they deserved, but it was never anything good. Horror movies really revel in the punishment that they inflict on wayward women. In the movie *Halloween,* the lead actress, Laurie, played by Jamie Lee Curtis, is saved from the attentions of the killer because of her sexual inexperience.

However, those reckless girls in the movie who lost their virginity are subjected to gruesome deaths. This is a prevalent theme in many movies. Hopefully, this isn't the movie industry's subliminal message to women that they shouldn't claim ownership of their own sexuality.

Sandy Camillo

Although disciples of Barbie don't acknowledge existence of women past a certain age, these women do exist, and wrinkles, sagging skin, grey hair, and drooping body parts are all a part of an older woman's reality. Society has decided that these characteristics are so repugnant that older women should be hidden from sight, especially in advertisements, movies, and television.

The words 'attractive' and 'young' are not synonyms and, yet, when a women ages, so does her perceived attractiveness. Telling someone that she looks young for her age is not a compliment as it implies that she is not young, and although she looks attractive most people her age don't. Totally ignored is an indisputable contradiction regarding the concept of aging. Everyone wants to live a long life, but no one wants to get old. Does this contradiction mean that people would rather die than become old?

It's interesting that, as teenagers, we can't wait to get older and fantasize about one day possessing the sophistication and privileges that come with added years. I recall the frustration I felt as a teenager when my carefully researched arguments about the justification for the war in Vietnam were ignored by my siblings as the ignorant ruminations of youth. I consoled myself by thinking that once I was older everyone would listen to my proclamations with great respect.

When did my joyful anticipation turn to dread at the realization that getting older wouldn't guarantee respect? Contrarily, the probability was very high that instead of my declarations engendering respect, they might be ignored as the ramblings of an older woman. Apparently, many random criteria, such as a woman's beauty, age and sexuality are all bizarrely considered indicators of a woman's character and worth.

The Journey of an "Invisible" Woman

Perhaps one of the strangest indicators is the use of hair length to gauge a woman's attractiveness and moral standing. For many centuries, various cultures have maintained that there is a strong tie between hair length and a woman's identity. In the early Christian Church, women covered their heads to indicate piety.

This practice was known as Christian veiling. For those of us who may have forgotten our bible classes, I Corinthians 11, in the New Testament references covering long hair for modesty. Apparently, long hair was considered seductive and the sight of it would incite men to ravage women.

Although, today, no one expects a man to froth at the mouth at the sight of a woman's hair, it is still implied that long hair enhances a woman's sexuality. Because of the ideologies surrounding hair length and sexuality, many young women hesitate to cut their hair. As women age, however, this belief that women must exclusively have long hair changes. Older women are now often encouraged to adopt a short hairstyle, as it is more appropriate for them. Does this changed exhortation infer that older women no longer have to protect their modesty because they are no longer attractive to men? We'll get a little deeper into this dilemma about hair in a later chapter but I guess that older woman can breathe a sigh of relief because no self-respecting rapist will look at them.

Although the media blithely continued to ignore gender equality in their portrayals of women, Mattel tried to make amends for casting a blind eye on women in professional roles. By 1995, Mattel was finally addressing the fact that women were making marks for themselves in professions that were traditionally dominated by men. The company wasn't completely altruistic in their recognition of women's professional advancements.

Part of their motivation to create a professional Barbie was to stay on top of the toy industry by adhering to the belief that they had to "follow the money." That meant that the new batch of Barbie dolls were doctors, dentists and firewomen. These dolls, however, were still stereotypically gorgeous young women wearing high heel shoes that emphasized their hourglass figures. Although Mattel was now marketing Barbie as a young professional with a high caliber career, they emphasized that she still looked fabulous while doing her job.

Mattel was constantly trying to correct the bad press about the disruptive influence of Barbie on a girl's healthy self-image and wanted to show that they had a strong social conscience. Although in 1980 Mattel came out with the first official African-American and Latina Barbie, it wasn't until 2016, that Mattel addressed the outcry for total diversity in its dolls by introducing the "So In Style" line of dolls. Barbie now had representative dolls from all religions, races, and cultures; but, aside from a one-time promotion for International Women's Day in 2018 celebrating role models, an older women Barbie was an anathema on Mattel's concept of feminine beauty. I guess producing a mainstream older woman Barbie was pushing the envelope too far for Mattel, as they didn't want to take the chance of frightening young girls with a depiction of their future selves. Even today, Barbie continues to influence a young girl's internalized feelings about who she is, and who she should grow up to be.

We have to ask ourselves if a woman's self-esteem diminishes once her perfect body, hair and face change with age and she sees herself through the eyes of a society that only worships youth; or will she rise up and declare, "Damn Barbie and Society, I'll never become invisible!"

CHAPTER 5
SPARE THE ROD, SPOIL THE CHILD

It wasn't just Mattel who was convinced that they had the power to mold a woman's body and personality. My mother could have taught them lessons. Her philosophy was that the end justified the means, and now that I think about it, Mattel had the same philosophy.

My mother would do whatever was necessary to shape her daughters' futures, according to what she thought was best for their happiness, even if it resulted in some cuts and bruises. Mattel's purpose was less lofty than my mother's goal. They would do whatever it took to bring in the money.

According to my mother, she based her philosophy directly on the word of God. She literally obeyed the dictate regarding the discipline of children that was contained in proverb 13:24 from the New King James Version of the Bible. However, although the words in the proverb were, "He who spares his *son* hates his son, but he who loves him disciplines him promptly" she was comfortable in widely interpreting the word, "son" to include daughter(s).

In my Italian family there was one established way to deal with a child who didn't listen, and my mother was the person in charge of doling out this punishment. Words don't do justice to the image of my short, little mother chasing me around the dining room table while wielding her metal serving spoon at me, but since I can't draw, you'll have to use your imagination.

Strangely enough I was the only one of my siblings who had to endure this form of what today would be considered child abuse. My brother was already knighted as the only son in the family, while my sister was the oldest and therefore untouchable.

They were respectively eight and ten years older than I, and were part of the generation that accepted certain barriers for women as the normal order of things. I, on the other hand, was determined to be my own woman and that meant knocking down all the barriers that my brother and sister resignedly accepted.

Needless to say, my mother felt obliged to follow the words of proverb 13:24 to demonstrate her love. We were like two bulls facing off before locking horns. My mother's temper wasn't helped by the fact that her hormones were raging because she was going through menopause. Sometimes she didn't know what to do with this recalcitrant child who considered Aretha Franklin's song, "Respect," her anthem for what she demanded from the world.

But getting back to the spoon-chasing scenario, to be fair, my mother never actually hit me because she couldn't catch me, but that didn't stop her from trying. My mother's objective was to reign in my rebellious nature so that I would fit into the 20th century definition of a proper lady. The only problem with her idea is that I didn't want to "fit in." I wanted to stand out and distinguish myself.

My desire to stand out was not only anathema to the wisdom in books like the 1950s guide for girls, "Betty Cornell's Teen-Age Popularity Guide" that offered guidance for girls who wanted to be, "poised, self-confident and shiny bright," but it also was a complete contradiction to my mom's upbringing.

She had spent her teenage years ironing her six brothers' shirts and cleaning her mother's house. If a shirt had a crease in the wrong spot, there was nothing comedic about the ensuing punishment that my mother endured. Her mother, who didn't speak a word of English, released her frustrations by cannibalistically biting her daughter. The last thing my mother wanted to do was to stand out; all she wanted was an exit out of her hellish existence into what she dreamt of as a normal life. That escape came via marriage to my father.

My father quickly amassed a fortune and enabled my mother to live the life of a lady. Once she had daughters of her own, her vision for us became set in stone. We would become educated and refined, and use these qualities to marry a wealthy man who would care for our children, and us. Her dreams were not ours, but we knew that she needed to hold on to her aspirations for us, even if she broke a few spoons accomplishing her goal. It was a better punishment than having teeth marks imprinted on our skin.

My mother wasn't alone in thinking that she could mold her daughters into becoming "perfect" women with modulated voices, and modest demeanors. From the middle ages to the end of the 16th century, the torture device of choice for men married to women who were too talkative and liked to gossip was the Scold's Bridle. A woman's husband would go to court and ask that the wife be ordered to wear the device. The device was an iron muzzle that enclosed the head with a spike pressing on the tongue.

This was seen as a sure way to cure talkative women of gossiping. You actually weren't able to speak at all unless you wanted to be left with a torn and bloody tongue. Some husbands would even attach a leash to the device and lead their wives on a walk of shame through town to guarantee that she was humbled. And the truly innovative husbands would go one step further and attach a bell to the leash so they would be guaranteed to attract the attention of a crowd. This device was considered so clever that it was featured in Shakespeare's play *The Taming of the Shrew*.

If a women's behavior towards her husband became egregious and uncontrollable because of her refusal to be subjugated, and the Scold's Bridle failed to rein her in, then her neighbors would take the matter into their own hands. In Elizabethan England it was actually against the law for women to invert the gender norms, (i.e., men in charge, women subservient), so the community would punish the woman by staging a Charivari—a mock parade in which the townspeople would walk with the woman, who was seated backwards on a horse or mule, throughout the streets.

To attract the most attention, the townspeople would create a discordant serenade as they paraded by, clanging pots and pans. The woman was seated facing the wrong way to symbolize her attempt to reverse gender roles through her assertive behavior (Marshall, 2014).

We can probably all agree that these attempts to break a woman's spirit are repugnant, and that any man that tried these techniques on a modern-day woman would be lucky to walk away from her with all his organs intact. In addition, in America, if a man uses corporal punishment on his wife, he runs the risk of spending some very uncomfortable days in a prison cell, perhaps receiving some corporal punishment of his own from his new housemates.

Although there is a consensus among civilized people that corporal punishment between adults is off limits, there is still controversy surrounding the use of corporal punishment between parent and child. Although research acknowledges that both nature and nurture influence a person's identity, there is still no consensus from the experts on the acceptable use of corporal punishment. Psychologists and other professionals are divided on the question of whether the benefit of corporal punishment might outweigh any potential hazards (Thompson, 2004, p. 539).

My mother wasn't able to channel my ambitions into acceptable female parameters by using corporal punishment, although she dedicated herself to trying, but corporal punishment is not the only thing that can be used to subjugate women. The word "corporal" is defined as of the body, or physical, and throughout history this physical type of discipline has proven effective in altering both men's and women's behavior. But there are other forms of behavior that can also break a person. We all read brainwashing stories with fascination, yet never consider the fact that every day there are certain methods used in brainwashing that are also insidiously used to denigrate women. Being told repeatedly that you're not strong, smart, pretty or thin enough, or that you're too aggressive, eventually erodes your sense of self. Media portrayals of women in submissive roles set the stage for maintaining restrictive barriers that limit a woman's professional expectations, and subtly encourage her to curb her ambitions.

When the media does portray women as bosses in the workplace, it's rarely complimentary. As for women who show managerial potential, The 1980 movie 9 to 5 is still depressingly relevant for women at work, as women continue to be underrepresented in management level positions. McKinsey's recent diversity report concluded that companies with a large percentage of women executives outperformed companies with fewer women in 2020. However, despite this fact, their study showed that more than a third of the companies in their data set had no women at all on their executive teams (Dixon-Fyle & Dolan, 2013).

Sandy Camillo

Women in male-female romantic relationships must be feminine (whatever nebulous meaning that has), attractive and nurturing. On the other hand, words used to describe a woman's ideal mate emphasize the inherent power in the man, who ideally should be tall, strong and muscular. Are these traits necessary because, to be a husband, and possibly a father, the male will be required to battle a tiger in the jungle? There definitely was no allusion to power as being a requisite trait for a suitable wife, or an employee in Judy, Violet and Doralee's job descriptions in the movie.

These controlling techniques can be insidious and as damaging as corporal punishment. They're not always recognized until the damage is done and a person meekly accepts the constraints that prevent them from fulfilling their dreams. Thinking back to my childhood, my mother was guilty of using both corporal punishment and mental conditioning to reconfigure what she considered were unsuitable goals for a woman, but her efforts didn't work, as I continued to break down doors that stood between me and my development into an independent woman.

CHAPTER 6
NOBODY PUTS BABY IN THE CORNER

My mother's strong-arm tactics didn't succeed in transforming me into her image of the ideal woman. My childhood and teenage years convinced my mother that God had put me on earth to let her atone for her sins. In her mind, the key words to describe my behavior were rebellious, defiant and above all spectacularly visible.

I was the baby of the family. My brother and sister were almost a decade older than me, so either my parents really wanted another child or I was a little accident. My behavior neatly fit into the definition of "Third Child Syndrome" (Kearney, 2018). My behavior epitomized the words, "the youngest child often clamors for attention, and will try hard to get it anyway she can." Not only was I the third child, but I was also the youngest. I guess that explained a lot of things about my fear of invisibility.

Once I became a teenager, I would always assert my presence in the most *in-your-face* way possible. This aberrant behavior was exacerbated because of unpleasant childhood memories of being ignored. As a little girl the words I heard most from my parents were, "be quiet; your brother is talking." Needless to say, as I grew older, I never shut up.

My conservative Italian family believed that a woman had total control of the home and children while the man's primary responsibility was to bring home the money. This belief meant that the men and women in the family should be provided with the tools required to perform their specific roles. Becoming a provider meant that a man was given every resource to accomplish his role in life and attainment of his role was the definitive end of the growth process. A woman was given the resources that she'd need to catch a man, and as a bonus, could attain a great education.

In my childhood home, special favors were given to the firstborn child, regardless of gender. This fact gave my sister special privileges. My brother was already entitled because he was male. That left me sitting alone in the corner, but not for long. My parents had clearly established the parameters for the social norms for their children to follow.

However, learning to cook, clean and take care of my man may have been a noble goal for my mother's generation, but it was not something that I wanted. Graduating from an elite prep high school further reinforced my belief that I could do anything.

So, when I was a sophomore in another preppy school, a women's college, I decided to create a bit of a scandal by eloping with my first husband. He was everything a mother feared, uneducated, poor, and sexy as all hell. This was something straight out of a teenage fantasy, and it was sure to make everyone take notice. And they did.

At the time, you couldn't get married in New York State without your parent's consent until you were twenty-one. There was no way that my parents would give that consent; so, my husband-to-be and I arranged to fly to a state that allowed minors to marry. We picked North Carolina because it was relatively close and the only requirement was a 24-hour residency.

As my husband-to-be and I sat on opposite ends of a cheap motel room to wait out the residency requirements, little did we know that a surprise was on its way. My mother could have worked for the CIA, as within hours of my boarding the flight to North Carolina, she had identified my destination, and she and my sister had chartered a plane to get to me. My family would do anything to make sure that their little girl didn't become "damaged goods." I guess that they envisioned me and my sexy boyfriend feverishly rolling around on a bed, engaged in passionate love making. They only hoped that they had arrived quickly enough to salvage what was left of my reputation. The reality was that both my husband-to-be and I were naïve young Catholic kids who still believed that going all the way was the quickest path to hell, and that was one place where we didn't want to go.

As we were sitting quietly in our motel room, the door burst open and suddenly my mom and sister were standing before us. I think part of me was glad to see that they came to rescue me from what in my heart I knew was a mistake and so, we made a deal.

If I abandoned the elopement and came back home, my mother would arrange for me to get married by a priest, in church, followed by a reception in a typical, over-the-top, Long Island, New York, wedding venue. It sounded like a lot of fun and definitely made me the center of attention; therefore, I told my husband-to-be, "Let's go for it." The seriousness of what I was about to do never entered my crazy, teenage mind. Needless to say, my little adventure became the topic of many dinner table conversations among my relatives. I would never be thought of as a quiet, forgotten bonus baby.

Sandy Camillo

The fairy tale drama of two star-crossed lovers eloping was soon over. Now we were married. Our cozy first apartment was actually a step above living in a tenement, but it was okay because I could play house with my handsome husband without anyone telling me what to do. I finally felt like I was in control of my destiny. Little did I know that my mom's surprise appearance in my North Carolina motel room was a harbinger of another surprise.

Three months after our wedding, that new surprise was revealed to me. I was pregnant, and what began as a fun filled, sure-fire way to gain attention from family and friends became a serious, life changing event. Neither my husband nor I had planned on ever ending the marriage, and now, with the introduction of an innocent third party, our union was irrevocably "till death do us part;" or at the time, that's what we both believed.

Soon, I was your typical young mother trying to balance family life with completing my educational requirements to obtain Bachelors and Masters Degrees. My mom insisted that I get these degrees because, "you never know what life brings," which, as it turned out, was a major understatement. It wasn't long before I realized that engaging in crazy stunts might provide me with fleeting moments of notoriety, but I'd have to look for other ways to express my individuality, now that I was a so-called grownup and I had another person in my life to think about.

When I became a mother, I understood that my life wasn't all about me. I was unique in my son's eyes because I was his one and only. But sadly, my husband no longer held that place in my heart, and my mother's warning about the uncertainly of life became my reality. I remember my mother's confusion when I mentioned to her that I was unhappy in my marriage. She couldn't understand what I was saying.

The Journey of an "Invisible" Woman

She asked me if my husband had cheated on me or beat me and implied that even those two issues could be overcome. I tried to explain to her that although my husband was a good man, that in itself wasn't enough to make me stay. In my eyes, marriage was more than a convenient living arrangement, it was an opportunity for two people to work together to achieve common goals, and there were no common goals left in my marriage. The time had come for my husband and me to part and get a divorce.

Although New York State didn't make it easy to get married, they did their best to make sure you stayed that way, once you tied the knot. At the time, there wasn't any no-fault divorce and my husband refused to consent to the divorce if we had to claim fault. It was up to me to come up with another solution.

The press of the day was filled with stories about Americans combining a quick and easy divorce with a weekend vacation in a tropical paradise. One of these utopias was Haiti, as it met all the qualifications; it was a beautiful island and there were very few restrictions for those people deciding to divorce there. Only one member of the married party had to be present and, "if you can say incompatibility of character in French, you're as good as gold" (Steely, 1975). My solution was easy; I'd go to Haiti for my divorce.

I wasn't alone in my decision to divorce in Haiti. It was the rage back in the 70s for hundreds of New Yorkers to fly weekly on party planes to Haiti for quickie divorces. This cultural phenomenon was even memorialized in the song "Haitian Divorce" by Steely Dan. It all sounded pretty exciting, so I arranged a flight to Haiti for my sister and me. When the plane landed, the passengers were instructed to disembark onto the tarmac, as this airport only had a small ramshackle shed as its terminal.

Sandy Camillo

We were told to stay together to wait for the bus to our hotel. We were sweltering in the 95-degree temperature and were becoming impatient to get to our air-conditioned hotel. Finally, what appeared to be an old school bus arrived, and we were all herded aboard to begin our 40-minute ride through dense jungle to the hotel. Needless to say, air conditioning was not one of the features on this bus, so by the time we got to the hotel we were all suffering, a bit, from heat stroke.

Suddenly, the jungle opened up and I had my first sight of the hotel. It looked like a castle, but one that had seen better days. We were ushered into the hotel lobby. I glanced around and I could immediately envision the hotel in its glory days. Massive crystal chandeliers hung from an elaborately frescoed ceiling and a variety of murals decorated the walls.

Unfortunately, peeling paint and cracked walls made the decor look like something resulting from the aftermath of a war. This once luxurious hotel had been transformed into the Heartbreak Hotel for the soon to be divorced. I was able to overlook the squalor by thinking about the great stories I'd be able to recount when I was back home.

After an uneasy sleep, having awakened several times with unhappy dreams, my sister and I went downstairs to board the bus to the courthouse for the legal formalities. Children pressed their noses against the windows of the bus as we slowly made our way through the narrow streets to the courthouse. Watching the crazy foreigners was probably a major form of entertainment for these children. Haiti was an impoverished country and children learned to amuse themselves in simple ways. We finally arrived at the courthouse.

As we, apprehensively, approached the entrance to the Courthouse, we noticed that it was guarded by soldiers with machine guns. My group of thirty nervous Americans assembled before the judge. We listened carefully to the French-speaking judge declare the words that we all hoped were the official end to our marriages. A glance at the divorce decree showed that it was written in French, so we had to take it on faith that everything was legitimate, and that we were, officially, divorced.

I discovered on the flight back to New York why these planes were called party planes. People were getting drunk and singing and dancing in the aisles. There were even some hook ups going on. I guess this is where the term, "gay divorcee" was coined. However, I was content to ignore all the partygoers, as I was just relieved to escape my loveless marriage. When I reflect back now on those times, I see my selfishness at not being able to consider my ex-husband's pain over the end of what he thought was a lifetime love.

The elopement with my first husband wasn't what most girls of my generation did, and neither was the process of my divorce, but both events confirmed for me that I'd always break down any doors that prevented me from achieving my goals. I'd never wind up again sitting in the corner. My marriage ended the way it had begun, with excitement and drama.

CHAPTER 7
I SAW THE LIGHT

Although my wedding and divorce were filled with excitement and drama, I was now a college student and things were quieting down as I adjusted to college life. However, I was different than most of the other students because I was also a single mother. I was aware that there was another major difference between me and other girls my age. These girls had practical wisdom of things that I knew nothing about.

Getting married at such a young age meant that I missed participating in most of the things that were associated with college, and I don't mean cramming for exams. I had no real-life knowledge of a typical college experience, like spending the weekend with a bunch of friends in a group house at the beach and staying up partying all night. I experienced these activities vicariously by imagining myself in television shows and movies featuring college students. The only time I had stayed up all night was to take care of my sick child. I wanted to make up for lost time, so the years following my divorce were spent in a frenzy of marathon dating, in search of my knight on a white horse. Luckily, my mother was happy to babysit, as it meant that she could have both my son and me back under her wings. She also secretly hoped that I would find a new man who could "take care of me."

The women of my generation held a different perspective than my mom's viewpoint about the reason for marrying. The feminist movement taught them that they could take care of themselves. These women didn't need a caretaker. They got married because they fell in love or thought they were in love. In the 1970s, many marriages were hastily arranged in order to save a boyfriend from serving in Vietnam. This altruism was only a small factor in my motive for getting married, as I believed that my marriage was a symbol of my independence, and the hoopla surrounding the marriage celebration satisfied my thirst for attention, even if that attention lasted for only a short period of time.

Also, I can now admit that the nuns had done a good job on convincing me that the path to hell was lined with girls who were no longer virgins, so the only way that I could experience the ecstasies of sexual union was to get married, and that was one experience that I was anxious to savor, so I married.

Many of these quickie weddings resulted in quickie divorces. Women had now started to claim the right to enjoy their sexuality. These women had survived failed marriages and were made stronger by the experience. The airways were filled with songs like, "I Am Woman" by Helen Reddy and "The Pill" by Loretta Lynn that embodied a woman's empowerment. Singles bars were numerous in New York City and were the then acceptable way for people to meet, until word spread that perhaps it wasn't the safest way. Women happily bar hopped until 1975 when the book, "Looking for Mr. Goodbar" was released.

The book was about a young teacher killed by a man she met while cruising the New York City bars. Fortunately, I was remarried before the book tainted the singles bar scene for me, but for many other women it was a reminder of their vulnerability.

It was a great time to be single, and I was enjoying the whirlwind life of a single woman in New York. Life was great until Ms. Native New Yorker met Luke, the Indiana Hoosier. He was a Rhodes Scholar, phantom jet pilot, lawyer, stockbroker and 6'3" hunk, with a face to light up a girl's heart. He was almost the whole package. He was just missing the white horse, because the horse he rode was black to match his heart, but to be fair, I didn't know this until I was over my head in love with him.

Luke used his mid-western charm to convince my son and me to move to Fort Wayne, Indiana with him. Although this wasn't like moving to the south of France it didn't matter because we were in love, love, love and, as we all know, love is blind.

This was also my chance to set tongues wagging again by leaving the Big Apple to move, with a man, to a small town in Indiana. New Yorkers didn't do that; consequently, I thought that this move really made me stand out. I never thought that out of sight is out of mind, and that once I was gone, people would quickly find a new topic of conversation.

At the time, although I had dated many men, I believed this was the first time that I had actually experienced the full glory of romantic love and was dizzy in anticipation of the joys to come. I wholeheartedly committed myself to the relationship, never surmising that it would have a negative impact on my self-esteem and identity as a strong woman. I threw caution to the wind in my eagerness to be daring and to distance myself from what I thought was a mundane existence, by getting into the U-Haul with my hero to make the trip to Indiana.

The novelty of being a big fish in a small pond quickly wore off. The romantic dinners in a rooftop restaurant

The Journey of an "Invisible" Woman

overlooking Manhattan were now, instead, an occasional visit to Fort Wayne's favorite local hamburger joint. I was far away from family and friends and finding a job and childcare wasn't going to be easy. Luke was my only oasis and he knew it. The sound of the black horse's hoofs thundered in my brain to the beat of my own depressing song, whose lyrics kept repeating, RUN AWAY, RUN AWAY.

Before long, I was convinced that, without Luke, I was nothing. The truth was that this was the first time there was something that I desperately wanted and was willing to compromise my convictions for, rather than engaging in a power play over who was the most subservient partner. In the past, it had been easy to give up some of my self-determination to be the ruler of the kingdom when I wasn't blinded by obsessive love.

Every time Luke and I were together he would point out my imperfections. He'd then tell me not to worry because he'd send me to magical doctors and fitness gurus who would make me perfect. I was advised to forget my career aspirations, because as his future wife, I'd be busy raising our children and getting involved in volunteer work. I was isolated and under his control.

If a girlfriend had confessed to me that her boyfriend played these types of mind games with her, I'd have pointed out that his actions were classic signs of emotional abuse, and yet I complied with all of Luke's suggestions, because he was a Svengali and I, a powerful ambitious woman, was under his spell.

One night, he giddily gave me his best news. Apparently, it was a no, no to be an Italian in Fort Wayne's social circles, but he was going to pull some strings so I would soon blend into Fort Wayne society, and believe it or not, he'd even get me admitted into the local Junior League. Instead of running into the street screaming in horror, I started to believe that maybe I was better off blending into the background, and then I would conform to Luke's concept of the perfect woman.

I wasn't just in love, but obsessed to the point of not knowing what I was doing, and not caring. My many years of self-actualization were reversed until I was no longer a self-assured, cosmopolitan New York City girl but instead a whiney, dependent shell of myself. And nobody found that attractive, especially Luke, and so, he said goodbye.

My 75-year-old dad drove a U Haul from New York to Indiana to save his daughter and grandson from the mess we were in, but my Indiana interlude wasn't quite over. We were back in New York, but as Luke was into drama as much as I was, he wrote to me to tell me he had made a terrible mistake and wanted me to come back to him. However, my father had made me promise that I wouldn't be in contact with Luke, as a condition of letting my son and me move back into his home.

Because our relationship now had the added element of cloak and dagger intrigue, things quickly got interesting again. I became the star of my own movie, but at the time, I foolishly thought my story was a romance, while it was actually a tragedy.

I loved my dad, but I was still addicted to Luke, and for this reason I guiltily disobeyed his order to give up Luke. I snuck away to be with Luke on the weekends, when he would fly into New York. My mom unwittingly became a co-conspirator in what she thought were my attempts to get over a bad relationship. She would do anything to get me back into the dating game by encouraging me to go out with friends, not knowing that the friend I was getting together with, was Luke.

The only two people who knew that Luke and I were still together were the two of us. Now, not only was I able to again experience the excitement of the chase, but that chase was made more exciting because it was a clandestine romance.

This situation went on for almost a year. Luke expressed his adoration of me on nightly phone calls and weekly letters. The only hitch to these declarations of love was that, once a week, he would break up with me on subsequent phone calls, at two in the morning. Luke acted like a person who was schizophrenic, or on drugs.

He really epitomized the guy who loved the chase more than the relationship and constantly endeavored to create increasingly bizarre scenarios to enhance its thrill. Either this motivation was egging him on, or I was just dating a real sadist. Probably both things were true. Any way you looked at it, I had to admit that a man was playing me like a yo-yo.

Although I hate to admit it, I was as bad as he was. I had a history of pursuing a relationship until I had a man who was entranced by me, and then I would lose interest. In this relationship with Luke, I couldn't get bored and take him for granted, because I never knew what he would do. It was the ultimate game, even though I knew that the real prince on the white horse wouldn't play this way. I was obsessed with someone whom I knew I could never fully have.

To add more spice to my life, I decided to ratchet up the drama a bit. Luke was a good Midwestern boy. He exercised and believed that his body was a temple. I, on the other hand, thought that cigarettes were ambrosia, but I kept that news to myself when I was with Luke. That was, until what was to be our last dinner together, in an old school New York Italian restaurant. We ordered our drinks. Mine was a martini and his was a glass of milk, as incredible as that might sound. Although he occasionally would imbibe with a celebratory glass of champagne, he prided himself on having no vices. Accordingly, he was particularly shocked when I then whipped out a cigarette and proceeded to vigorously puff on it, with a finesse that I had practiced for years.

Luke demanded that I put the cigarette out, but I was determined to make this Custer's last stand and assert my newly found control over our relationship. Now, if this were today, I would thank him for caring about my health, but back then cigarettes were a sign of sophistication, not death. So, I stared him straight in the eye and said, "NO." However, my victory was short lived, as he got up and left the restaurant, leaving me with the bill.

Many women can recount stories about interactions with men like Luke. Some of those stories involve public figures and are widely posted by the media. Although no one wants to suffer from someone else's misfortune, these public revelations illustrate that emotional abuse can happen to all women regardless of social or economic status and can be detrimental to a woman's self-esteem and her personal and professional success.

One such story, particularly, stands out as a demonstration of a powerful woman's humiliation at the hands of the man she loved. Anthony Weiner was a politician who was forced to resign from his congressional seat after a sexually suggestive photo that he sent to a woman via Twitter was publicized. His wife, Huma Aberdin, held the powerful position of vice chair of Hillary Clinton's 2016 campaign for president. This was a woman who exerted great political power in the world and yet, was powerless when it came to asserting herself with her husband.

Weiner, who used the name Carlos Danger when sexting to various women, denied what he was doing, even though there was extensive proof of his misdeeds. Huma not only stated that she believed Weiner but also, even after he continued to send explicit texts and photos to young women, said that she was proud to be married to him.

The Journey of an "Invisible" Woman

How could she possibly be proud of a husband who sent a text to a young girl saying, "Would you let me hold your hair while you gagged on my c***" (Miller, 2013). Huma finally saw the light and divorced Weiner. Although Huma's story doesn't excuse my pitiful reaction at mistreatment by Luke, at least people weren't watching my shame on the seven o'clock news.

I never saw Luke again. It took me years to realize that Luke loved the challenge of trying to break a strong-willed woman and to recreate her into his own Barbie doll. He believed that a woman's place was under a man's thumb, and she deserved to be crushed if she tried to get out from under his finger. He was the one that got away, and it took many years before I realized how lucky I was that he disappeared. I vowed to myself that I would never again have my identity compromised by someone else's idea of who I was. I finally saw the light.

CHAPTER 8
THE "OTHER," OTHER WOMAN

Unfortunately, some women and men establish their power and control over a loved one by doing things that ultimately hurt the loved one. This is sometimes the case in a relationship between two lovers that involves a third party. The third party is commonly known as the Other Woman.

History is filled with tales of these types of intricate love relationships. A good illustration is the story of Anthony and Cleopatra. They carried out a torrid love affair in spite of not one, but two of Anthony's wives. Cleopatra is a classic example of a traditional "Other" woman. The Other woman is usually understood to be a married man's lover. However, it makes sense to somehow modify this word, "Other," to include some unconventional distinctions in the meaning of this word. An "Other" woman might be a mistress or also be a second wife or a wife-in-waiting, and each of these roles conveys a different meaning.

It's accepted that a mistress is a woman having an extramarital relationship, especially with a married man. Generally, there is no expectation of marriage between a man and his mistress. A wife-in-waiting is someone who has graduated from the status of mistress or lover and is simply

The Journey of an "Invisible" Woman

waiting for a divorce to be finalized so she can take her rightful place as a wife. Of course, the word "second wife" is self-explanatory. These women are all "Other" women and yet their roles are quite different.

There are numerous examples of wife-in-waiting women in our everyday lives, but few stories involving average people are as sensational as when they involve a wife-in-waiting in Hollywood. Jennifer Lopez was briefly a wife-in-waiting before she married Marc Anthony. She and Marc made plans to marry as soon as his divorce was final, which they did four days after it was finalized. Jennifer's relationship to Mark was more than just a casual lover.

Perhaps, the relationship of Brittany Spears and Kevin Federline best captures the distinction between a lover and wife-in-waiting. Brittany and Kevin got engaged while Kevin was still engaged to a woman who was pregnant with his second child. Brittany waited and then she wed Kevin. She was indeed a wife-in-waiting. The responsibilities of a mistress, second wife and wife-in-waiting are somewhat different, but one thing remains the same, and that is that each of these women must publicly put her man on a pedestal.

Did I mention that one of the requirements to be a successful "Other" woman is taking acting lessons? Your man probably thinks that he is a god among mortals. Not only do you have to second this opinion but you also must convince him that being with him makes you the luckiest person in the world. Now, maintaining this illusion may cause you to choke on laughter at times, but remember, your performance doesn't have to be academy award winning. You only have to be convincing enough to make him forget the castrating interactions between him and his ex. Anything that massages his ego makes him happy to be with you.

Sandy Camillo

I recall a time in my life when I was the "Other" woman. I adopted this new personality during my entire relationship with Luke, the knight on the black horse, whom you just read about in the last chapter. You learned how I eventually saw the light, but I'll explain to you my perspective when I was an "Other" woman in an unbalanced relationship.

I met my love at the point in his divorce when everything had transpired but the final 60-day waiting period after the court filing; therefore, technically, I wasn't a married man's mistress. My profile would best be defined as being a wife-in-waiting. I fell under this man's spell and became convinced that my path to happiness could only be found in his arms. And what arms he had! If he were a woman, people would say that he was stacked, as the manly term buff, didn't quite capture the whole picture. He would be my trophy wife, although he didn't quite meet the criteria of being just eye candy, as he also was financially successful and intellectually gifted. This relationship would definitely elevate my image in the world as a woman was often judged on the quality of her mate.

Needless to say, I played my role of "Other" Woman with aplomb, never letting my true thoughts about my love slip out. If you remember my over-the-top ravings about Luke's magnificence, you can understand why I was mesmerized by him but, I also was a dyed-in-the-wool New Yorker. This meant that I considered anyone outside of New York a bit unsophisticated.

Thinking back on this time in my life, my assumption that my boyfriend lacked urban polish and refinement because he lived outside of New York was very hypocritical, as I, personally, knew that not every New Yorker was cultured. Many of my New York relatives had never stepped foot in a museum, gone to the ballet or attended a performance at the Metropolitan Opera.

The Journey of an "Invisible" Woman

To put it kindly, they might be called "rough." Because my duty as an "Other" woman required me to bolster his ego, I had to be cautious not to infer anything demeaning about his style. Maybe I could just take him down a small notch to make myself feel a little more confident when I was with him.

Perhaps one of my biggest criticisms of him was that his Midwestern taste buds were quite different from mine. I grew up as the daughter of a gourmet food distributor and an Italian mother. My dad would bring home chocolate covered ants, fried grasshoppers, caviar, and other exotic foods as special treats, while my mom thought that eating was the raison d'être. In her eyes, you didn't eat to live; you lived to eat.

My Indiana boyfriend had 100 different recipes for casseroles and thought that green Jell-O was avant-garde. He loved to cook, so I had a choice to make. I could criticize him for his plebian tastes or embrace his down-home cooking. As I was still the "Other' woman, I, of course, praised his creations to the roof and instead ridiculed my family's obsession with epicurean cuisine. As dopey as it sounds, I got my sustenance just from being with him because, remember, I was still the "Other" wife-in-waiting woman.

Before I moved to Indiana, my hero constantly told me that he was going to save me, and that meant taking me away from the "awful" city that I lived in, and this was of course, New York City. What made this sentiment really ridiculous was that he told me this while we were sitting in a sophisticated, glamorous restaurant, sipping champagne, 45 stories above the city looking out at the twinkling lights. This was hardly a textbook description of an awful place to live. It was more like being the prince and princess in a fairy tale.

Sandy Camillo

I guess that I forgot to tell him that, to me, there was nothing as spectacular as what we were seeing. But I wanted to be with him, wherever, or so I thought. So again, I looked into his eyes and told him that I couldn't wait to disappear with him, as I wanted to be wherever he went. At this point, I began to wonder if I should press my boyfriend to hasten our march towards the altar, as the duties of an" Other" woman were beginning to exhaust me.

And then I got a surprising phone call. Mr. Indiana's ex-wife wanted to tell me a few things. She then proceeded to wish me well in my relationship with her soon to be ex-husband and began to fill me in on all of the things that I could look forward to in a marriage with him. I was polite and listened, and then I heard something that really rang a bell.

Every time after we finished making love, Mr. Indiana had a strange habit of declaring that his performance would really show his "ex-wife a thing or two." He explained that she used to denigrate his lovemaking skills, but my exuberant praise of his sexual prowess made it apparent that he was a master of his trade.

I was no expert in this area, but I did have a few experiences with other men that made me understand that my lover was no stud, and his ex-wife's put-downs were true; for this reason his ex-wife's revelations came as no surprise to me. I was a pretty good actress, or liar, depending on how you wanted to see it, so I moaned and groaned like someone deliriously possessed and our interactions continued to be filled with my declarations of awe about his lovemaking.

Although my actions were, undoubtedly, duplicitous, the real person that I was hurting was myself. It would be very difficult when I was no longer the "Other" woman, but was now the wife, to criticize my love for the things that I praised him for in the past. I was putting myself into a purgatory that might last many years. But as you know by now, my relationship with Luke didn't last. Although, when he dumped me, I felt like I'd never laugh again, I did recover and roared back with renewed confidence to enjoy an exciting social life, vowing never to date men on black horses again. But not all "Other" women only hurt themselves.

Divorce is difficult for everyone involved, but when there's a conniving "Other woman" second wife in the picture, substantial damage can occur. My ex-husband's second wife took her job as an "Other" woman seriously, and probably managed to restore my ex's self-esteem, which was destroyed when I divorced him, but this was at the expense of our son.

As sometimes happens, my ex and I had a brief rekindling. During this time, he told me that this woman revealed to him when they were dating that she couldn't stand our son. After we separated from each other again, my ex married this woman.

We all know that sweet nothings are not the only things that can be whispered into someone's ear as they sleep. Wife # 2 convinced my ex that he must stop seeing our son once they married, as he was a reminder of his past love for me. And he did. She might have, initially, done her duty as an "Other" woman bolstering my ex's ego, but in the end, their marriage shattered, and so did my ex's relationship with his son.

This situation was something that was beyond my ability to control and made me feel helpless and invisible. I was filled with anger at my ex-husband and his new wife. It was beyond me to understand how my ex's relationship with a woman could cause him to sever ties with his child. This was something that reinforced my belief that women could be ruthless, if it benefitted their needs, and men could often act spinelessly to accommodate a woman's demands. The real loser in this game was my son. The day would come when I'd have to explain why his father was alive but didn't choose to see him, and I knew that for my son's sake, I'd put a positive spin to the horrific betrayal, I just didn't know how.

Obviously, one of the first guidelines that an "Other" woman should remember is that innocent bystanders should never be hurt. After that guideline is followed, there are a few other qualifications that a woman needs, to be successful in her role as an "Other" woman. The "Other" woman must remain inconspicuous at all times. Your love must believe that the sun rises and sets only on him. Even if your inner voice is screaming out for you to tell him that you could have solved in five minutes the problem that he's been working on for two hours, you remain silent.

Your role commands you to live in the shadows, while the one you love makes his mark on the world. The only way that you can survive this invisibility is to remember that it is temporary. One day, you'll no longer be an "Other" woman and you'll be able to reclaim the essence of who you really are. But never forget that, even though you're no longer an "Other" woman, ultimately you will become an older woman, and when you do, you will, again, have to face the threat of becoming invisible in the world.

CHAPTER 9
MADONNA, AKA, THE BLESSED VIRGIN MARY

Now that you're no longer the "Other" woman and have comfortably settled into your new position as the "Wife," you might wake up one morning and suspect that the nausea and tiredness that you're experiencing is more than a little virus.

Although you learned about the birds and the bees many, many years ago, you're still surprised to see the little blue line appear, indicating a positive result on the pregnancy test. This news will either be joyously celebrated by you and your partner or will cast a veil of gloom over your plans for a carefree, unencumbered life.

A woman's pregnancy unabashedly announces to the world that she is no longer a chaste, innocent person. Christian women are told to model themselves after the mother of God, the Blessed Virgin Mary, but Mary was a hard act to follow, as not many of us can get pregnant without giving up our virginity.

I guess that we'll have to admit that although we may be wonder women, we, unlike Mary, still need a man to conceive a child, even if the union of our egg and his seed takes place in a laboratory. Despite how much our men love and appreciate us, women still have to carry the frequently miserable burdens of pregnancy on their own shoulders.

Some women have partners who suffer from a little understood malady named, Couvade syndrome. This is a situation in which otherwise healthy men, whose partners are expecting babies, experience pregnancy related symptoms such as weight gain, food cravings, nausea and vomiting. Nonetheless, these men will be spared the thrill of forcibly pushing or having cut out of their bodies a watermelon sized human being; that adventure is one that only the mother gets to enjoy.

I still remember starting my first labor with the claustrophobic sensation of being held prisoner in my own body. The culmination of my pregnancy felt like being carried along in the midst of a torrent of water as it cascaded from a massive waterfall. Although Mary must have been honored when the angel told her that she would give birth to God, it is probable that her contemplation of the less than pleasant actualities of childbirth also caused her a lot of anxiety.

Pregnancy and childbirth are usually commonplace events and most women never experience the scrutiny that Mary underwent, regarding her impending motherhood. Religious conservatives (Verde, 2017) portray Mary's husband, Joseph, as a geriatric man of at least ninety years of age. This concept of a grey bearded, grandfatherly Joseph underscores his non-sexual relationship with Mary. However, modern scholars have thrown a wrench into the theory of the antiquated conservative concept that Joseph was a frail, elderly old man. Today, many of these scholars believe that Joseph and Mary were the same age when they married.

Apparently, early church theologians thought that if Joseph was portrayed as much older than Mary, then her perpetual virginity would be better understood, as, unlike a virile young man, an old man past his prime would not be tempted to have conjugal relations because his libido would have already dried up.

In this sense, an old St. Joseph is a safe St. Joseph" (Catholic Straight Answers, 2021), and the most that Mary would have had to endure, regarding her purity, would be incredulous stares and snide comments about the veracity of her child's miraculous conception. If one thing is indisputable about Mary's life, it is that she would never be seen as an invisible woman.

Looking back in history, women should jump for joy that they live today, as many long-ago birthing practices were barbaric. Before the mid-1800s, women weren't given painkillers during labor, and there were harsh penalties for women who relied on folk medicine to relieve the pain. In 1591, a woman was burned at the stake for taking a painkilling herb while giving birth to twins (Epstein, 2010). Until the early 1900s, maternity wear consisted of wearing tight corsets that were thought to crush reproductive organs and suffocate babies.

Epstein points out that chainsaws were actually invented to cut and widen a woman's pelvic bone during childbirth, and this was before the invention of anesthesia. I bet that made a woman think twice before getting amorous with her partner. There are many books that contain pregnancy and childbirth horror tales filled with bizarre rituals and superstitions. Women were told to drink mare's urine and to soak her insides with manure mixed with stag's antlers to increase her fertility (Schuder, 2020, p.3). If we think that we became much better off in later decades, then how do you explain a patent that was filed in 1965 for a machine that would spin a pregnant woman around at 7G until the baby was flung out by the force? (Epstein, 2010)

Sandy Camillo

Although modern childbirth is not as exciting as it was in the past, I'm sure that we all know some interesting stories. I gave birth to my first child at the age of 20. Throughout my pregnancy I enjoyed the adulation of my family and friends. Every part of the experience highlighted my important role in bringing a human being into the world, or so my hormone-affected emotions convinced me.

I felt like I was floating on a cloud high above the inconsequential activities of the rest of the world. I was mother earth and nothing could top that! Unfortunately, my return to the real world was quick and ugly. LABOR... they don't call it that for nothing! My first birth experience illuminated many realities of being a woman and mother. In my ninth month, I recall feeling frightened as to what was ahead of me and thinking that the worse part of it was that I couldn't stop it from happening.

This was truly a situation that left me feeling out of control. All of the encouragement from my parents and husband was meaningless, because no amount of determination and effort on my part could make my labor any easier. It was just me, me alone. I had spent so much of my life emphasizing my singularity and identity, and now I just wanted to escape from myself.

My firstborn made me sweat it out for 21 hours before he decided to come into the world. When he was born, the attitude of the medical world towards childbirth was, "Drug 'Em Up.'" Although that may sound idyllic, it was anything but that. Most, but not all hospitals, allowed fathers into delivery rooms. My hospital, unfortunately, did not, and therefore I was alone.

Perhaps, they realized that the drug nicknamed "twilight sleep," which was conscious sedation, would make any interaction between mom and dad impossible, especially if given in large amounts. Therefore, the Hospital determined

The Journey of an "Invisible" Woman

that there was no point in allowing a woman's partner to take part in the delivery process, since the mom was virtually deaf, dumb and blind while under the spell of twilight sleep. This drug was abandoned when it was noted that some time after giving birth, some women started to remember the traumatic effects of their childbirth experience, and were not happy with their memories.

I was one of those unlucky women who, as my amnesia dissipated, had small snippets of memory come back to me. I recalled being alone in a small, squalid room, thrashing on the bed and screaming for someone to do something to stop the pain. I lay in that room for 21 hours and at some point, during that time, I started hallucinating about scary-looking aliens staring down at me while babbling questions in an indecipherable language. As I came out from under the drug's effect, I was able to begin to distinguish fact from fantasy.

I realized that during my long labor, there were never any actual threats to my safety from alien life forms, but that didn't change the extreme fear that I must have felt while sedated. The drug's promise of a pain free labor proved to be a fallacy. Meanwhile, my life-altering experience didn't cause a ripple in the minds of the hospital personnel, as they viewed what I had endured as a daily, commonplace event. To them, I was just one more person in a long line of young pregnant women who came screaming into the hospital, asking for attention because in their own eyes they were someone special.

The revelation that, to the hospital personnel, I was just a typical complaining, entitled woman, was especially hideous because I'd dedicated my entire life to establishing my uniqueness. To make it worse, my hospital stay extended into Thanksgiving Day, and on that day I was alone. My family had decided to skip their visit and instead they stayed at home to enjoy their feast. It appeared that, once again, I was the forgotten third child.

Not every woman's pregnancy ends with the woman getting a photo of herself groggily struggling to sit up in bed while holding a little bundle of joy. The other side of this coin is the pregnant woman who, for whatever reason, finds herself having to terminate her pregnancy. In 1970, abortion, prior to the 24th week of pregnancy, was legalized in New York State.

This was three years before the passage in 1973 of Roe V. Wade that decriminalized it for the entire United States. This new legislation meant that women no longer had to self-induce abortions by using hangers, or by throwing themselves down the staircase or having them done by incompetent practitioners with questionable motives.

One of my close friends, Elizabeth, was fortunate that abortion was declared legal a few months before she decided to terminate her pregnancy. She was a Catholic, and had been raised to emulate Mary the Madonna, and yet she was determined to stick to her decision. She made an appointment with her regular gynecologist, and in a few days, was checking into the hospital where her doctor did his surgeries. Although what Elizabeth was doing was totally legal, the doctor and staff treated her as if she was a criminal and this treatment magnified her Catholic guilt over what she was doing.

Elizabeth often repeated to me a story about her daughter and Gloria Steinem. Her daughter had attended a speech given by Ms. Steinem, in which she candidly reflected on the illegal abortion she had at the age of 22 and inferred to the audience that this abortion allowed her to become her best self. Elizabeth and her daughter discussed how it would be possible for a person to become their best self if they did something that they believed was morally wrong. Adhering to the tenets of their faith, they concluded that if life began at conception, then abortion was the act of killing.

They also admitted that, just like when considering euthanasia, there were sometimes reasons to kill; but, unlike Gloria Steinem's opinion, this act wouldn't make them their *best* selves, and for them, would only result in feelings of guilt. Elizabeth's guilt resulted in recurring dreams, featuring Mary sadly shaking her head and weeping over her decision to end a life. Pregnancy, resulting in either the birth of a child or its termination, unalterably affects the course of a woman's future in ways that men never encounter.

The transformation of my life occurred after my first child; a son was born. "Me" became "We." This "we" was different from the "we" of marriage. In marriage, a man and woman become a couple, sharing a life and responsibilities, but with each maintaining their own identities. In the relationship between a mother and child, the mother is the nurturer; she provides unconditional love to her child.

This love provides the foundation for the physical, emotional, and social development of a child. Unlike marriage, there is no divorce that can end the relationship between mother and child, no matter how difficult the relationship. Actually, saying that "me," became "we," after my son was born is not quite accurate as a description of our relationship.

Part of my essence became part of my child, so what once had belonged only to me, was now also part of him. You might think that this sounds freaky or that this idea could be incorporated into a plot for a sci-fi movie, but there's no better way that I can describe the intensity of this newly created bond.

The lifestyle change brought about by having a child drastically altered my priorities. I realized that attaining the pinnacle of success was a multifaceted goal. I would continue to tirelessly work to attain professional prominence, but this accomplishment wasn't any longer the only objective in my life. The world might finally see me as a shining star, but there were many stars in the sky; in my son's eyes I wasn't just any bright star, but the only one, and to me that was real success.

Unlike Mary, my birthing experience didn't end with having one child. I did it three more times, and with each one my life expanded. Maybe I would never become a famous person, but because of my children, the story of my life would never be forgotten.

CHAPTER 10
THE GOOD MOM

If all the pregnancy and childbirth horror stories haven't convinced you take an oath to never become a parent, then you're ready to talk about how motherhood can diminish a woman's ability to excel professionally and personally.

You don't have to be a mom to understand the sentiments in this chapter. You just need to open up your heart and acknowledge the hypocrisy that exists in certain values revolving around motherhood. Society venerates a woman who chooses to become a mother, and yet it expects her to give up her ambitions once she becomes a mother and be satisfied, assuming the responsibilities of a puppet monarch of a small domain. I gave birth to four children, but if I chose to remain childless, I would have still been the same person mentally, emotionally and morally.

You notice I didn't say physically because the sagging skin on my stomach would repudiate my words. Although parenting my children was a time and energy consuming job, I never lost sight of my plan to establish myself as a person who wields power and influence in the world.

The subject of motherhood is fraught with conflicting emotions because women experience many feelings when contemplating becoming a parent. There is a vast dichotomy between society's vision of motherhood and a woman's innermost thoughts about the experience. But you are entitled to your choice, regardless of whether your desire is to have a child and be a stay-at-home mom, remain childless, or be a mom who works 24/7 at a high-powered profession. There is nothing that innately controls what you will do, or how you will do it.

Throughout history the concept of maternal instinct or "baby fever" has fostered the idea that women are specially wired to yearn for motherhood. It wasn't until the 1960s and 1970s that this idea was challenged and the pendulum swung to the other side. *The Dialectic of Sex,* written in 1970 by Shulamith Firestone, sparked controversy with the radical statement about motherhood that "subjugation of the self to the needs of others is the antithesis of liberation." (Firestone, 1970).

Women began to doubt the directives passed down through generations that they not only should be mothers, but they should also ache for that privilege. Men, on the other hand, had been taught that one day they might become a parent, but they shouldn't lose sight of the first priority in their lives, which was their profession.

There is clearly confusion in a woman's mind about how her role as a potential mother would coexist with her professional aspirations. Perhaps, she chooses not to be a mother at all, or is unable to biologically give birth and instead decides to adopt a child. If a woman decides to become a parent, does that mean that she has agreed to substitute her determination to ascend the corporate ladder for pretending excitement at spending endless days watching the Disney Channel with her children? A man's desire to have children would probably evaporate if this were his fate.

The Journey of an "Invisible" Woman

Social mores deem it unnatural for a woman to lack "nurturing" qualities. Although society makes a point of praising women who have broken through the glass ceiling, eyebrows are raised if that woman is a mother. Obviously, she is neglecting her "real" work.

Anthropologist Sarah Blaffer Hrdy has done research that disputes the theorem that women are born with the maternal instinct. She maintains that bumps in the hormone oxytocin result in parent child bonding in, not just biological mothers but also adoptive parents, fathers, and grandparents. She cites experiments to illustrate the "maternal instinct" fallacy by using female virgin lab mice, who after hearing the cries of young mice pups, would respond by either ignoring the pups or cannibalizing them.

The mice were then injected with oxytocin. They stopped cannibalizing and learned to care for the pups. The scientists then injected the male mice, and they too became nurturing caretakers. The maternal instinct for these creatures was created in a laboratory. As Hrdy contends, it was not present because of an inborn special gender trait (Gibbens, 2018).

Ignoring scientific research, in the hopes of proving that a woman is genetically ordained to eagerly anticipate tending children as her primary duty in life, I've heard people authoritatively comment that all female mammals are naturally nurturing. A great example of the fallacy of this assumption is seen in nature, when we study the parenting habits of the male marmoset. The mom gives birth and then the male marmoset immediately takes over the caretaking duties once the baby marmoset is born (Byner & Pappas, 2011). I'm sure that many women would jump for joy if men could take parenting lessons from the male marmoset, but it's unlikely to happen anytime soon.

In the 1950s *Leave it to Beaver* world, everyone took seriously the cliché that the mom's place was ideally in the home. Following this mandate wasn't a problem for a woman who had married a "man of substance," but depressed economic circumstances would sometimes demand that women be required to work out of the home.

If this was the case, their opportunities for employment were usually limited to blue collar, service or clerical jobs, as these were considered fitting positions for a woman. Today, a woman has many career choices and both parents often work out of the home because of escalated financial need or professional aspirations.

Nonetheless, after the birth of a child, questions regarding caretaking decisions are usually directed to just the woman, underlying the implication that caretaking is her real job. Magically, society transports her back in time and in an instant, generations of sexist ideas and structures become the basis for a judgment of her actions.

Social norms stipulate that a man must return to work after the birth of a child or he's a slacker, yet the same benchmark is not used when understanding a woman's relationship between family and career. A woman's love for her children doesn't preclude her longing to achieve prominence in her professional life.

Yet, because of gender discrimination, a woman's character is judged defective if she rejects the traditional role of woman, as the main caregiver. She is also viewed as heretical for admitting that she adores her child, but that she would take a bullet to the head before she'd want to stay at home with her child full time. The best caretaker for a child is the one who can ensure the most successful outcome in the child's emotional and intellectual development, and the requisite qualifications to achieve this goal aren't specific to the gender or biological relationship of the caretaker to the child.

The Journey of an "Invisible" Woman

Extensive research has been conducted regarding the significance of caregiving as it relates to the socio-intellectual development of the child. Olson, Bates & Bayle's article in *Developmental Psychology* states, "mother-child cognitive interactions predict mental and verbal development in children" (Olson& Bayles, 1984). In addition, in Borstein's research it was found that "parental speech directed to young children is crucial for early child development" (Bornstein, 1992).

Would a child's mental and verbal development suffer if the word "caretaker" was substituted for "mother" in Olson, Bates & Bayles statement?

Many women decide that they need or want to leave the caregiving duties to someone else. As of 2019, nearly 30 percent of infants and toddlers attend home-based childcare as their primary arrangement, while 23.4 percent of children under the age of five are in some organized child care arrangement, which includes day care centers, nurseries and pre-schools (Paschall, 2019).

When I was a young mother, I was certain that my formal education would enable me to ensure the exponential growth of my children's intellectual advancement. In my teacher training courses, I learned the latest trends in child development and was eager to use them in parenting my children. But after playing Chutes and Ladders for the fiftieth time with my first child, I realized that I would be trusting my children's intellectual and emotional development to someone else, because the siren call of a stimulating a career was beckoning to me.

The guilt started to overwhelm me as I worried that, perhaps, my children would get the short end of the stick because I selfishly was thinking of my own gratification. I knew that many paid home child caretakers have a minimal education and, or speak English as a second language.

Although, these caretakers appreciate the importance of literacy and intellectual development, they might not be able to provide the same intellectual stimulation to my children as I could.

I also knew that children needed to be raised in a happy environment if they were to thrive. If I gave up my career, my misery would supersede any academic enrichment that I could offer to them. Does this mean that the responsibility of raising a "perfect, super achieving" child lies totally with the mother, even if this responsibility means that to be a "Good Mother" she must put her professional ambitions on the back burner.

Generations of women have been told that they could climb as high as they wanted on the ladder to personal and professional prominence. The one caveat that wasn't mentioned was that once they became mothers, it would be expected that they direct their energies to caregiving and accept that their personal dreams needed to be delayed or forgotten.

There are fantastic women who willingly choose to be home caregivers, to personally experience those once in a lifetime moments happening in a child's life, and this may fulfill their dreams; but this is a choice that they should be free, and not coerced, into making.

There is no evidence that shows the desire to receive affirmation for accomplishments is less present in women than in men and yet ambition in women is sometimes viewed in a negative light. Studies of gender such as the Bem Sex Role Inventory reveals that the two basic traits of femininity are that femininity exists only in the context of a relationship, and that a woman must be providing something for another person. Ambition is not ranked as a top feminine trait. Many ambitious women scream out in anger when confronted with this failure to acknowledge their willingness

The Journey of an "Invisible" Woman

to strive for the attainment of some type of achievement, such as power, honor, fame or wealth.

If a woman decides that she wants to be a parent but not a full-time caretaker, can she withstand the guilt that might arise from her not being everyone's definition of a "good mother"? A woman might escape these vague feelings that she has not quite fulfilled her duties as a parent, but instead be filled with anger over the unbalance in society's attitude towards her and her husband's parental responsibilities.

As a working mother, I had to overcome many obstacles in my career, not to be assigned to the infamous corporate "Mommy track." I was never able to accept the guilt over my parenting choices, but I think in the eyes of my children, I was a "Good Mom" because I am, and will always be, the person who loves them just because they exist.

CHAPTER 11
I (DON'T) GOT YOU, BABE

No two women are the same. Some of their differences are obvious because they are easy to discern. Some women are wives, mothers, single, childless or are an Other woman. You don't have to guess about their relationship status, as it's not something that people attempt to hide. However, some women have things going on in in their lives that are never seen by others and that segregate them in a special place where few women want to visit. And yet, for many women, this ugly place is a part of their lives.

We are all influenced by what we hear and see in different media communications. Many of these narratives focus on the activities of famous people and expose misogynistic relationships between famous women and the men whom they love. I was intrigued by what I've learned about three of these women who were so famous that they are immediately recognized by just their first names: Cher, Paulina and Tina. Seemingly, they had it all—wealth, beauty, and fame—but under all the glitter were women suffering from low self-esteem and humiliation.

Sonny and Cher were one of Rock and Roll's hottest couples of the 1960s and 1970s, and their duets, "I Got You

The Journey of an "Invisible" Woman

Babe" and "The Beat Goes On" were sensational successes. But everything wasn't kisses and happy days for the couple, and because of their problems; they eventually split up as husband and wife. Although Cher's success in her career had eclipsed Sonny's success, she always felt that she was the subservient partner in the relationship.

Cher was quoted saying, "He treated me more like a golden goose than his wife." She also claimed that Sonny had constantly demeaned her looks and intelligence, yet she stayed with him for eleven years. She cited "involuntary servitude" as the reason for the split; nonetheless, Cher said that Sonny did a good job of looking after her.

Why would a woman with money and public adulation endure treatment that she equated to enslavement? Although Cher was successful in the eyes of the world, she apparently subscribed to the notion that she needed a man to take care of her. My mother would have approved. Cher's father was a drug-addicted gambler who divorced her mother and abandoned Cher when she was ten months old.

Cher's search for a father was fulfilled when she met Sonny. Not only was he much older than she, but also according to Cher's mother, Sonny was the spitting image of Cher's father. Conveniently, Sonny was more than eager to fill the role of father, and even did his best to replicate her birth father's mean personality. As Cher explained about Sonny's demeanor, "He could be real tough; I couldn't stand on my own two feet and talk back to him." Sonny was eager to take care of Cher, as long as she did what he said.

Sonny's and Cher's relationship perfectly illustrates a woman's willingness to lose her true self in the pursuit of love. As so often happens, Cher was blinded by love and was unable to recognize that Sonny wasn't just controlling her emotions, but he was also playing games with their finances, games that Cher was destined to lose.

Sonny had formed a corporation that he named after Cher. That sounded like a loving act, however, she discovered that 95% of the company was owned by her husband, with the remaining 5% held by their lawyer. Sonny had also convinced Cher to sign a restrictive contract that prevented her from taking any jobs without him, because he recognized that she was the main attraction.

She would be released from the contract only if she participated with Sonny in performances in shows with an anticipated $1,000,000 in revenue. Her identity was now totally entwined with his, and he was tightly holding her future in his hands. But maintaining control of Cher through money wasn't enough. He also attempted to gain sole custody of their child. And yet, even with all of his disgusting behavior, when Sonny died, Cher read the eulogy at his funeral and effusively praised Sonny at the ceremony.

Cher had fame and money, but she constantly questioned her self-worth, and had to work hard at convincing herself that she could be successful without Sonny. Her perseverance in working towards success in her career never wavered, and eventually she became known as the Goddess of Pop, because of her embodiment of female autonomy in a male-dominated industry. But it didn't come easy, babe.

Famous woman might be worshipped by the world, but behind the scenes these same celebrities might meekly accept a subservient role in their relationships with their partners. Paulina Porizkova was the Golden Girl and Super Star model of the 1980s. After establishing herself as a top model in Paris, she made a name for herself in the United States when she posed in swimwear in *Sports Illustrated*. She eventually landed many multi-million-dollar contracts with major beauty and fashion icons.

You'd definitely think that this lady could hold her own in maintaining her self–esteem, but you'd be wrong.

The Journey of an "Invisible" Woman

Apparently, her 28-year marriage to Ric Ocasek, the front man for the rock group, The Cars, led her to doubt her worth. In describing the collapse of her marriage, Paulina quotes words in the poem "Bride" that was written by Maggie Smith and published in the New Yorker on January 27, 2020. These words are applicable to many of us:

"How long have I been alone in this house, but not alone? Married less to the man than to the woman silvering with the mirror."

Believing in the strength of their marriage, Paulina had put her life's earnings from modeling into the marriage, which is a common theme in many marriages. The co-joining of assets is interpreted as an expression of trust, but that trust is never tested until kisses turn into curses. Paulina and Ric's days of kisses eventually came to an end, and in 2017 the couple started divorce proceedings, but strangely enough, continued to live together amicably. Suddenly, her husband had to undergo surgery for life threatening cardiovascular disease.

Although the marriage was at its end, Paulina remembered the love that they had shared, and therefore she decided to take over the task of Ric's aftercare. Days slowly passed in Ric's recuperation. Several months after Ric's surgery, Paulina and their two sons were getting dinner ready and looking forward to watching TV together, later that evening. She decided to bring Ric a cup of coffee in his room and was horrified to find him dead in his chair.

Paulina became even more horrified when she found out that Ric had been busy, prior to his death, writing her out of his will. And yet, instead of outrage at her husband's duplicity, Paulina commented after his death that she couldn't imagine a life without him, as "being with a man who possessed me, who fully possessed me, was really comforting."

Was there something unique about Paulina's life that made her welcome being controlled by a man? Her early years had been difficult. She was born in Czechoslovakia and, as a toddler, she was separated from her parents and not reunited with them for seven years, after a lengthy legal battle with the Czechoslovak authorities.

At the age of fifteen she was discovered and started modeling. She quickly rose to fame as a model, author and television and movie actress. These achievements are the very definition of the accomplishments of a successful woman and yet, Paulina became more dependent on Ric, the older she became.

Also, remember that this is a woman whose combined net worth with her husband in 2019 was 80 million dollars, with much of this money coming from her achievements. Yet now, after her husband's death, she would have to fight for what was rightfully hers.

Perhaps, when Paulina married Ric, she chose to take a step back from being in the limelight and instead let her husband bask in its light, thinking that their love would then become a perfect fairy tale.

However, at the age of 54, she realized that society no longer considered her a young woman, and that her glory days might be behind her. In an interview, Paulina said that, as an older woman, she had been dismissed from the table. Her words, poignantly, describe a woman's sadness at her recognition of her waning importance in life.

There are numerous famous women whose names are immediately recognizable to each of us and yet these women chose to carefully dim their light so their partners can shine more brightly. Perhaps one of the most moving stories about one of these women involves the magnificent Tina Turner. It's doubtful that there's anyone who hasn't seen a movie, television show or read a book detailing the mental and physical abuse she endured from her husband, Ike.

The images of her bloodied and broken body are indisputable evidence of her victimization, but these physical attacks would eventually mend. As horrific as this abuse was, the verbal assaults and humiliations were what destroyed her spirit. Ike's domination of Tina was so complete that Tina even received orders as to what she should eat. She complied with even this form of debasement, until the day that something inside of her snapped and she said, NO! and claimed her identity. Even fame and fortune doesn't guarantee a woman's ability to assert her selfhood.

Like Cher, Paulina, and Tina, there are many women who subjugate their needs to others because of a romantic relationship; then there are some who do so, because they think that it is the only way to advance in their careers. Thinking back to the Roger Ailes sexual harassment fiasco at Fox news, it becomes clear that even seemingly powerful women fall prey to male misogynists who only view women as pretty playthings to be used and then disposed of when a new model comes along.

Thank God for the "Me Too" movement, which has shed light on numerous women who chose not to disappear into the background when their "services" are no longer desirable.

In the chapter, I've used three highly visible women to show the damage inflicted on a woman's self-esteem, as the result of toxic relationships, but this destruction is even more common in the lives of average women. My friend, Mary, was one of those women. She wouldn't accept that her husband was having multiple affairs, even though he was constantly seen all over town with his sweethearts.

One day, her parents saw Mary's husband on the street, engaging in a passionate kiss with one of his other women.

Sandy Camillo

Finally, Mary was forced to take action, but told everyone that she wished she never knew anything about her husband's infidelities so that she could still be with him.

She felt that she truly didn't exist without him. When they got married, Mary took the words, "and two shall become one flesh" to heart; only what she didn't understand was that it meant that the two are now joined together, not that one person has disappeared.

An article in Psychology Today reports that research shows that women lose twice as much self-esteem as men after a breakup, but, because they search for what went wrong in the relationship, they develop great perceptivity regarding future relationships.

On the other hand, a man's testosterone levels drops when he enters a relationship with a woman and another hormone, oxytocin, is released, which makes him more susceptible to bonding, but once he decides to exit a relationship, the testosterone goes back up and he's back in the game.

Although both genders suffer from a breakup, a man is quicker to start a new relationship, because he is hormonally influenced to do so, while a woman remains busy analyzing every minuscule thing that she may have done wrong.

However, there is an upside to all of this for a woman. Because a woman spends hours in self-reflection, she will hopefully know what warning signs to pay attention to in her next relationship, but awareness doesn't always lead to corrective action.

When Mr. Indiana dumped me, I made a promise to myself that never again would I lose myself to another person. After returning from my Midwestern interlude, my friends remarked that I seemed different, and I was. I remembered that, as a young girl, I thought that I had a very special place in the world, and I became determined to claim that spot for myself again. I may not be Cher, Paulina or Tina but I'll make sure that before my light is extinguished, it shines on as many people in the world as possible.

CHAPTER 12
THE DEADLINE

I was back in New York from my short residency in Indiana and trying to get over the heartbreak of finding out that my knight on a white horse was more like a devil on a donkey. But now I was a woman with a newly awakened sense of her value, and I knew that value commanded a high price in the game of love. The starry-eyed, naïve young girl was gone and in her place was a sophisticated, slightly jaded woman determined to take her rightful place in the world.

When I wasn't working or taking care of my young son, I was spending my time dating half of the bachelors in New York. I was caught up in the thrill of finally experiencing what most people did while in college, as my college years were spent as a wife and young mother and my social life revolved around the children's playground.

Now it was my time to dazzle New York with my presence. I was young, educated and I knew that the world was mine for the taking. All I needed was the perfect mate. Once I could check this accomplishment off my list, I'd be able to get on to the task of making my mark on society. Looking back on these thoughts, I laugh at my typically youthful foolishness at that time, in believing that I had the blueprint for success.

Although I certainly wasn't lacking in ambition, I didn't have a clue about the number of obstacles that I'd have to overcome to achieve my goals. Yes, I was educated, but it was a textbook education. I was attractive to men, but lots of women were pleasing to men. I had a lot to learn about the real world and there were some major surprises coming my way.

Therefore, I continued my marathon dating. Although all of these bachelors were eligible to date casually, they didn't have the characteristics that I believed were essential in a husband and father. Even though it might sound strange that I was thinking about marriage at such an early point in my new dating career, you have to remember that I also had a five-year old son.

For me, daddy qualities were an important trait in a boyfriend, and that trait wasn't easily unmasked. In addition, after my experience with Mr. Indiana, I avoided like the plague men who were narcissists. A man's good looks might initially be exciting, but intellectual stimulation, trustworthiness and kindness were more important in the long run.

Is it possible that I was finally maturing and using my head as well as my heart as I searched for a new partner? I knew the type of man I wanted, but it didn't mean that a man with such specific qualifications was easy to find.

Despite what may be perceived as a difficult task, it was easier than I thought to eliminate the oddballs. For instance, there was an interesting man with a Ph.D. from New York University. He was intelligent, handsome, sexy, and down to earth. He seemed to have the whole package until he explained why he was working part time as a janitor, instead of holding a high-level position in medicine, law or corporate America.

He said that he had the perfect job because it gave him the chance to occasionally sleep during the day and this was very important to him, as he might still feel groggy from snorting too much cocaine the night before. Obviously, he wasn't husband or daddy material.

Another potential match seemed too good to be true, and as it turned out it was. This man checked off all the right boxes to qualify as a potential mate. He was smart, funny, humble, cute, respectful, and held a steady job. What more could you ask? Unfortunately, he taught me the lesson that everyone has secrets and some of them were dating deal-breakers. His secret was that he was particularly excited about dating me, because without my knowledge, he was also dating my sister. Apparently, dating sisters was the fulfillment of one of his major fantasies.

It didn't take long before my sister and I shared a conversation about the great guys we were dating. We realized , quickly, that it sounded like we were actually dating the same guy. This discovery wasn't as easy back then as it would be today.

Back then, there were no cellphone cameras to capture a potential pervert's image on Instagram or Facebook. Our guy was also shrewd enough to use a different name with each of us. To confirm our suspicions, we had to come up with a plan to positively unveil his true identity. I invited our mutual boyfriend to my apartment to watch television.

As we sat together holding hands on the sofa, my sister suddenly popped out of the closet. It was interesting to watch our guy jump up and begin stammering his protestations against the unfairness of our trap. Either he was more than a little nuts, or he really didn't think that he did anything wrong, because he had a distorted sense of morality.

The Journey of an "Invisible" Woman

We asked him to leave, using his own two feet or we'd carry him out. Nobody messed with two Italian sisters. Our mutual boyfriend was lucky to escape his little adventure with all his parts intact.

I was beginning to think that I should remain a single mom and just enjoy the New York City dating scene. Prior to my entanglement with Luke and subsequent move to Indiana, I was employed as a director at a top rated, two hundred student preschool.

This was an achievement for a young woman just out of graduate school, but I had abruptly resigned from that position to follow my man. Now that I was back in New York, I was ready for adventure. For me that meant putting aside my background in education and finding a position in a field where I could spread my wings and experience the excitement that was New York City. In my mind, this meant that my search should focus on something involving the media, as one of my lifetime passions had always been to be a journalist.

Unfortunately, any job that I'd be able to get was entry level and had nothing to do with becoming a mover and shaker in any part of a communications organization. I was hired rapidly and just as rapidly quit two low ranking jobs. The first of those jobs was working at the *Village Voice* newspaper, in the hope that it would satisfy my interest in being a journalist. Instead, I actually spent each day placing classified ads for people.

The second job was promising, as I was hired as an editorial assistant at Cambridge Book Company. There was just one problem, and that was that the job pretty much consisted of doing nothing all day. The other assistants loved having endless free time to relax and read their personal books, but I was going crazy with boredom.

Sandy Camillo

Finally, there was hope. I was offered a job at International Famous Agency (IFA), a theatrical management company. Although I was overly qualified for the position, I was hired in the accounts payable department, where all I did was balance accounts.

As I was juggling numbers, I could hear snippets of conversations between the agents about the latest movie star signed up by the agency, and my adrenaline raced to be part of this world. Little did I know that my employment at this organization would not be a beneficial step up my career ladder. However, my position at IFA would play a pivotal part in my finally identifying the perfect man to be my husband and the father of my children.

I was in no rush to quit this latest job, as each day at work provided me with a new opportunity to daydream about various scenarios that would place me in the center of the action at the agency. For example, I envisioned an agent stopping at my desk to ask me if I ever thought about acting for a career.

OK, so maybe I wasn't quite that mature yet, if I thought that I was now even a small part of this glamorous world, but I considered this job as a stepping stone to my eventual fame and fortune. I didn't know what would make me famous, but I knew it would happen. I guess you could add the word delusional to my dreams, but I was very young and the greatest challenges of life were still ahead of me. But before I'd be able to meet those challenges, I still had to find the perfect mate.

Valentine's Day was for lovers, but the year that I worked at the theatrical agency, I found myself alone on that holiday. A friend from work and I decided to go out for a drink to celebrate. The company had given out hearts filled with candy to everyone, so my 19-year-old friend decided that we should bring our candy with us to share. Keep in mind that

The Journey of an "Invisible" Woman

in 1975 the legal drinking age in New York was 19. Although my friend was therefore "legal," she wasn't an experienced drinker. After visiting the first bar, which was rather quiet, my friend decided that we needed to find somewhere more exciting.

Our next stop was Brandy's, which back then was a popular singles bar with live music. By now, my friend was pretty smashed and was going from person to person sharing her candy. Feeling somewhat responsible for her welfare, I closely watched her so that no one would think that they were going to get more than candy from her. My chaperoning duties were over when she finally decided to call a taxi and go home.

During our stay at Brandy's, I had remained seated at the bar next to a very quiet young man. We exchanged a few words about the silliness of youth, although we were also being slightly ridiculous, as we were only 7 years older than my friend. As it got later, the alcohol started to kick in, and as sometimes happens when people are drinking, this man and I started to talk seriously about life and past relationships.

The young man that I was speaking with had remarkably brilliant blue eyes, and something clicked when I looked into them. I felt drawn to him in a way that I hadn't felt in a long time. I questioned myself to be sure that I wasn't just romanticizing the moment because I was hypnotized by those dreamy eyes, but it quickly became clear that he cared about what I was telling him and somehow shared many of my dreams. Blue Eye's name was John.

Our conversation revealed that his cousin worked at the same agency where I was working. In a city of millions, this connection seemed significant and elevated him from stranger status to friend. As it was raining, I found myself offering him a ride back to his apartment. In today's culture this would have been comparable to walking down a dark alley in a dangerous neighborhood, but in the 1970s, people in singles' bars thought that forming instant relationships was normal.

However, I wasn't completely trusting, after my experience with Luke. I couldn't wait to get to work the next day, to ask John's cousin about him and verify that he was legitimately a good guy and not another schmuck.

When we got to John's luxury building on the Upper East Side, Blue Eyes pecked me on the cheek, said goodnight and got out of the car. He was either one of the few remaining gentleman left in New York, or I wasn't attractive to him. In any case, he made a definite impression on me that night, and I had the foresight to give him my phone number.

I expected a call the next day, but it never came. I thought that we had hit it off, but my radar must have been wrong. Two weeks went by before the call came. I shocked myself by saying yes when he asked me to meet him in a restaurant in the City in an hour. The dating playbook made it very clear that a girl had to play hard to get, and clearly, meeting shortly after being invited out violated all the dating rules.

But quite honestly, I was intrigued by his aloofness, and agreed to meet. Blue Eyes told me later that he purposely held off calling me immediately, as he gathered from my stories that I was a bit bruised from my previous relationships.

On our third date, Blue Eyes asked me to marry him. I told him he had six months, and that if we weren't married by then, the relationship was over. I was willing to remain single, but if Blue Eyes really loved me, then he loved me, and we should get married. I had a son, and my days of playing games had to end. If I wanted to reach my professional goals, I needed to get back on track to

The Journey of an "Invisible" Woman

developing my skills and accomplishments with the support of the right man.

There were two things that I really loved in life. One was my family and the other was my little red fiat convertible that I never let anyone touch. Shortly after I met John, my father invited me and my son to accompany him and my mother on a business trip to Europe. Even though I had known John for only a few weeks, something was telling me that he was the real deal, and therefore I agreed to leave my little red Fiat with John during my absence. Now, John had my heart and my car, and we had our deadline.

CHAPTER 13
A PROPOSAL, ITALIAN STYLE

It looked like John was determined to make my designated deadline and one day soon I would be a married woman again. A big difference this time around is that I'd have a man walking with me down the road towards success rather than trying to pull me down a road leading away from my dreams. I wondered whether John would plan a traditional or creative proposal.

These thoughts eventually led me to become curious about the entire concept of a man's proposal of marriage to a woman. I was startled to realize that a proposal is one of those rare times when a woman eagerly and willingly takes second seat to a man. The proposal is the first test of many in a marriage. Woman imagines the proposal as a magical experience. On the other hand, many men naively believe that the process simply involves their nervously uttering the words, "Will you marry me? To make matters worse, many women use romantic movie proposals as a barometer to judge the perfect proposal.

Unrealistic expectations about proposals penetrate a woman's psyche very early in her life. Most of us remember Prince Charming's proposal to Cinderella. Men might smugly point out that Charming ultimately didn't say much more than the words, "Will you marry me?"

But if these men want to hold up Charming as a role model, then they'd need to also experience the hell Charming had to endure in order to find and be with Cinderella. Movies successfully provide the quintessential inspiration for grand romantic gestures through their portrayal of memorable proposals.

My friends and I have spent many hours together, debating which movie proposal is the best embodiment of the ideal declaration of love. After several heated discussions, we finally agreed on these several finalists for best movie proposal:

Walk the Line, when Johnny Cash proposes to June onstage in front of 7,000 people.

The Wedding Singer as Robbie serenades Julia over the loud speaker of a plane with a song he wrote, "Grow Old with You".

Love Story when Oliver says he wants to marry Jenny. She asks "Why?" and he says "Because."

When Harry Met Sally as Harry proposes to Sally under the wire at midnight on New Year's Eve saying he can't wait another minute to spend his life with her.

However, we were still having difficulty picking our winner from the list of these great proposals. During one of our chats, we agreed that the traditional words, "Will you marry me?" are sometimes not even used in the most impressive proposals, and yet the man's intent to marry is still clear in his use of other endearing words or grand romantic gestures.

As my friends and I continued our discourse, we couldn't help but notice that we hadn't made any reference to the elephant in the room. One of my friends remarked that it seems that the man has all the power and control in a proposal since he is the initiator of the event. I reminded her that, although it's true that the man asks for a woman's hand in marriage, nonetheless, she retains ultimate control of the situation, because she is the one who rejects or accepts the proposal.

I'm sure that, like me and my friends, you have a favorite movie proposal that, for a moment, makes you forget all your ambitions and swoon as you're caught up in the depiction of love's raptures. Although I wish you could share your pick with me, I'm sure that you'd like to know which proposal was declared winner of the debate. Which one do you think we picked?

Before I announce the winning proposal, I should probably tell you that my friends and I cheated in our choice of best proposal. We picked one that wasn't a finalist and wasn't even technically a proposal, as the objective of the winning proposal wasn't marriage. Despite this, we were convinced that the entire movie was a monumental declaration of a man's love for, and commitment to, his true love.

The movie, for those of you who didn't guess (although you wouldn't know unless you were a clairvoyant) is *The Notebook*. Take a look at Noah's words to Allie. He said, and our hearts fluttered, "So it's not gonna be easy, it's gonna be really hard. And we're gonna have to work at this every day, but I wanna do that because I want you. I want all of you, forever. You and me. Every day." (Cleary, 2019, p.1). Noah captured the essence of what every woman in her innermost core wants to hear from the man she hopes to spend her life with. If a man ever wanted a cheat sheet to guide him in melting any woman's heart, he'd just have to plagiarize Noah's words expressing his devotion to Allie. Of course, he'd need to be sure to clean up some of the grammar to get rid of the wannas and gonnas.

Although real life proposals will probably never compare with the mesmerizing drama of movie proposals, the story of my proposal might be considered a type of unusual tragicomedy. Clearly, the story of my proposal may not be ready for prime time. It could, however, possibly be a contender for a filler on late night television, as people aren't too choosey about what they watch, when they're almost comatose at four o'clock in the morning.

Let me set the stage for you to explain the slightly bizarre background of Blue Eyes's proposal to me. Our proposal began like a dream with two lovers gazing into each other's eyes over a candlelight dinner, but quickly morphed into a Greek tragedy starring Italian actors.

Getting married in an Italian family was not only an event between the bride and groom, but also an occasion to establish relationships with the couple's families. The success of many Italian marriages often depends on whether the family accepts the proposed mate.

My first husband didn't measure up to any of the requisite educational or social qualifications, but even that could be overlooked if he possessed the most important characteristic, and that was being of Italian ancestry. Unfortunately, he scored a zero in all categories. And then came Blue Eyes, who checked off all the boxes, but after my divorce, my parents had raised the ante. Now, a suitable mate for their precious daughter would have to be a candidate for sainthood.

After a very brief whirlwind romance, my boyfriend, Blue Eyes, innocently asked me when would be the best time to meet my parents to tell them that he wanted to marry me. Although my parents thought John was a pure Italian because of his last name, he was actually part Scandinavian.

He would proudly tell me that he was Scandinavian from the waist up but Italian from the waist down. He really admired those Valentino type Italian lovers.

I think because he had watched the Godfather too many times, he thought of himself as a modern-day Michael Corleone and was determined to imitate Michael's Italian proposal, to please my very Italian parents. He was also a real Viking. My immediate response to his exuberant desire to do the right thing with my parents was, "NEVER!" He simply smiled and told me that he would drive home from work with me the next day to have this fateful conversation.

To the average parent, the thought of an eligible young lawyer asking for their daughter's hand in marriage would be good news, especially when that daughter was divorced and living with them, with her five-year-old child. However, in my mother's eyes, she had not only gotten her daughter back home, but was also blessed with the additional bonus of an adorable child to love. My Italian mother lived for her family and hated the thought of any of us leaving her.

Her recurrent dream was of her parents, siblings, children, and grandchildren all living together under one roof. Of course, aside from her husband, the people all had to be related by blood, so in-laws were not part of this ideal scenario. My mother now had part of that dream come true and she wasn't going to give it up without a fight. Knowing her attitude, I suspected that John would not get the reception that he was hoping for with his announcement.

I woke up the day of the big meeting, thinking of the many ways I could delay the inevitable confrontation that I knew was coming, between my parents and my boyfriend. I didn't have the money to escape to a foreign country, and jumping off a bridge seemed a little extreme. My hours in the office flew by, and before I knew it, I was in John's car on the way to my parents' home. I tried, for the last time, to convince him that he didn't actually need to ask them for their permission to marry me, but since he was Italian, he knew the rules and couldn't be dissuaded. I held my breath, and we went into my parent's house.

Prior to his encounter, John had spent many evenings sitting at the kitchen table, as my mother happily fed him until he was stuffed to bursting. She fed her family as an expression of her love and was happy to extend that hospitality to everyone who entered her home, but that didn't mean that you were one of us.

When we came into the kitchen that apocalyptic night, my mother briefly glanced up from her cooking and told us dinner would be ready in a few minutes. She was cooking, and she considered this job one of the most important duties of a wife and mother, and therefore she didn't want to be interrupted.

My boyfriend told my mother that he wanted to speak to my father before we all sat down for dinner. There were two things that were immediately working against us that night. My mom and dad were in the middle of one of their "we're not talking to each other" fights that could last for days.

In addition to this, we were asking my mom to delay her dinner, and that was tantamount to asking the sun not to shine. My dad was down in the basement in his recliner watching television and wouldn't come upstairs. This was not a good start.

After much begging, I finally got my dad upstairs and seated at the table. My mom was at her station in front of the sink. My boyfriend began his speech. He got as far as the words, "I love your daughter and want to marry her..." before the first pot hit the floor. My mom would never think of throwing something at a person, but the floor wasn't off limits. This action was accompanied by her screams for John to get out of her house as she lunged across the table, as if she planned to grab him by the throat. Throughout all this, my dad sat silently at the table, as if stunned by my boyfriend's words. I hustled my boyfriend out the door. In the background I could hear my mother and father agreeing, "That boy had some nerve."

"Well, I think that went well," said John, and with those insane words he left, saying he'd see me tomorrow. I went upstairs to sleep. Instead, I stayed up half the night having alternating visions of myself as an old maid or the wife of a clearly delusional husband.

The next day, after work, John called to say he'd pick me up as usual. When I got into the car, I realized I didn't know where we were going, as there was no way I could imagine bringing him home with me. "I wonder what your Mom is cooking tonight," asked John, apparently not on the same wavelength as I. Although I begged and threatened him not to go home with me after the prior night's craziness, John continued towards my home.

As he purposefully walked through the door, he wrapped his arms around my mother and said, "Hi mom, what's for dinner?" My mother responded, "I made your favorite pasta for you tonight. It will be ready in just a few minutes." John had acknowledged my mom's authority, but he had also held his ground, and for that, she respected him.

She figured it was better to add another person to the family than to fight what was obviously going to be a losing battle. My mother and John continued to enjoy many hugs and pasta dinners together until the day she died.

CHAPTER 14
$$$ SHAME

By now it should be obvious to most of you that I constantly fought my parents tooth and nail to declare my independence from their rigid doctrines, which attempted to set the appropriate lifestyle for a "proper' woman. There were however, many instances where I had to admit defeat.

Although I ultimately did what I wanted to do, my parents' influence colored my decisions with touches of guilt if I veered too far off the course of their guidance. This guilt arose if I chose to date the "wrong" type of man, neglected some of the more mundane duties of motherhood and marriage, or even coveted an employment opportunity they considered beneath my intelligence.

However, my parents' influence had, perhaps, the most pervasive effect on my attitude towards money and its relationship to a person's social class.

There is considerable disagreement among sociologists on how to measure social class, yet most sociologists agree that wealth is a useful factor for grouping social classes, and that "having more money means having more power or opportunities." Woman often find themselves becoming more and more invisible in the workplace, because of their reluctance to acknowledge the importance of money in their careers.

My parents were first generation children of immigrants. Therefore, they were acutely aware that money was the key that opened many doors in America. However, they also knew that lack of money could engender greed and jealousy in people, so they occasionally went overboard in their efforts to dissuade their children from flaunting any signs of privilege.

Their eagerness to appear self-effacing evokes images of Hebrew men and women following the ancient custom of indicating humility before God by wearing sackcloth and dusting themselves with ashes. However, I always got a little confused by the inherent contradiction existing between the intent and practice of this custom.

Wearing sackcloth and ashes would certainly make a person stand out in a crowd and yet, calling attention to oneself seems to be the antithesis of humility. I have a feeling that if my parents were Hebrew, they would have wholeheartedly adopted the sackcloth and ashes custom, while nonetheless secretly continuing to enjoy the luxuries money can buy.

Today, anyone walking down the street or getting on a bus wearing sackcloth and ashes would be labeled homeless or insane. Nonetheless, many people commiserate with others who feel shame about their appearance, humble homes, or personal inadequacies. However, there is a shame that is rarely acknowledged about having, or wanting money.

So I have to ask this question, why is the discussion of money so taboo and shameful for some people? It wasn't until the death of my parents that I decided to reveal the secret rituals our family practiced to enjoy money, while still upholding a belief that the accumulation and discussion of money was somewhat unsavory. I only hope that my mom and dad are not somewhere in the afterlife shaking their fingers at me, because I washed their dirty laundry in public, but I guess I'll have to take that chance.

As a child, I was taught that it was "low class" to discuss money. My immigrant, Italian, family believed that if you had to ask how much something cost, it meant you couldn't afford it, and admitting that—even if it were true—was shameful, and shouted out to the world that you were nouveau riche, a designation that my parents dreaded like the plague. You became a detective when shopping, in an attempt to surreptitiously find a price tag, so you could escape the indignity of asking the price. The words, "How much is that?" equated to uttering dirty words.

This money shame haunted me throughout my early years. Although my family didn't talk about money, my mom loved expensive things. Her favorite store was Bergdorf Goodman's department store. I remember cutting the Bergdorf label out of one of my coats, so I wouldn't be embarrassed if my friends saw the label, and then knew that the coat cost a lot of money.

We lived in a middle-class neighborhood in Queens, New York. Bayside was aptly named, as it was a beautiful town by the bay with well-tended homes, in short, the fruition of the American dream. For the most part, the residents were the children of European immigrants who worked hard to earn enough money to raise their families in a suburban environment close to Manhattan.

Having the status in our neighborhood of being a big fish in a small pond made our family very influential. However, despite the times when I wanted to be the center of attention, I was like all teenage girls; I longed to be just like my friends, and they didn't shop in stores like Bergdorf Goodman.

I didn't consider the dichotomy in my wish to stand out while also fitting in, because in my teenage mind there was no contradiction in wanting to be the leader while wearing the same grungy clothes that my friends wore. A teenager's style had no rhyme or reason behind it.

My father helped perpetuate the misplaced sense of shame that I felt. For example, he drove a modest Oldsmobile station wagon that he changed out every two years, but he always bought the same brand, model, and color car. I asked him why he didn't try another brand, or at least change the model or color and he said, "then everyone would know that I'm buying a new car." His pants came from a catalogue not known for its fashion sense, but the pants were cheap and in his eyes, that was what counted.

My father, who grew up living with his parents and eight siblings in a two-bedroom tenement apartment, now had the money to buy that tenement building; yet he was ashamed of striking it rich. In my family, it was okay to be proud of your education, family, and job success, but having money was something that was kept to yourself.

I remember my mom telling me that she had no idea what my father earned. She only knew that he was the provider, and would take care of his family. She never wrote a check and using a credit card meant you didn't have the money to pay for the things that you wanted.

When my father died, my mother's naiveté was a liability. Since, in my mother's eyes, money grew on trees, she didn't understand that if you spent it too fast it might disappear. Upon my father's death, it became my brother's turn to make sure that my mom always had a fresh supply of cash. Thankfully, he was a successful attorney and had the resources to easily take over this responsibility.

It was unthinkable to my mother that she would have to deal with the dirty details of maintaining a cash flow. In her mind, men were the breadwinners and women needed to take care of their men. Even though that old time way of

The Journey of an "Invisible" Woman

thinking would sound ridiculous today, women still find it awkward to have conversations about money. I'm always amazed when I hear about women who leave all financial negotiations in their husband's hands when it comes to the important things like the purchase of a house or car.

Although leadership status was a primary goal in my career, I secretly harbored the aspiration of making a six-figure salary. There was only one problem, and that was the thought of haggling over a salary made my stomach turn. I knew that I was worth a substantial salary, but I didn't want to ask for it. I guilelessly believed that my employers would be so blinded by my spectacular abilities that they would shower me with money.

Many surveys, such as those taken by the wealth management division of UBS bank and staffing firm Randstad US, show that women suffer more than men from money shame, especially when it comes to salaries and investing. UBS bank indicates that women leave investment decisions to their husbands. Randstad reveals the shocking news from the results of a survey of over 1,200 women that "60% of women say they've never negotiated their salary-and many quit their jobs instead" (Leonhardt, 2020, p. 1).

This is surprising. as there have been laws for many years that guarantee financial opportunities for women, such as those regarding equal pay. In 1963, the Equal Pay Act was passed, which stipulates that women get equal pay for equal work, followed by Title VII of the Civil Rights Act of 1964, which bolstered the Equal Pay Act. Most states eventually passed similar acts, but the reality is that, as of March 2020, overall, women are paid 82 cents for every dollar paid to men and yet women remain hesitant to demand their just share of the pot.

Women have been raised to believe that it's "un-lady-like" to bargain over money. This fallacy casts a large shadow over a woman's ability to successfully engage in salary negotiations, and results in a discernible difference in negotiation skills between men and women. Society not only perpetuates the myth that men are naturally aggressive but also encourages the misconception that men seem to intuitively know how to use this aggression to negotiate in their best interests.

However, there is no innate ability in a man's nature that gives him an edge over a woman in negotiations. Men are convinced because of erroneous gender norms that it's not only acceptable but also expected that they view negotiations as a form of battle. These same norms declare that a woman's place is not on the battlefield and therefore an aggressive woman is called a bitch, and that's something that women are taught is shameful.

Pay equity workshops have become popular to help women, and there has been an uptick to the number of women holding C-suite executive positions in corporations with substantial salaries, but this achievement hasn't been seen in all industries. Women still accept this unbalance as part of the natural order of things and continue to feel embarrassed when asking for compensation for what they are worth.

I recall my own salary negotiations for a high-level corporate job within a company where I was working. The interview was rolling along and it looked like I'd get the job, but then the moment came that I dreaded. I was asked to name a number and blanched at the thought. Suddenly, my parent's training kicked in and triggered in me the fear that my image would be sullied if I looked "money hungry." I recalled that a fellow employee had reminded me of the outrageously high salaries of the leadership team, so I knew that the money was there to be had. I also realized that I possessed unique skills that were of major importance to the organization.

Now all I needed was the confidence to convey that importance to the organization by requesting the substantial compensation that I thought I was entitled. Finally, I drew up the courage to throw out a fair number, and to my surprise, they agreed to my request without the slightest resistance. I had confronted my reluctance to admit that money mattered, and was rewarded for my efforts.

This hesitancy to admit the importance of money in our lives becomes even more problematic as we get older. After retirement, asking to be compensated for your worth becomes more of an issue for both genders, especially for women. How many times have you heard retirees comment, when asked about why they want to return to work that, "I'm not doing it for the money, I just need something to do?" Money shame is pervasive and undermines our self-worth. Why not proudly say, "I want to work for the money and all the things that I can do because of having it." It's fascinating how, once a person reaches a certain age, the assumption is made that they would love to volunteer without compensation to perform the same work that previously came with a paycheck.

Many nonprofits rely on volunteers to perform duties that are done by employees in for-profit organizations. This altruism is an essential factor in the successful operation of these nonprofits. But the real question is whether retired people are volunteering out of a desire to promote the wellbeing of others, or because of a last-ditch effort to establish their self-worth.

Although portrayals of white-haired older people happily biking through a lush field, or gazing out over the ocean is a popular marketing concept of retirement, often, the more sobering reality is that many older people are devastated over their loss of purpose and identity.

Retirees who have spent their entire lives equating purpose and identity with money, suddenly, find that there's shame in admitting the sense of inadequacy that they experience when they can no longer command financial compensation for their abilities.

A report by U.S. News and World Report (2010) shows that money is the overwhelming reason that older people return to work, and according to the American Senior Alliance those findings haven't changed. These findings are rarely mentioned in conversations about post retirement employment. Evidently, money shame is an underlying motivation that leads to the denial of the important relationship between money and a person's sense of purpose in life.

Now that my parents are gone, I no longer have to remember their exhortations to always present a modest demeanor to the world even when enjoying the fruits of my own labors. Although I can finally boast about my accomplishments and subsequent prosperity, perplexingly, I still find myself maintaining a low profile when talking about anything smacking of affluence in my life.

In my never-ending search for visibility, I've become convinced that it's true that money can't buy you love but it can get you lots of great things, many of them intangible, that will enhance your self-esteem. There's nothing intrinsically shameful about having money but as my parents would say, "Stop bragging."

CHAPTER 15
FLYING BLIND

By now, you must have surmised that I like to be the leader of the pack and in control of my own destiny. These traits, combined with several phobias, create the consummate control freak, who is basically afraid of anything and everything.

As I mentioned in the chapter $$$ SHAME, money can buy you lots of great things, and flying off to exotic vacations is, certainly, one of them. But, when I look back on the trip to Italy that I took with my parents just before my marriage to John, I realize that this form of enjoyment might not be quite so fantastic for someone like me, who always needs to be in charge and in command of her own fate.

The trip to Italy was my last chance to travel alone with my parents. I was a young, unmarried woman who, at this early stage of her life, believed she was quite a gift to the world. But somehow this news wasn't communicated to the airline staff.

I recall being herded onto the plane without being asked if I needed help carrying my heavy designer carry-on bag. Keeping in line with my parents' almost religious fervor to reject any forms of obvious entitlement, all of us were flying economy class. It never entered my mind that a spur of the moment trip to Europe for a family of five was the very definition of entitlement. I fantasized that, once beverage and food service began, I would be sipping French champagne and eating caviar, but instead, the flight attendant only offered me a complimentary bottle of water.

I couldn't imagine why I was being treated like everyone else on the plane instead of the princess whom I knew I was. The rotten food service was then amplified by the response that I received when I requested a down pillow which I, haughtily, emphasized, needed to be at least 95% down. The flight attendant gave me an incredulous look, as if I had just asked her to sell me her first-born child. How could I be expected to sleep during the nine-hour trip if my pillow was as hard as a rock?

But who was I kidding? I knew that I'd never go to sleep, because if I did, then who would be alert to any problems that might arise during the flight? My memories of this flight convinced me that, if I were to continue flying, I had to work on developing the same sense of control in the friendly skies that I possessed when my feet were planted firmly on the ground.

Before I go any further in my fear of flying saga, I need to come clean and confess that, although I did accompany my parents on a trip to Italy, that's the only true fact about my behavior on that trip. I may sometimes act a little egocentrically in my quest to remain visible, but I'm not an actual narcissist. Also, if I'd actually acted the way I described on that flight, my parents would have demanded that I get off the plane.

To me, airline travel is the perfect storm that combines loss of control with a fear of anonymity, claustrophobia and a dramatic death. It reduces those of us who are not celebrities and fly commercial to nameless, faceless, minions.

The Journey of an "Invisible" Woman

On my trip to Italy, my sense of entitlement obviously colored what was typical treatment afforded most airline passengers into something that was demoralizing and demeaning. This anonymous status reminded me that, in certain situations, I wasn't viewed as anybody special. During the nine-hour flight to Italy, I was just another passenger who had to be flown from point A to point B.

This understanding triggered in me a foreboding presentiment that as I got older, I might find myself perpetually destined to exist in this type of obscurity. I can't imagine the insufferable prospect of, permanently, leading a life without significance.

Sometimes the best way to confront frightening things in life is to transform them into make-believe. With this new insight into a possible solution to overcome the fears that threatened to diminish my ability to fully enjoy life, I began to bubble over with excitement at the thought of engaging in this new fantasy type exercise.

Movies are a good example of something that provides us with various imaginary situations in which we can vicariously reassert our power and control. Some people watch horror films, because they enjoy feeling really intense emotions, like terror.

Also, the fictional nature of horror films affords viewers a sense of control by placing a psychological distance between them and their fear. According to a theory credited to psychologist James Gross of Stanford University, the activation of this feeling is called emotion regulation.

Emotion regulation is applicable to many types of fictional experiences. I decided that my first experience using the technique of emotion regulation would be to use my imagination and make up my own worse case fictional flight scenarios. By doing so, I would let my imagination elevate me into a world of fantastical thoughts about air travel, which no matter how nonsensical, would be under my control.

Therefore, let me share with you one exercise that I used, to I activate my imagination and create my harrowing flight fantasy. I've interspersed some actual aviation information into my fictional narrative to counterbalance my frequent personal reflections, so let's fly.

My musings begin with my arrival at JFK airport in New York where I, immediately, search for the waiting area near my gate. After I locate the waiting area, I take my seat with dozens of other passengers who are sitting quietly, entertaining their own neuroses about the trip to come. Now, none of us are masters of our own actions. Instead, we become submissive and ready to obey the commands to sit, line up, and generally to do whatever the flight attendants demand of us. We're like captives on a pirate ship, steeling ourselves for the final walk off the plank.

Common sense tells me that air travel is one of the safest modes of transportation. I remind myself of this fact as I stand on line to board my plane and yet, just to be on the safe side, I surreptitiously glance at the other passengers to catch a sign of any mental instability that might have been overlooked during the check in process.

Suddenly, a voice is heard over the speaker system, "The flight to Miami will be late taking off," and a collective groan is heard from the passengers on line. Everyone scatters and cell phones are whipped out of pockets, as some travelers notify friends and families to start dinner without them. Other travelers call hotels to tell them to hold rooms for what could possibly be a very late arrival.

The simple announcement of a delayed departure can trigger a variety of scenarios in the mind of an imaginative passenger. Is it a simple maintenance issue that is causing the delay or is a temporary fix being applied to an airplane that has made one too many flights?

Although the sun is shining at the departure airport, perhaps a decision has been made to delay the flight until a series of tornadoes moves out of the flight path. To the suspicious mind, images of drunken pilots and called-in bomb threats increase an already tense mood.

There was an article that appeared many years ago in a magazine that advised fearful flyers never to read about or view photos of airplane crashes. However, even without media input, it is very difficult today to insulate yourself from the ominous possibilities of air travel.

How many ways can you rationalize the need for removing your shoes when going through security, other than acknowledging their possible use as containers for explosives? Or do you start to become uneasy while undergoing the latest hand scanning for bomb-making residue? These thoughts can make a normally sane person flip out; but don't feel bad, because you are not alone. The fear of flying, or aviophobia, is one of the most common phobias, "with an estimated prevalence ranging from 2.5% to 6.5% of the population," (Ducharme, 2018, p. 1).

What determines your level of anxiety as an airline passenger? People fly for business, pleasure or as the result of an emergency, sickness or death. Upon debarking, expectations of what awaits you upon arriving influences your emotions when flying. For instance, if you are going to visit your mom in the hospital, the entire trip will be spent anticipating her condition. On the other hand, it's already party time if your destination is a beautiful tropical island or reunion with a loved one.

We all know people who can never relinquish control of any situation, as well as happy souls who are content just to be alive. If we fall into the first group, as I do, we become anxious when abdicating our control, but we've learned to employ different methods, usually of an alcoholic nature, to sooth our anxiety.

If felled by a serious illness, we still maintain the right to choose the doctor who will care for us, and to research his or her qualifications. This provides the patient a modicum of power, but when we fly, we've pretty much given up all authority regarding our welfare to someone else. We have no idea into whose hands we are placing our lives.

People with controlling personalities experience an uncomfortable sense of helplessness when they become simply part of the pack. And unless your face appears routinely on the front page of magazines, you will become just another anxious face in the crowd while waiting to board an airplane. This descent into anonymity is contrary to all my aspirations.

Although social equity is seemingly established while everyone is sitting together in the gate area waiting room, waiting to board, it vanishes when the magical words, "boarding first class" are heard. The reality then surfaces that there are four classes of people who fly: the wealthy, the famous, the frequent flyer road warrior, and everyone else. The fourth class quietly watches while the privileged few elbow to the front of the line with a superior smile on their faces.

The fourth-class passenger's self-esteem plummets to new lows as they contemplate what the words, "first class" means. They wonder if they're not in it, then does that mean that they are "second class?" And what does that imply? I was raised to believe that I was meant for excellence. Could you be excellent if you were second-class? None of these thoughts help to relax me or any of the other already disgruntled passengers. Enough rumination, now let's resume my fantasy flight.

The Journey of an "Invisible" Woman

I have spent the two hours waiting to board my flight thoroughly studying my fellow passengers, and I am finally satisfied that there are no terrorists on board. After I get on the plane, and as I'm walking down the aisle, I notice out of the corner of my eye that someone, who is already seated, is hacking away, with what is certain to be a highly contagious virus, while several rows further back is a young family with four children, all under the age of six. Possible death or certain torture. Which of these passengers would you want to sit next to?

Finally, I am seated in my almost perfect seat, and before I can take a deep breathe the pilot speaks on the intercom. In a soothing voice he tells us to relax and enjoy the ride, but all I can think about as he speaks is the possibility that this could be the voice of a severely depressed person planning to fly him and us into oblivion.

They always say that taking off and landing is the most dangerous part of flying and, apparently, our pilot seems to feel an obligation to fulfill that saying. Without warning, the plane starts to shake as if it's going to break apart. Passengers' screams can barely be heard over the ear-splitting noise of the plane, and now I think I'm smelling smoke.

Just when I think that it can't get any worse, things quiet down. I pull out a book to keep my mind busy during the three-hour flight to Miami. Several hours after takeoff, I notice that we seem to be flying in circles instead of lowering our attitude in preparation for landing. As I get ready to press the call button for the flight attendant a voice comes over the intercom to tell us that we would be circling over our "new" arrival airport for an additional hour, because of weather.

I had no idea what they meant by "new" arrival airport, but I would soon find out. Our new airport turns out to be in

New Jersey, a state not even close to the geographical direction in which we were originally going. We finally land, and I think that once the weather clears in Miami, we'll be on our way again. However, I am mistaken.

After waiting another hour, the plane begins to back out, and we finally prepare for takeoff. I am relieved that the long ordeal was finally over, or so I had thought. Suddenly, the plane comes to a screeching halt and the Captain's voice can be heard, thanking us for our patience, but he's sorry to say a minor glitch has come up, and we must return, again, to the gate.

As we slump back into our seats, we wonder what the code words, "minor glitch" really mean. Will we have to disembark and go through the entire boarding process again, or will we be quarantined on the plane for hours, because of a rumor about the possibility that a passenger onboard harbors a contagious disease? Imagine the newspaper headlines! My family will finally have the chance to see my name in the news.

But maybe I'm getting ahead of myself, and I should just ask that pleasant-looking soul across the aisle if he has some extra happy pills that he can share with me, so I can relax and contemplate my next steps, in regaining my autonomy as a powerful woman in control of her own destiny.

I had survived the worst-case flight scenario that I could envision in my emotion regulation exercise. I was now ready to put this great tool to work on creating fantasies that focus on dealing with obstacles that actually threaten my visibility in society.

CHAPTER 16
THE WILD WEST

Although I attempted to break loose from my family to try out life in the Midwest with Mr. Indiana, my heart was always saddened by the thought of leaving the place in which I was born and raised. I am a born and bred native New Yorker and I, like many other New Yorkers, believe that anyone living outside of New York is unsophisticated, and a bit boring. Based on my attitude, it's probably not difficult to understand that I was more than a little shocked when my husband Blue Eyes, announced that his company, JAXX, Inc. would be relocating to Dallas, Texas, and so would we.

This move would make my husband the sole breadwinner in the family until I found employment. I knew that I had to think of this as an adventure and swallow my trepidation at leaving New York. Two of my four children were babies and I had no job or support system in place, so it looked like this move would give me a taste of living the 1950s life of a suburban mom that my mother always prayed for me to have.

This would be the first, and I hoped last time that I would have to swallow my pride and follow my husband's lead. The only thing I knew about Texas was what I'd learned from watching cowboy movies and a television show, popular when I was young: *Dallas*. Although I wasn't stupid enough to believe that everything I saw on television was real, I couldn't imagine that the creators of Dallas wouldn't, at least, try to include some authentic Texan touches to the show.

I took some bits and pieces from the show to paint a broad picture for myself, of what I imagined was a typical life in Texas.

Now that I had gathered at least a few impressions of what to expect, I felt a little comfortable embarking on this journey to a place that one day I would probably have to call my home. I began to review all the information that I'd collected about life in Texas, and concluded that most people had double first names like Sue Ellen or just use initials, like J.R., and the men were either cowboys or rich oil magnates living in luxurious mansions with their beautiful, perfectly groomed wives. I was partially correct in my reflections about life in Texas, but I still had a lot left to learn.

My husband's company, JAXX, offered a free "look see" trip to Dallas for its employees, to locate a house. I was game for this new experience, so before I knew it, I was on a flight headed to Dallas. As the plane's altitude dropped, I caught a glimpse of the area from my window.

My mother, aptly, had named me Sandy, as I loved the sandy shores of the New York ocean, but what I saw outside my window as the plane taxied into the Dallas, Fort Worth airport made it very clear, that not only was there no ocean, but also, what little vegetation existed appeared scraggly and sparse. The flat topography took my breath away, but not in a good way.

JAXX made every effort to entice its executives to relocate, so they arranged a number of excursions, mixed in with the house hunting. I was excited to go on a tour of the

The Journey of an "Invisible" Woman

mansion depicted in the show, *Dallas,* where the super-rich Ewing family lived. Once I actually saw the house, disappointment replaced my excitement.

As typical, when filming a television show, the broad lens of a camera is often used to make certain enhancements to the location. But what I was looking at wasn't simply an enhancement; it was a total fabrication. They might as well have used a computer-generated image, but I guess computers weren't yet that advanced in the late 70s.

The humongous mansion in the show was actually a cottage, with a swimming pool that could, possibly, accommodate a really short person floating on her back. It's amazing—the magic that wide-angle lens cameras can do. If this was an omen of things to come, it wasn't a good one.

Headquarters for JAXX were planned to be built in a suburb of Dallas, twenty–five minutes from the Oklahoma border. Therefore, our search for a home began in this area. In another twenty years, this suburban area would become a central residential hub with an abundance of shopping, housing, businesses and entertainment; however, during the time of our "look see," all our eyes could see were cows roaming on empty plains with nothing in sight except a sign, announcing the future site of JAXX.

After driving around for some time, we finally saw a long dirt road with a marker indicating the addresses of a few of the homes that we came to see. At the end of this road was a community of houses that could have been constructed using a giant cookie cutter. Every house was identical to the one next to it. The thought entered my mind that anyone living here better not get drunk and then try to find their house, as they might find themselves making an unexpected visit to a neighbor. I didn't think my quest for recognition would be welcomed by the residents of this cookie cutter community.

Sandy Camillo

After this initial house hunting excursion, we drove back to our hotel in silence. Blue Eyes had made a previous trip to Dallas, and thus surmised that our trip might not end well, so he had wisely decided to book our stay in the most exclusive hotel there.

Neither one of us wanted to be the first to bring up our feelings about the home search, so I excused myself and went into the bathroom, where I immediately slumped to the floor and sobbed my heart out. My New York sensibilities were injured by the thought that I would now become a country bumpkin, quietly living out my life, gazing at roaming cattle.

The next day we, stoically, got into our rental car to look at another neighborhood. It looked like things might be turning around. We found a neighborhood that could have been posted in an ad for houses in a suburban New York City bedroom community, if that community's residents were all homogeneous with no hint of economic, cultural, or racial diversity.

It was nicknamed the "Bubble," because of this appalling characteristic, which wasn't discernible until you became a resident. However, the biggest selling point of this neighborhood was that each house was built in a distinct architectural style to distinguish it from its nearby neighbor, and mature trees surrounded the homes.

This was as close as we would get to replicating the type of suburban community that we'd become accustomed to back East. Time was running out for us to make a decision on where we would live. We warily bit the bullet and chose "The Bubble."

We soon found out it wasn't just the homes that distinguished our new neighborhood from other areas of Dallas. We soon found out that The Bubble was where the first families of Dallas lived. My new neighbors were people whose names you read in the newspapers. Participating in social activities was considered an important part of a resident's networking duties, and was even expected of young children.

Women dutifully attended gala benefit events and planned far in advance to groom their children to participate in cotillions and debutant affairs. Everyone seemed to be motivated to succeed in one way or another. This was a community of go-getters.

Maybe this community's energy would act as a catalyst for my ambitions. I was ashamed to admit that I had impetuously judged a state and its citizens, based on fictional accounts in movies and on television. The foolishness of my assumptions is highlighted when I think back on my emotional collapse on the hotel bathroom floor, after observing cattle grazing in a Texas field. It was naïve to equate a state's sophistication with their commerce. To be fair, New York State also has a robust cattle industry, and yet I managed to live in New York for many years without constantly erupting in tears.

We discovered that not all Texans were cowboys and cowgirls and that the clichéd depiction of a Texan in cowboy boots and jeans was, in reality, a rare sight. Although in New York one can attend the Opera wearing dress jeans, in certain parts of Dallas wearing jeans for anything other than cleaning out your garage was frowned upon.

Even though I liked to be noticed in all situations, I decided not to buck the tide, and no longer ran out to pick up a container of milk in my sweats. Instead, I chose my supermarket outfit as carefully as I would for an evening dining out.

In New York, I was considered a man magnet. Consequently, I experienced quite a letdown when I realized that I no longer stood out as an attractive woman in this city, where women made maintaining their beauty an important priority. During my time in Dallas, it was a rarity to meet a woman in the Bubble who worked outside the home.

Her attractiveness, social standing in the community and her husband and children's successes determined her identity. Women in their 30s and 40s held onto a sorority mentality that demanded that they bend over backwards to conform to the social standards established by their circle of friends. Since individuality was not a prized trait in Dallas, I sensed that my uniqueness might not be fully appreciated by my new friends.

There was a 1972 movie called the *Stepford Wives* that was about a woman who suspected that submissive wives in her idyllic Connecticut neighborhood might be robots created by their husbands. I watched that movie several times, because I was enthralled by the theme, never imagining that one day I'd encounter anything even slightly resembling such subjection of women in real life. But that day arrived. It was the first day of school at my children's preschool, and I witnessed a scene that might have been taken directly from the *Stepford Wives*.

All the mothers were driving Suburbans and wearing pinafores, with huge bows sitting atop their identical hairstyles. They quietly walked their perfectly dressed children to the school door, never raising their voices beyond a controlled decibel and smiled at each other while showing off a dazzling array of perfect white teeth. This was creepy and portentous of things to come.

Because, at the time, a Dallas woman's identity was so closely tied to her children's achievements, a great part of her daily life was filled with making sure that her child was the best in school, athletics and his or her social relationships. This meant that encouraging your child to study, enjoy a sport or develop friendships was not enough. Special tutors needed to be engaged; endless hours of practice were promoted to guarantee acceptance into "special youth leagues," and diligent attention was given to filtering out undesirable friends.

Children as young as 10 years old attended Cotillions to learn how to dance; while their anxious mothers canvassed the group to identify potential desirable future mates for their child. My upbringing and drive had made me a little more self-centered. Although I adored my children, I also knew that one day I wanted to be recognized for my own achievements, outside of motherhood. Therefore, I couldn't understand why these educated women were content in living their lives vicariously, through their children.

Obviously, my attitude regarding the values of Dallas women was bound to identify me as a feminist and therefore, an outsider. Even if I kept my thoughts to myself about what I perceived as their weaknesses, it was indisputable that the minute I opened my mouth to speak there was no hiding the fact that I was a Yankee. Many of my conversations ended with my being asked by another mom to say something to her friends. At first, I didn't understand this request.

However, I soon got the message when, after uttering some inane statement, I would hear a bunch of these ladies giggling at my New York accent. Perhaps their joking wasn't quite as innocent as it first appeared, as apparently, my attitude towards gendered roles threatened the cushy lifestyles they had embraced, in exchange for abandoning their empowerment as women. I was an oddity in this land of y'all, but I was definitely visible.

The years went by and we were now at the end of the 90s. I had made some good friends in Dallas who were able to overlook my Yankee roots and feminist leanings. Dallas was changing, and its women were beginning to assert their unique identities.

Sandy Camillo

They were now not only stay-at-home moms, but also attorneys, doctors and women working in innumerable professions. Although at the time of our move, JAXX was one of just a few companies to choose Dallas for relocation, it later became a center of corporate relocations, and diverse neighborhoods became common. If one wanted to see a cowboy, the only way to do it was to watch a western on television, or go to one of the tourist attractions in Fort Worth.

Despite all the changes that have taken place, there was one thing that hasn't changed. It is that Dallas women still pursue their quest for physical perfection, and the trophy wife still exists. It was, and still is, very difficult for a woman to stand out in a crowd in Dallas, unless she is young, and exquisitely beautiful. Maybe, one day that, too, will change.

CHAPTER 17
THE BOY WITH THE PENNY UP HIS NOSE

I was no longer that young, or exquisitely beautiful, like some of my Dallas friends, but I knew that I could distinguish myself in other ways. We had been in Dallas for over a decade and I had started writing and selling real estate, while always remaining alert to possible next steps on my career track.

I knew that it was probably time to put my academic degrees to use. Although I didn't want to fulfill my mother's dream of making education my career, I wasn't going to kick a gift horse in the mouth either, and a job as an elementary school principal was practically flung into my lap, so I took the job.

Leadership status can be a real ego trip for a young woman, particularly one who loves the limelight. When I accepted my first role as a school administrator, I was looking forward to my impending prominence as a leader. It also felt good that I wouldn't just be climbing the ladder to my own self-actualization, but also, I would have a hand in determining someone else's destiny.

As a school principal, I was responsible for setting teacher, staff, and student objectives. My decisions had a major impact on the emotional and intellectual development of many children. In my mind, my new position as a school principal wasn't just another job, but fulfilled a grand vision of myself as a prominent person in the field of education. I would become a modern-day Maria Montessori. With this noble mission beckoning me, I was determined I'd be the greatest principal in the state of Texas.

As I mentioned many times before, I was raised to believe that the world was holding their breath, waiting for me to do great things, although I recognized that not all children grew up with the type of positive reinforcement that I had received.

I took to heart the words of Dr. Seuss who said, "Why fit in when you were born to stand out" and was determined that not only would I live by these words, but I'd also help each of my students to discover their unique selves. However, not every person finds themselves standing out in the world in a good way. Many times people find themselves through no fault of their own, being recognized for all the wrong reasons. Society cruelly labels "different" people as oddballs, weird or eccentric.

Although this chapter is focused on a devastating incident in a boy's life, the underlying moral is also applicable to girls. Both girls and boys need to remember that being the center of attention in a crowd has its advantages and disadvantages. Depending on the circumstances, the crowd may acknowledge you as a leader or your uniqueness might intimidate them and cause them to strike out against you, to assert their own dominance. Although I always longed for attention, some children find themselves becoming a victim, due to unwanted attention.

I'm going to share with you a story that highlights the damage that a single social interaction can have on a child's self-esteem and the effect that this damage has on a person's

The Journey of an "Invisible" Woman

ambitions. If someone is constantly belittled it's doubtful that they will develop the confidence required to achieve their goals.

Thinking back on my early school days, I now understand the major influence that my interactions with teachers had on my self-image. Therefore, before I recount my story, I need to warn parents about the foolishness of putting all their trust into the hands of their child's teacher. Most of us are tempted to share cute anecdotes about our children with their teachers, but maybe parents should think again before doing it. Elephants aren't the only creatures with long memories.

The story of "The Boy with the Penny Up His Nose" is always good for a little laugh, unless that boy happens to be your child and you have just returned from a harrowing trip to the hospital to dislodge that penny. As if this frightening experience isn't enough, you probably wouldn't be thrilled to learn that the school is now using your son's ordeal as a cautionary tale to warn other children about the danger of putting objects in their nose.

Unless you want your child to be teased about this incident for years to come, it's better to remember that some information has no value to anyone outside the family circle. But if you really believe it's no big deal if your child is the target of a joke, the story I'm about to share with you, Dan's story, might change your mind.

Dan's teachers knew that he had been having problems fitting in with his classmates. He and his classmates were just entering their teenage years, and were experiencing the onset of puberty and all of its associated mood swings.

This was a time of stress for any child entering early adolescence as they began the search for their identity, and Dan would have to face additional impediments in his search. Dan was a sweet child who would frequently stop by my office to wish me a good day. Because of our frequent interactions, I took a special interest in his development.

There were many things that made Dan different from his classmates. He was struggling academically, and exhibited all of the behavior symptoms of severe attention deficit hyperactivity disorder (ADHD). In Dallas, athletic ability was prized, but Dan was physically awkward and clumsy at most sports.

He was the very definition of class pariah. When his classmates weren't teasing him, they avoided him. He just didn't fit with their adolescent standards of friendship.

Each year, the eighth grade went on a weekend trip to celebrate their last year in elementary school. I, unenthusiastically, was accompanying several teacher chaperones on this memory-making adventure in the mountains of New Mexico. Dan and I had become best buddies during this fun-filled trip. I had breathed a sigh of relief that the trip was over and no one had tormented Dan during our weekend stay. Little did I know that I should have held my breath a little longer!

The exhausted chaperones finally got their charges on the bus for the long trip home. Typical of adolescents, the students considered the bus ride an ideal setting for some romantic boy and girl interactions, as well as the perfect opportunity to stage many practical jokes. Thus the chaperones were kept busy keeping an eye out for boys and girls sliding down in their seats to engage in some kissing and who knows what else. They never imagined that the stage was being set for a heartless joke on Dan.

All weekend, he boys had been planning an epic trick to play on Dan, on the bus trip home. They arranged to rig the bus's bathroom door so that, although it appeared to be locked, it would open when leaned on from the outside. Once Dan was inside the bathroom, a classmate would burst in on him. This would be guaranteed to embarrass Dan and would be just one more mockery he would have to bear. The boys thought that Dan had been the perfect bullying victim since Kindergarten, so why should they lighten up now?

The boy who masterminded the joke gathered several students to witness the result of his creativity. The door was pushed open and Dan was mortified to see his classmates staring at him. What should have ended with an apology became the beginning of a traumatic experience for Dan. Some of the most disreputable students decided to take advantage of his peripheral status in the group by fabricating what they saw when Dan was exposed in the bathroom. As if being observed while using the bathroom wasn't bad enough, these students now spread the rumor that Dad was engaged in a sexual act of self-gratification when he was interrupted.

Dan was horrified. He was already carrying the weight of the world on his shoulders and finding himself in such a humiliating situation was the final straw. He frantically started making telephone calls to the students, pleading his case, and trying to convince them that none of the story was true. Instead of things quieting down, the students were now dividing into pro and con Dan teams. The parents became involved, and soon Dan's parents, who were once part of a close-knit parents' group, were no longer invited to social events.

Dan had tried to fit into his peer group and yet he was left to stand alone. His resulting depression took a turn for the worse when Dan negatively reacted to the anti-depression medication he was taking. He started talking about suicide and was sent to a residential facility for a week. Dan was eventually able to return to school and he even developed friendships with a few students who had not been involved in the practical joke.

My response to this nightmare was to suspend the students involved in spreading the malicious rumor about Dan, as well as permanently removing them from the football team. These students might have been bummed-out by their punishments, but the harrowing memories of their eight-grade trip would not permanently affect their lives. Dan and his family, however, would definitely never forget his eight-grade class trip, but for all the wrong reasons.

Dan was different, but this didn't give anyone the right to harass him. He stood out from the group, but not in a way that was accepted, and at his tender age he couldn't possibly understand the fragile nature of the social hierarchy existing even in elementary school. The in-crowd would always pick a victim to bully and once you were declared "it," the in-crowd would mercilessly go in for the kill. In this case, Dan was "it."

It's not just students who develop social circles at school. Parents also form friendship groups, and Dan's parents were part of one of these groups. Typically, everyone in the group acted as if they were part of one big family, until they weren't. As we all know, sometimes there are jealousies and disagreements in families and these things also exist in many parent groups. As a result, I found myself spending a good deal of time acting as a mediator between the parents involved in Dan's saga.

During this mediation process, I learned that parents need to be careful about, not just what they tell their children's teachers, but also what they tell their own friends, as depending on the circumstances, family anecdotes can sometimes take on new meanings.

For example, when Dan had to go to a residential facility to recover from the students' brutal bullying on that fateful trip, the parents of the students that bullied Dan cried out that their children should not be blamed for his breakdown. These parents said that Dan always had issues and his breakdown was inevitable. They further said that this was the truth, because Dan's parents told them so.

Dan's story might seem like a one-off situation that most people would never encounter, however even things that seem perfectly normal in a family's dynamic might sometimes seem odd to outsiders and become the cause of a child's degradation. For example, little Johnny's preference for bubble baths over an invigorating shower may stem from hearing five of his sisters rave about how great those baths are, rather than gender confusion.

Even those friendly conversations between parents can turn ugly and become ammunition used in a battle to protect your child. A perfect illustration of this situation is demonstrated when a fight happens between your daughter and your friend's daughter, both of whom were once best friends.

Your friend remembers that you complained to her that your daughter's temper erupts very quickly in disagreements with her siblings. She decides to bring this fact to the attention of the teacher when discussing the fight that took place between her daughter and yours. No matter how close a friendship you have with someone's mom, when push comes to shove, that mom will always fight like a tiger to protect her young.

Although science has stated that it is a fallacy to attribute the traditional concept of maternal instinct just to women, real life experience shows us that in most cases it is the mother that becomes a prizefighter when her child is harmed. To understand this idiosyncrasy, we need to acknowledge the influence of false gender norms that set expectations for women's behavior.

As a school principal, I truly enjoyed the fulfillment that came with my role as a mediator. But unlike in most mediation, I was also in the unique position to stipulate that my decision, whatever it might be, was the final word on a matter. Although this meant that the loser might wind up hating me, I was elated with the power that I derived from playing judge.

Growing up, I was in a constant struggle to live my life according to motives that weren't the product of distorted external forces. As an adult observing Dan's tragedy, I experienced a reawakening of my understanding of the darker side of childhood. This understanding reminded me how easily self-esteem can be destroyed.

Although education was not my dream profession, my helping Dan made me understand that I could still be a person of influence and power in my little educational microcosm. Actually, I didn't just help Dan, but he helped me in a more profound way. Although I still appreciated getting accolades from others, I now realized that the key to being somebody special and attaining the most elevated status could come from a quiet act of caring.

Although I still couldn't say Y'all, I knew that this Yankee had made a lasting impression on the lives of many people, certainly, at least, on one named Dan.

CHAPTER 18
WORKING NINE TO FIVE

I really took my search for self-fulfillment seriously. I held jobs in so many diverse industries that I could have written a woman's guide to career opportunities, and maybe I'll do that next. In my quest for success at something exciting and high profile, I tried my hand at being a teacher, an editorial assistant, a classified ad writer, a nursery school director, a corporate paralegal, an accounts payable clerk, a realtor, an elementary school principal, a freelance writer, a receivership specialist and a governance/compliance consultant.

One could say I was really well rounded or had a major case of attention deficit disorder, or that I was just frantically searching for that one job that would satisfy my ambitions.

I pursued some of my many jobs because they touched on the periphery of fulfilling my lifelong dream of becoming either an attorney or a writer. However, my educational background acted as an important catalyst for my employment as a teacher and administrator.

Remember all those degrees that I was able to obtain, because my mother became my full-time babysitter? To a certain extent, she believed in women's equality and knew that, without financial security, a woman would never obtain that equality, and would remain subservient to others, especially to the men in their lives.

Although my mother was innately intelligent, she was never given the opportunity to advance beyond a high school diploma. This made her determined to do everything that she could, to see that her children attained the highest educational levels possible. Unfortunately, the usual career pathway for most women of my generation was for us to become teachers, nurses or secretaries. This is not to say that these weren't great professions, but the fact is that women weren't encouraged to be doctors, accountants, scientists, or engineers and therefore few of them took these career paths.

Gender bias against women in STEM occupations was evidenced in gender-stereotyped publicity photographs of young female contestants in the Westinghouse Science Talent search of the 1950s. Although these girls had successfully accomplished academic tests to compete in this talent search, the photos showed them holding up banquet dresses and wistfully gazing at the Hope diamond on a visit to the Smithsonian in order to emphasize that this was where their interests truly lay.

As I was basically a good girl, and my parents had not only paid for my education but were also taking care of my child, I obediently followed their wishes and the adage given to girls of my generation to enter an acceptable career in education, nursing, or secretarial work. Each summer my parents also made me take secretarial courses and enrichment classes so that I would be a step ahead of my classmates. I was so busy with my studies and being a mom that it was easier to just fall in line with my parents' agenda for my future; but something kept prodding me with the thought that their plans might not align with my true desires.

The Journey of an "Invisible" Woman

My parents were driven to make sure that I was highly educated so I could be financially independent, but they also hoped that I would marry again, so I could stay home and become a lady of leisure. They never considered the possibility that these two goals were polar opposites, or that I had another vision for something more exciting and high profile for myself.

I spent quite a bit of time considering career options that were designated appropriate for women in my generation. I fainted at the sight of blood and I wanted to be the boss, not the assistant, so nurse and secretary were out of the picture. Therefore, since I was out of alternatives, I took my first job as a teacher. On my first day of work, I could feel the blood surging through my veins in excitement as I got into my car to drive to the school. I knew that this was my chance to make a difference in someone else's life.

My idealism, however, plummeted when I reached my destination in a very, very depressed area of the Bronx. Previously, my only experience with this New York City borough was my once-a-year trip with my father to Yankee Stadium, to cheer on my favorite baseball team. My father and I would always park our car in a garage no further than one block from Yankee stadium and then make a mad dash into the stadium.

This was the only time that we got up close and personal with this borough. During these brief excursions, we saw enough to know that the area surrounding the stadium was slightly impoverished and possibly dangerous.

Other than this once-a-year experience, I was also able to see bits and pieces of the Bronx from a car window while driving on the Cross-Bronx Expressway en route to New Jersey via the George Washington Bridge. Everywhere I looked, I saw burnt out buildings and graffiti. These compressed glimpses of areas in the Bronx tarnished my impression of the entire borough.

However, this exposure didn't convey the extent of the squalor that I now saw, when I arrived at my newly assigned school. I was a spoiled, naïve girl from suburbia who was suddenly thrust into an educational world very different from the idealized environment depicted in educational textbooks. I was also only 22 years old, so I had a lot to learn about the world outside of my privileged stomping grounds.

When I arrived at the school's location, I noticed that I'd have to navigate through a maze of abandoned cars in order to enter the building. Not an auspicious beginning, but I weaved, successfully, through the maze and got inside the school. The first thing that I noticed when I entered the building was that it was dark, very dark! Then I saw that the windows were boarded up, because vandals had smashed them.

Suddenly, I heard a cheerful voice calling my name and a friendly looking person quickly whisked me into the administrator's office, where I was given a briefing along with my classroom key. I then met my co-workers at an orientation meeting and was surprised to see that most of them were novice teachers. I was soon to find out why this was the case.

I spent much of my first week at the school alternating between threatening and cajoling my 6th grade students to behave. They were like jack-in-the-boxes, constantly jumping in and out of their seats, and the concept of classroom silence was unknown to them. Apparently, I needed to study Jean Piaget's theory of cognitive development more seriously to know how to help these kids. So, I muddled on, interspersing some pearls of wisdom along with the basic rules of school behavior. Much of my dialogue with the students consisted of the phrases, "Stop It, Sit Down, Be Quiet" with the

The Journey of an "Invisible" Woman

occasional, "Get that gum out of your mouth." The final straw that broke my back was the day I walked into the hall, to see the principal nonchalantly stepping over an 8th grade girl, who had decided to take a nap on the hall floor.

It would be a monumental task for a young teacher to achieve any educational goals in an environment that accepted chaos. I realized that there were no experienced teachers in the school because the administration couldn't retain them. I dejectedly gave up my dreams of making a difference in this school, and walked away after three months. Now I had to find a new career.

When I was a little girl, I must have watched a lot of Superman movies, because I was enthralled with Lois Lane and dreamt of being a reporter like her. I had images of myself dashing off to cover the news about a tornado wiping out a neighboring town. It also didn't hurt that there were little sparks going on between Lois and Superman.

The weird thing is that I was also determined that someday I would become a lawyer like my older brother and could see myself passionately defending an innocent client in court. I bounced between these two dreams, until I was forced to face reality. That reality was marriage, divorce, and a child.

Although I was only in my early twenties, I had already divorced my first husband, and that divorce made me acknowledge that I would have to make adjustments to my career objectives. I was now the sole breadwinner for my little boy and me, and all my degrees in education were meaningless in the legal and journalistic worlds.

It was time to buckle down and accept the fact that, maybe, I needed to forget my vision of myself as a superstar lawyer or writer, and embrace the image, instead, of doggedly working at a job that I had no interest in doing.

Sandy Camillo

I knew that I really didn't enjoy teaching children. Maybe having my own child at such a young age made me crave the company of adults. I needed to find something that was akin to running my own business, but which would utilize my training as an educator. Therefore, I accepted a job as a director of a pre-school and actually enjoyed the work.

Part of my enjoyment was probably because the owner of the school was a gorgeous, brilliant scientist, whom I quickly started dating. This job sufficed as a means of supporting my child and myself, until I met Mr. Indiana, and my obsession with him became a job of its own. After I moved back from Indiana, I came to my senses and knew that it was time to focus on what I wanted to be when I grew up.

Although interrogating an important witness in a courtroom was something that I would probably never do, my second husband, the lawyer, presented me with a new opportunity to enter the legal arena. He suggested that I become a paralegal, as at the time, there was no required certification. And that's what I did. But the only problem was that, although I was a paralegal, I actually thought of myself as a lawyer in training because, if you remember, I was raised to think that I could do anything.

Somehow, I managed to secure a position with a Park Ave law firm in New York as a corporate paralegal. My credentials were good, as previously I had been employed as a paralegal at the largest legal services company in the United States. Also, keep in mind that at this point of my life I was very young and was judged attractive by men.

These attributes considerably ratcheted up my desirability factor when I applied for a job in a field that, in the 1970s, was comprised of a disproportionate number of male chauvinists. The lawyers worked hard and played hard. Office flirtations were common and all the women in the office were fair game for the lawyers. I knew how to play the

The Journey of an "Invisible" Woman

game, so I managed to appear unaffected by the sexist office banter while preserving my morals, but it wasn't easy.

The managing partner of the firm, Mr. G, firmly believed that women should only be employed in subservient roles, regardless of title, which meant that all women were fair game for intimidation and degradation. Actually, he had a God complex when he dealt with everyone in the firm, whether they were men or women lawyers, secretaries, or paralegals. His modus operandi, when conversing with a young associate, was to stand toe to toe with him or her and then proceed to hurl the vilest curses imaginable at them.

These young lawyers would take this garbage as their careers depended on his goodwill. It was only a matter of time before my turn would come for a confrontation with Mr. G and, when it did, I knew that I was up for the challenge. So, challenge him, I did. Little did Mr. G realize that under my feminine persona lurked the heart of a tiger; but it wasn't too long before the tiger came out of its cage.

Most of the time, Mr. G. ignored the secretaries and paralegals, as in his eyes, he considered them too low on the totem pole to be noticed. After only a short time, I was promoted to a paralegal supervisor and was able to continue my never-ending quest to stand out above the crowd.

The day came when a big project that I was coordinating came to Mr. G's attention. It was now my turn to stand toe to toe with him. Apparently, he was an equal opportunity employer when it came to dishing out abuse, so he got up in my face and started to curse at me.

Feeling confident, I pulled myself up to the tip of my 5'4" height and got even closer to him. This was before the "Me Too" days, and therefore I knew that I was on my own. I told him that if he didn't back off, he'd live to regret it. I had no idea what I meant by those words, but, apparently, they worked. I don't know if he thought he had a potential lunatic on his hands or if he really did respect me.

Strangely enough, after the confrontation with Mr. G., I found myself with a new responsibility. All new associates with the firm had to come to me for training in the basics of practical law, such as drafting certificates of incorporation and bylaws. What a rush, maybe I couldn't be a lawyer, but I could be in charge of one.

My legal work at the Park Avenue firm was short lived when I found out that I was pregnant, and that my dream of becoming an influential power in the world would again have to be put on hold. After giving birth, I decided that it was time to move on to a new career, as I no longer found paralegal work stimulating, and I really wanted to be the lawyer, not the assistant.

One morning I woke up and understood what I was destined to do and that was to be the head honcho of an organization. I would be in control and everyone would have to listen to my proclamations. That would be heavenly. All I had to do now was to find this job nirvana. This might be a little difficult since women had tremendous competition in their climb up the corporate ladder.

Fortune 500 companies reached a record high, while having only 33 female CEOs in 2019. It was difficult to find a job that would utilize my educational qualifications while also fulfilling my desire to be an important somebody. I decided to try something completely different from my previous jobs, therefore I got my realtor's license, but quickly realized that I hated sales.

We moved to Texas and my hiatus from employment continued. Around this time, a friend begged me to help her out of a jam. This friend was principal of an elementary school and was desperate. School was to start in two days and one of her teachers had suddenly quit. I hesitated,

The Journey of an "Invisible" Woman

because I never totally squashed my fantasy of one day becoming a great writer or attorney instead of an educator.

My mind still had flashes of me interviewing the CEO of AOL for an article in the New York Times about a new discovery called the World Wide Web, that would revolutionize the way that we communicated with each other, or seeing my name noted as attorney of the year in New York magazine. Notwithstanding my trepidations, it was time to be realistic. Although I had sworn to myself that I would never again teach, my friend really needed the help, so I said I'd help her, even if only for a few months.

A few months soon became a year, and then I was made an assistant principal, and suddenly I knew the career direction that I would take. I got my administrative certification, became a school principal, and was finally the queen of my very own universe; but I forgot that many queens have to bow to a king. The school's king was the parish pastor who hated women and answered to no one but God. This resulted in many angry confrontations, in which the pastor would constantly remind me that I was inconsequential in the grand scheme of things. The queen was sitting on a throne made out of sand, and the sand was constantly shifting.

I had finally attained my golden moment, even if it were a little tarnished. I had the dream job, a great family, and my health. Nothing could bring me down. But life had other ideas. Within the space of a year, I was involved in a major lawsuit with my school, my husband's job was phased out, and three of my four children moved cross-country. It was a fast slide from the top of the mountain to the bottom of the valley. I began again. The major difference now was that, although my abilities had not changed, my age had.

Technology is a gift to society but it can be detrimental to an older person seeking employment. Job applications prohibit questions about a person's age, but an HR person merely needs to Google someone's name to ascertain their birth date. I was now at that age where roadblocks appeared for older women starting over in their careers. It looked like there weren't just roadblocks for me to drive around to continue in my quest for self-actualization, but I might soon be hitting a brick wall that I wouldn't be able to penetrate. This brick wall had graffiti on it that said, "TOO OLD."

At that point of my life, I realized that I might have to accept the fact that there was something that I couldn't control merely by determination and hard work. Although aging is a fact of life, and death is the only alternative, it's still difficult to accept that age would now define the parameters of my potential achievements, and when the world looked at me now, they would only see an older woman.

But the story didn't end here, as before I knew it, my life would take some strange and happy paths.

CHAPTER 19
WHERE ARE YOUR ROSARY BEADS?

The saying "No good deed goes unpunished" is a fitting phrase that aptly describes the resulting fiasco that emerged from an act of kindness to a friend and propelled my return to the world of education. As I hinted in the last chapter, my good deed backfired on me and I became deeply entrenched in a career that I not only disliked but that also would result in litigation.

However, before I can share the story of this debacle with you, I need to acquaint you with some important idiosyncrasies of growing up Catholic. The somewhat eccentric practices and beliefs of the Catholic religion are crucial to your understanding of what comes next in my career as a Catholic School Principal.

Most children believe that they don't learn anything in school that is applicable to life in the real world, and I was no exception to this train of thought. I never guessed that the rosary and Catholic rules and rituals would eventually play a big part in my life. Every good Catholic school student knows how to pray the decades of the rosary as well as they know their own name. We had cheap everyday rosaries, fancy rosaries for when we wanted to show off among our friends and special commemorative rosaries.

For those of you who didn't get to experience this Catholic practice, let me explain to you what is a rosary. The rosary refers to a form of prayer that uses a string of beads or knots to count the required prayers. The 'decades' are sets of ten Hail Marys. One Lord's Prayer, followed traditionally by one Glory Be, which precedes each decade. Traditional rosaries also have a crucifix. Five decades are recited per rosary. As you can imagine, the practice of saying the rosary could be quite time consuming and would almost always eradicate all impure thoughts from your mind.

The rosary is significant to Catholics, as it is considered an important part of the veneration of the Blessed Virgin Mary in the Catholic Church. She isn't only considered the mother of Jesus Christ, but also is thought to be a direct pipeline to Christ; although, during the 16th century, the Protestant Church considered worship of the Virgin Mary idolatry and an act of heresy. Therefore, if you were Protestant, you definitely didn't use a rosary.

In the past, all Catholic school nuns had worn distinctive religious habits, depending on their order, but they had one thing in common, and that was somewhere on their person was a rosary. I was a bit rebellious in high school. I remember a particularly intimidating looking nun barreling down the school hall towards me with fury in her eyes. I knew that I was in trouble, but for some reason all I could focus on was her rosary swinging from her habit. Maybe I was fervidly praying that Mary would magically intercede to stop my coming punishment.

History reveals that it wasn't only nuns who wore rosaries. In the '30s and '40s in Los Angeles, Chicano youth wore rosary beads, to highlight their Hispanic heritage. The rosary became a fashion statement in the late '70s in the

The Journey of an "Invisible" Woman

Goth and Punk subcultures, reaching into high fashion in the late '80s and early '90s.

Madonna highlighted this fashion trend in her, "Like a Virgin" video. Purists have denounced the practice of wearing rosaries as jewelry, but the Church states that it is permissible, as long as a person's intent is to do glory to God. Obviously, the use of rosaries as a street gang symbol contradicts its purpose as a spiritual tool. So how did a little string of beads affect me?

When I was a child, all Catholic schoolteachers were nuns. We knew these women were nuns because they wore habits with rosaries prominently attached. By the time I was in college, lay teachers were also teaching in Catholic schools and nuns started wearing regular clothes. Nun's habits might be gone, but rosaries were always somewhere on the nuns.

Although my return to education began when I innocently helped my friend by filling in as a teacher in her school, it wasn't long before my leadership skills were recognized and I was hired as a Catholic school principal in a parish in Dallas. At that time, feminism was just exerting its influence on society. In 1972, the magazine "Ms." debuted, and women quickly adopted the magazine's name to use as an honorific with their last name.

It became the accepted form of address for women, regardless of their marital status. In past jobs, I proudly claimed my identity as an independent, strong woman by using this new title. However, in my position as a school principal, I believed that this anonymity was a bit standoffish and contradicted my belief that approachability was an important trait for an administrator. Therefore, I dropped the prefix preferred by feminists and introduced myself to everyone by just my first and last name, minus any title.

During my first days on the job, the question being asked by everyone about me was, "is she or isn't she" a nun.

However, because I wasn't giving out any clues, the staff and students couldn't tell from my name if I was or wasn't a nun. In the old days, the dead giveaway, aside from the intimidating habit, would be that I'd be called "Sister," but modern times changed all that. The one hint that would point to my possibly being a nun was to find evidence that I wore a rosary.

Then again, even that proof wasn't 100% irrefutable. Perhaps a woman really dug Madonna (the singer, not the Blessed Virgin Mary) and decided to imitate her propensity for using the rosary as jewelry. I could also be secreting the rosary away beneath my clothes. Finally, one of the older students couldn't take it anymore and bravely decided to blurt out his question to me. "Where Are Your Rosary Beads?" he asked. With a wink at him, I answered, "In my handbag."

Now he had a real dilemma, as he couldn't demand to see the rosary. In addition, he realized that having a rosary would only give him insufficient proof, as it didn't prove I was a nun, it only proved I was a Catholic. After a few days, I decided it was time to end this little game and let everyone know that I was a married woman, not a nun.

Since this was a Catholic school, there was a strict leadership hierarchy. At the top of this hierarchy was the Pastor, who only answered to God or his representative on earth, the Bishop. In the past, school principals, just like teachers, were only nuns and they reported directly to the Pastor. Both nuns and priests take vows of obedience to the hierarchy of the Catholic Church.

The ranking between priest and nun requires that the nun show complete subservience to the priest. Since I wasn't a nun, this robotic acquiescence to the priest was anathema to my way of thinking. However, my years of Catholic school had instilled in me a never-ending sense of guilt and therefore I was torn on how I should behave. In the end, as it turned out, there would be fireworks.

I was invited to meet weekly with the Pastor and his staff of ten, to discuss school and church activities. At first, I thought that this was a great example of democratic management, resulting in all of us working together to achieve great things for the parish.

My assumption was proven wrong when I realized, after several meetings, that these gatherings were an excuse for the Pastor to regale his little fiefdom with his wise declarations about everything. He had no desire for input from his staff and he made it clear that he would have a heavy hand in every school decision, from important ones like curriculum design and teacher hiring to ones as simple as choosing lunch menus. This was definitely a bad sign.

There were seventy teachers and almost nine hundred children in my school. My substantial leadership position could definitely establish me as a mover and shaker in the community. Now, all I had to do was get the Pastor to recognize my autonomy.

I must have been incredibly naïve back then. Otherwise, I would never have thought that this man, who began his career as a military chaplain and then continued to rise to prominence as a major fundraiser in the Catholic diocese, would view me any differently than he did an obedient nun. In his mind, his word *was* God's word, not just 'like' it.

Little struggles happened daily, as I tried to balance adhering to the Pastor's arbitrary directives with my desire to do what was educationally correct. The students all came from very wealthy families and their parents had extremely high scholastic expectations for their children. In the parents' eyes, every one of their children deserved a spot in an elite private high school. Unfortunately, there were only a handful of these schools within commuting distance from their homes and even worse, the parents were specifically insistent that their offspring attend only two of these schools. The Pastor wanted something too.

He coveted the acclaim that would come to his parish if these two schools took a high number of the school's students. More importantly, he knew that the students' parents would dig deeply into their pockets and generously donate to the parish in gratitude for this accomplishment.

There's no magic in education. Teachers teach and students are supposed to learn. There are numerous tomes that each claim a certain educational theory works best, but in the end some students will do better than others and educational theories go in and out of favor. Standardized tests are supposed to measure if a student has achieved a certain standard for each grade.

The test is meaningless if the system cheats, whether it is the student or teacher doing the cheating. The year that I took over as principal was the year that the first 8th grade would graduate to high school. In order to accede to the desires of the parents and the Pastor, past principals had cast a blind eye to the common practice of not enforcing any time limits to testing. This practice led to the first major confrontation with the Pastor, and in the end, I persevered, and all future tests were timed.

The next issue was much more serious, as it involved misdirection of matched funds. Catholic schools can take a corporate matched fund and use it for educational purposes; most times a church cannot. One of the Pastor's henchmen came to see me at the end of a school day to ask if I'd seen a certain corporate check. I told him I had. I then reminded him that the check in question had to stay in the school's account, as a parent was donating the funds to the school from a corporate matching plan. He said he wanted the check, and in a threatening voice told me to hand it over to him. I told him if he persisted harassing me, I would call the IRS to have them explain the situation to him. I didn't hear from him again, and I reminded myself that this is how a strong woman behaves, but the worst was yet to come.

The building that contained the school and church was featured in Architectural Digest for its avant-garde design. The only problem was that, although it was aesthetically beautiful, it wasn't quite functional. When it rained, a waterfall appeared in my office that, although charming, left mold in its wake. I was soon to find out that this insidious problem existed in many of the classrooms.

The unique design of the school included an individually self-contained air conditioning system in each room. The facility manager was a friend of the Pastor and was in charge of all maintenance for the building. He was instructed to mitigate the mold problem by placing swimming pool chlorine tablets in each ceiling air conditioning unit. Unfortunately, the manager, who previously had been a soldier in the US Army without maintenance experience, didn't realize that the gas produced by the chlorine tablets was poisonous.

You'd think that the skull and crossbones on the label would have given him a hint about this danger. But either he didn't care about the warning or he was too stupid to understand it, and my students started getting sick.

I kept asking about the situation but wasn't told anything further about the chlorine, only that everything was being handled. Finally, in exasperation, I directed some parents whose children were getting sick to ask the facility manager what was going on. One of the parents went to his office and did just that, and a few minutes after that meeting, he stormed into my office with the facility manager's container of chlorine tablets, clearly marked with a skull and crossbones.

The parents had quite a different reaction from that of the facility manager, at the sight of the skull and crossbones. There was no room for doubt in their minds about the seriousness of the situation. It was Show Time, so I picked up the phone and called the Health Department. I was ordered by the Health Department to immediately shut down the school, and before I knew what was happening, my 15 minutes of fame had begun.

All the local news' outlets rushed to the school. The Pastor told me to go home and not to speak to anyone. Of course, I didn't comply with his request, and soon his directives were public knowledge. My celebrity among the other school principals was instantaneous. I was their champion.

I received numerous calls, thanking me for speaking out about what I later found out was just the tip of the iceberg of wrongdoings in the school district. I lasted a few more months at the school, until my rebellion became too much for the pastor to take and I lost my job. I sued, and he paid, and I took my rosary and went home.

CHAPTER 20
TWO FOR THE PRICE OF ONE

You probably learned more than you ever wanted to know about the Catholic Church in my last chapter. However, I forgot to mention the important fact that all nuns take a vow of poverty when they complete their novitiate training and enter the religious life. Yet, Diocesan priests don't take a vow of poverty.

This is an interesting point to consider, as this inconsistency seems to contradict the Bible's exhortation in Galatians 3.28 regarding fairness and equality that, "There is neither Jew nor Greek, there is neither slave nor free, there is no male and female, for you are all one in Christ Jesus."

Apparently, some people who dedicate their lives to serving God choose to ignore the dictates of the Bible and instead agree to accept economic gender inequality. Therefore, it shouldn't surprise us when the average person shuts their eyes to this injustice.

Similarly, I'd imagine that if you saw a sign in a store window that said, "special offer, only available to MEN—two cupcakes for the price of one" you would feel shocked, outraged, and curious as to the underlying reason for such unfair treatment towards women. It's unlikely that in real life you'd encounter such an egregious demonstration of gender bias.

And yet gender bias against women is often viewed as an inevitable price of doing business in a society where only a lucky few women manage to break through the glass ceiling. I was one of those few lucky women who had been able to achieve success in my professional life despite this unfairly balanced power structure, but my triumphs didn't come without a struggle. I had to kick and scream much of the time to assert my right to be judged on my abilities. However, my good fortune is not bestowed on all women.

A woman's age, appearance and sensuality have a major impact on her status in society. Many women throw up their hands in despair when they encounter these artificial and arbitrary qualifications, and accept whatever cards they are dealt, out of fear of retaliation or provoking anger from their bosses, friends or families. Others struggle to maintain their rights and turn to legal resolutions or entreaties to the public for action.

The 1987 movie *Wall Street* symbolized the intrigue and financial manipulations of stockbrokers and corporate raiders. It memorialized a bastion of male exclusivity where a locker room atmosphere, not always comfortable for women, prevailed. Men were the hard drinking, cursing, cocaine snorting power brokers and women were the accessories. Although Victoria Woodhull and her sister, Tennessee Clafin were the first female stockbrokers in 1870; it wasn't until 1967 that Muriel Siebert became the first woman allowed to buy a seat on the floor of the stock exchange. To underscore this male dominated environment it wasn't until 2018, fifty-one years later, that Lauren Simmons became the only full-time woman equity trader at the New York Stock exchange.

Obviously, the situation was ripe for a push back from women to establish their place on the street. There were many old discriminatory practices that had to be abolished and one of these practices was known as occupational segregation. If women weren't treated the same as men for the same work, their only option would be to go to court to get satisfaction.

In 2009, Bank of America bought Merrill Lynch and assumed its responsibilities and liabilities. One of these liabilities occurred in 2013, when a 39-million-dollar settlement was paid to women brokers resulting from a gender bias suit.

News of this settlement sent a huge ripple through the financial community, as Merrill Lynch, with its iconic bull, epitomized the power of Wall Street. The claim was that Merrill Lynch discriminated against women in regard to equal wages, promotions and account distributions. These women had been quiet for many years, until finally they demanded to be acknowledged and judged on their accomplishments, not their gender.

Now, the tide is starting to turn on Wall Street, as evidenced by the appointment in 2018 of the first woman president of the New York Stock Exchange, and placement of the Fearless Girl statue in front of the exchange, but we still have a long way to go.

The world of finance is not the only place where women are compensated less than men for their contributions. In 2019, an esteemed economics team determined that male actors earned $1.1 million more per film than female actresses with similar experience. This pay gap is even greater if the market value of the actress is based on beauty for the calculation of her compensation. But perhaps the most egregious disparity between compensation for male and female actors and actresses results from the use of age as an important determinant in judging that beauty.

Sandy Camillo

Although the $1.1 million pay gap, affecting actresses until they reach middle age, is outrageous, the disparity for women actresses after the age of 50 jumps to an astonishing average of just under $4 million per film, in favor of men actors. This gap even affects top line actresses like Meryl Streep. The obvious conclusion is that a man ages like fine wine, but as a woman ages, she turns moldy like an old piece of bread.

If we lose at something, we've all been taught that we need to be a good sport and not be rude or angry about our loss. But it's difficult to take that adage to heart if the cards are stacked against us; accordingly, laws exist to ensure our rights and protect us against such abuses. For instance, sports are as American as mom's apple pie, and yet their games are not always fair. Title IX is the federal law that prohibits discrimination on the basis of sex in educational activities that receive federal assistance, including sports. Even though Title IX doesn't cover Olympic athletes, it did make these athletes sensitive to this type of discrimination, and determined to do something about it.

In 2019, twenty-eight women on the U.S. Olympic women's soccer team filed a 67-million-dollar lawsuit against the U.S. Soccer Federation (USSF) demanding pay equity for members of the team. The USSF responded to the suit by stating that "pay for women is fair because men are bigger, stronger and faster."

Based on this reasoning, I guess it follows that salaries for men playing on the same basketball and football teams should be based on height, size, and strength rather than ability.

The reaction to that should be interesting. These women Olympic athletes simply demanded that their accomplishments be judged on an equal playing field with

The Journey of an "Invisible" Woman

the male athletes and not be diminished because of their gender.

Recently, there was an article in the news that compared the 2020 salaries for superstar basketball players Sue Bird and LeBron James. They both had 17 seasons in the industry and had each won 4 championships in their own leagues. Yet, Sue had earned $215,000 while LeBron topped out at $37.44M. These outrageous disparities in salary engendered a heated discussion between my husband and me.

He said it was a simple business decision, as the WNBA doesn't raise the amount of revenue that the NBA does and that's why there can't be parity in salaries between players in the different leagues. I had a simple solution to this argument. Salaries should be based on ability, not gender, and that means women must be allowed to try out for the same opportunities as men.

If the NBA is where the money is, then a woman who exhibits the same or better ability as a man must be allowed to compete in that league and receive the same monetary rewards. No one is suggesting that a socialistic process be adopted that evens out the playing field by distributing the same monetary rewards to all players, regardless of ability or merit.

However, if Sue is as good a player as LeBron, then the same revenue will be generated to see her play, and she should receive the same salary and bonus as he does. Although it won't happen overnight, hopefully the mindset of basing the distribution of financial rewards on gender instead of talent will change.

This idea might seem radical to some people, and could even get their hackles up. It's possible that even Sue Bird would disagree with my proposal, if her interview with Mary Holt of *USA Today* indicates her true thoughts. Her statement that she doesn't think "we should get the same money as NBA players" but instead, wants the same media coverage and the corporate sponsors, "so we can build the business; and then when it's really good, like the NBA is, then we can get that money" is startling and yet not too surprising.

Women have been taught to soft peddle their demands and that good girls must learn to wait for things. I doubt that LeBron would be so understanding if the situation was reversed. My reaction is to say, "Show me the money!"

You might feel good about yourself right now because you're neither a financial guru, movie star nor Olympic athlete, but this financial inequality affects even those women with regular lives, and inequality starts at a young age. A 2021 Boston College's Cooperation Lab study has shown that a gender gap in the art of financial negotiation emerges in girls as early as age eight. The study found that "girls asked for less than boys when negotiating with a man,' and that 'we should be teaching young girls to advocate for themselves in the context of negotiation from as early as elementary school." Perhaps Sue Bird's teachers needed to encourage her to better develop her negotiation skills.

There are many new programs such as Work Smart and Start Smart that have been created in the past few years to help college students and women already in the workplace learn how to develop skills to successfully achieve their financial goals. However, as Boston College's study notes, we need to take action to address this gap in a woman's skill set early in her life, as these skills are requisite to the attainment of many of her objectives.

When I was a school principal, I encountered this pay equity discrimination when it was time to give teachers raises. The protocol in my school district required that I review the proposed raises with the superintendent prior to distribution. I was a firm believer in merit raises and had prepared a chart, noting teacher accomplishments to back up my rationale for these raises. My presentation was cut off by the superintendent's comment that he hoped that I gave priority in distributions to the male teachers. I was a little confused, and asked for a reason.

He blithely responded that men had to support families, and therefore should get greater raises than women. I managed to shake off my incredulity and reminded him that we have some male teachers without wives or children to support and many teachers who are single mothers. According to my supervisor's reasoning, I needed to allocate raises based on marriage status and family responsibilities.

Following my supervisor's reasoning, I'd no longer award the most meritorious teacher, but instead would apportion raises according to gender and family status. Married men with children would get the most money, and that amount would increase depending on the number of children. Single men better get married quickly if they wanted to earn more money and if you were a woman teacher, you needed to find a big, strong man to take care of you and beef up your income. This was ridiculous and discriminatory!

Some of my friends are afraid to challenge the status quo and ask for equality with men. Part of their reasoning is that woman will be forced to behave identically to men if they demand equality. Women envision themselves in full body armor on the front line in some horrendous war. It's possible that if the draft was reactivated, women in a truly equal society might be conscripted.

However, just as in all human activities, physical characteristics would be used as criteria for enlistment and active combat. Israel has drafted women since 1948, with 7% serving in combat positions as of 2016. Israeli women wanted formal and substantive equality in their military service. Is this everyone's dream or nightmare?

Sandy Camillo

Equality is not like an item that a woman can choose on a restaurant menu; rather it must be visualized as a fine mist floating over the ground, wrapping itself around everything that it touches. There can't be any societal barriers that impede a woman's opportunity to reach her full potential in life, whether that means having several million dollars in the bank or living in a little cottage with or without a husband and children.

Sometimes this means that we must swallow our fear and take the good with the bad, as long as, in the end, a woman retains her true identity and rightful place in the world.

CHAPTER 21
AIN'T NO STOPPING US NOW

It always amazes me that women are able to score so many victories over the seemingly insurmountable challenges presented to them and still come out the other side with their identities intact.

They may constantly get knocked down but always seem to find a way to bounce right back up. We always hear stories about heroic deeds of celebrities, nonetheless, that unassuming looking person in line next to you in the supermarket sometimes has equally remarkable things going on in her life. My two friends, Linda and Diane were two women who refused to accept societal customs that demeaned women.

They would never blend into the wallpaper when entangled in volatile situations that occurred in their professional or personal lives. I often think about them and all they have done to promote equity for all women.

It was 1979, and Linda and Diane were at the beginning of promising careers. The tenets of the Woman's Rights movement were firmly entrenched in the minds of these young women, who believed that they could do anything and go anywhere. Linda and Diane thought back to the first time that they heard the disco hit, "Ain't no Stopping Us Now" by

McFadden & Whitehead, which contained the following lyrics:

Ain't no stopping us now;
There's been so many things that held us down,
But now it looks like things are finally comin' around,
I know we've got, a long, long way to go, And where
we'll wind up, I don't know."

The song's lyrics spoke to their souls and were a musical expression of their affirmation of the obstacles that hindered a woman's path to success, and captured their hopefulness that things would finally change. Unfortunately, these two women would encounter a number of setbacks before they would attain their personal goals.

Back in the '70s, social and business institutions still harbored long held prejudices about a woman's place in the world, but office buildings weren't the only place where deals were done and fortunes were made. To the casual observer, a golf club was a place where people went to entertain their hobby of playing golf and for dining with friends.

But behind that façade of innocent entertainment, well-heeled men were engaged in tense, frantic business networking. You might notice that I referenced only men in my allusion to surreptitious business dealings on the golf course and that is because some, not many, golf clubs are still considered one of the last bastions of male misogyny. They operate under the antiquated premise that, even if women play golf, they're not interested in the career networking potential that men enjoy through club membership.

It would be interesting to hear them explain the gender disparities in membership benefits to powerful women CEOs like; Susan Wojcicki, of YouTube, Marillyn Hewson, of

The Journey of an "Invisible" Woman

Lockheed Martin, Mary Barra of General Motors, and Ginni Rometty of IBM. You might be thinking that not all of us are CEOs of major corporations who have the clout to influence institutions to change their discriminatory practices, but that's because you haven't met my friend Linda, who considers the anthem, "Ain't No Stopping Us Now," the motivation behind her actions when confronting injustice.

Linda held several academic degrees and many prestigious positions as chief administrator in state government offices. She served on dozens of state civic organizations, received many awards from community organizations, was a board member of several national advocacy organizations and was recognized in her community as an effective advocate for change. She was the total package, and oh, yes, she also had a 15-golf handicap. Linda loved what she did, so after staying at home a number of years to raise her children, she returned to work.

During the years that she was a stay-at-home mom, she would spend an occasional weekday afternoon playing golf at the club that she and her husband had enjoyed belonging to for ten years. However, when she returned to work full time, she was unable to play on weekdays and made what she thought was a reasonable request of her private club. She asked to pay the same membership fee as her husband, so she could tee off with him on the weekend mornings, but the club refused, because she was a woman.

I can't think of any woman that would appreciate being called a "WORM," and yet in many private golf clubs this is the term used to designate a married woman's status at the club. A WORM (Wife of a Regular Member) designates the woman as a guest at her own club. Linda had achieved professional success in her chosen career, and yet she was considered a WORM or second-class citizen at the golf course where she, as well as her husband, were members.

Linda was an activist, and after spending many years fighting for the rights of others, she knew that it was time to fight for her own rights.

It was a lonely fight because other club members were afraid of retaliation if they supported her efforts. At one point, her husband was even asked to keep his wife quiet, but he wasn't intimidated and neither was Linda. She did her homework and pointed out to the club's management that when a male is admitted to a so-called private golf club in New Jersey, the club's Board of Directors knows not to limit that member's access to the playing course because of that member's religion, national origin, color, marital status, nationality, or age.

These clubs are careful not to engage in any discriminatory practices, and yet that's exactly what those golf clubs have been doing to women—discriminating against them because of their gender.

Undeterred, Linda decided to use her expertise to lobby the New Jersey legislature to take action to stop the discriminatory treatment of women at New Jersey private clubs. She also realized that the inequitable allocation of playing times pales in comparison to some of the other repulsive tactics that many clubs used to segregate women and men's membership benefits.

Some clubs also have men-only dining rooms, and often prevent women from voting on club rules. And, when a couple divorces, or a male member dies, the club often orders the woman to clean out her locker, ignoring her status as a club member. Linda delineated these vile practices to members of the New Jersey legislature and demanded that a bill be introduced to eliminate them.

Linda also noted that these restrictions hurt women's efforts to be equal in the business world. For example, while men can invite their business clients to play golf at almost any time, women cannot—a practice that has created "a grass ceiling" of sorts. Linda knew what she wanted and she knew how to get it.

A bill for mandatory equal membership rights for men and women at private clubs was approved by the New Jersey legislature, was signed by Governor Christine Whitman and became law in 1997. Linda's perseverance and achievement were reported in many media articles, including the New York Times, Sports Illustrated and New York magazine. She had made it clear that her rights as a woman couldn't be ignored.

Although Linda spent most of her life living on the East Coast, don't be fooled into thinking that her story would have been any different for a woman living in any other part of the country. Women are given subliminal messages to remind them that they are not, and will never be, equal to men.

Sometimes these messages aren't just vague references to expectations for appropriate female behavior, but are blatantly used as a basis for denial of a woman's rights, which leads me to Diane's story. Like Linda, Diane never had to guess if her gender adversely influenced decisions affecting her professional career, because during most of her life, prejudices against ambitious women were openly accepted.

Diane's early years in Nebraska weren't spent participating in activities at an elite country club. She spent her spare time in high school working at a Dairy Queen and in college she was proud to snatch another female-appropriate job doing babysitting.

This new opportunity would increase the meager salary that she received from Dairy Queen to a whopping seventy-five cents an hour. She was an ambitious woman who knew that she'd never be satisfied living within the social parameters set for women when she was a young girl in the

1950s. Therefore after college and graduate school, she began her quest for self-actualization and realized that this might mean moving to wherever the most opportunities existed for women.

She thought that obtaining a Master's degree would be a positive step in enhancing her opportunities, only to find out that she was now overqualified for jobs considered "fitting" for women.

It was now 1970, and although, at the time, women made up only 4% of the legal profession, Diane thought that taking up the law was a path that might serve her well. This might seem like a strange choice for Diane as, at the time, the common perception was that, "While entry into the medical profession might be justified as a natural extension of women's nurturing role, the law was clearly an all-male domain, closest to the center of power that was not to be invaded or changed by females."

She was a great student and was at the top of her class in Law School, but she was naïve in her assumption that her sterling grades would take precedence over any gender discrimination or that academic success would be the key to opening the door to obtain a great legal job. After she graduated from Law School, and was waiting to take the bar exam, she applied for a summer job. She didn't get the job, but instead got her first taste of what lay ahead for her as a woman seeking employment in the legal field.

The summer job that Diane didn't get in 1973 was with the National Labor Relations Board in Kansas City. She was told simply that they didn't hire women. It looked like she would have to move again, in her search for employment, so she went to Washington, D.C., because she thought that there would be an abundance of available legal positions in this legal mecca.

The Journey of an "Invisible" Woman

Before too long, Diane admitted to herself that hidden prejudices against female attorneys might make it difficult for her to attain her ambitions. When she applied for a job with the U.S. District Court, she was told that they couldn't offer her a job because it was unseemly for a woman to be politically active.

They contended that she had demonstrated this unfeminine trait by, at one point in her career, running for the U.S. Congress. Today, this comment is no longer just ridiculous and discriminatory because of its unfair treatment of women, but also would be grounds for a lawsuit. Diane finally found a job that she loved at the Legal Educational Institute, where she was so highly regarded that she designed seminars for use by government lawyers and managers.

Thinking that she had overcome the lack of parity existing in the perception of a male and female's legal abilities, she confidentially asked for a promotion, but was told that this would be impossible until a man was promoted first.

Despite this setback, word had spread about Diane's great legal skills. As a result, she was recruited to become the Deputy Director of the Freedom of Information Office. This was the top career grade for a government lawyer and a major achievement for a woman.

She finally thought that she had found a home, until the office was abolished during the Reagan Administration and the Department of Justice downgraded her powerful position. She was then re-assigned to paralegal work, but chose to resign and to handle legal affairs at a non-profit, female friendly organization.

Soon, her heart and soul called her back to government work, and she found herself working as a litigator for the Defense Office of Hearings and Appeals. Shortly thereafter, her litigation skills led to her being called to become an

Administrative Judge. Finally, she had found a place where her strength as a woman was seen as a positive quality, and she would never again be asked to maintain a low profile because it was more appropriate for a woman. Linda and Diane believed that ultimately, there was no stopping them, as "things are finally comin' around."

CHAPTER 22
SEPARATION

As I mentioned before, sometimes a woman must take the good with the bad to reach her full potential in life. I always knew that I wanted children. I realized that this role would involve not only the initial nine months of wearily carrying around a basketball inside of my body and at the end of that time enduring hours of excruciating pain laboring to try to get rid of that basketball, but subsequently participating in numerous activities with my children that I considered mind numbingly boring.

Scientists might have disproved the concept that women naturally have a maternal instinct and yet, I knew that being a mother was part of who I wanted to be. So I took the good with the bad and carried that basketball around with me, four times. I would be a mother until the day I died, and yet the significance of this role would change many times in my life, and one of those times was when my children had become adults.

It's every mother's goal to raise her children to be independent, but sometimes the satisfaction derived from her success at establishing her children's independence is negatively counterbalanced by the realization that if she does her job correctly, one day her child will leave the nest and the nature of the ties between mother and child will irrevocably alter.

It was the last summer that my daughter and I would spend together before she graduated from college and moved away. We had moved cross-country from New York to Texas when my daughter was a young child, but our family all loved the ocean, and we spent one month each summer in a rented house on the beach, back East where I had grown up. My daughter and I were sun worshipers and would spend lazy days on the beach lying in the sun, and nights staying up until the early morning, watching old movies.

All of our extended family still lived in New York. Consequently, each year during this month at the beach, we would visit my mother and rekindle relationships with many of my other relatives. Our visits were also an opportunity to show my relatives how great my life had turned out. They all thought that, because of my rebellious nature, I'd ultimately wind up a bitter, lonely woman sitting in a dark café, espousing feminist rhetoric to a handful of like-minded fanatics.

To my relatives' chagrin, their illusions about my life were completely off the track. I was definitely engaged in the feminist movement through my work at a women's advocacy organization, but the peer group that I was working with was comprised of over 100,000 female activists—definitely a lot more than a handful. As far as being lonely, my husband and four children made sure that loneliness was a condition that I never experienced. But we didn't see these relatives the last summer before my daughter graduated from college, because it was the beginning of the last of many things.

My mom had died a few months before our yearly stay at the beach and, therefore, there would be no visits to see her this year. Although I had flown back to be with her during her last few days, the memory of her death was still very fresh in my mind and cast a pallor over what had always been a wonderful time for my daughter and me.

Our lighthearted days at the beach now became days for us to reflect on mother-daughter relationships. My daughter knew that I called my mother at least once a day, so she pledged that she would be there for me, as I had been for my mother. She said that maybe sometimes she might forget to call, but she'd always answer the phone when I called her.

This was a major commitment for a college student eager to establish her own independence. I think that her grandmother's death was a reminder to her that one day she would have to say goodbye to me forever. In the rush of daily life we can forget that life is transient. As the clock ticks away on our shining moments, we must force ourselves to face the reality that our accomplishments will rarely be remembered beyond our lifetimes.

And then, the realization hit me hard, that my children played a big part in my visibility as a woman. I had spent so much time and energy resisting the archaic notion that a woman's role was in the kitchen with crying children clinging to her apron, that for many years I had hidden an important truth from myself.

I now had to admit that, for me, being a mother was something I became not because I should, but because it satisfied a need in my soul. In my desire to reject the sociological role of motherhood because it was defined as a "restrictive institution established to perpetuate a social system designed by men" (Rich, 1976, p. 804). I'd also rejected a part of me that made me who I was.

My daughter is the youngest of my four children and the only girl. The things that my mother taught me about the importance of believing in myself seem to come naturally to her. Perhaps the actuality of growing up with three brothers presented her with a do or die situation. She either asserted herself or got left behind.

No one could tell her that she couldn't do something as well as the boys because then she, invariably, would push even harder to prove them wrong. She had yet to experience some of the restrictive boundaries that society delineates for women.

The summer was over and soon my daughter went back to school for her last semester before graduation and I went home to Texas. Although I always knew that the day would come when she would leave home and begin her own life, I still became breathless at the thought that this *leaving* was only a few months away. All mothers hope that their children become independent, responsible adults but after spending many years helping our children pursue that goal, it is a sobering thought to realize that, for this to happen we must separate from our child. My daughter's three siblings had already left the nest, so you would think this separation would be easy, but it wasn't. When you love someone it's natural to want to be with them and hold them in your arms.

There was an age gap of nineteen years between my first and last child, so it would be accurate to say that a good portion of my life had been spent raising children. My daughter was the youngest child, and with her departure I could just worry about myself again.

That moment of separation was near. In two months, my daughter was graduating from college and moving to Boston to start working at her first real job. I was feeling mixed emotions that were swinging between elation at the thought of finally being free and sadness at the loss of this part of my life. As I look back on some of the times that my daughter and I shared in the past, I remember groggily answering the telephone at two o'clock in the morning to hear my daughter crying that her car was towed or that her boyfriend said something unkind to her.

I wanted to protect her and make her world a happy place, but sometimes things just happened that I couldn't control, such as the sorrow that I felt the day she left for her last semester at school.

The day she left for the last semester at school before she started her own life's journey reminded me of the excitement and joy that I felt the day that I left my family home to marry. I never stopped to think that, perhaps, my mother was feeling sorrow that I was leaving her. As my daughter packed her last few items of clothing, I saw in her face the same happiness that my mother must have seen in my face, so many years ago.

I suddenly realized that her happiness was natural and no reflection of her love for me. I only wished that I could turn back the clock and appreciate some of the shared experiences that I found irritating when they occurred. I think back on the frustration of finding out, just as I was getting dressed for an evening out, that my daughter had worn my favorite dress and left it dirty and crumbled in the back of my closet floor.

How ridiculous I was to get angry over this inconsequential inconvenience. It's strange to think that this little girl, who'd once depended on me to take care of her every need, could now rely on herself.

After my daughter's departure, it occurred to me that I had always depended on her to share with me her passion for life. When I felt low, she could send me into a fit of laughter just by exaggerating a facial expression. Going to the supermarket with her became an adventure. Instead of just grabbing a few mundane Idaho potatoes we mulled over whether to pick a Rose Finn Apple Fingerling or a Russian Banana Fingerling to satisfy her interest in learning all she could about exotic food products.

Sandy Camillo

Children no longer settle down in the communities in which they were raised. Soon I wouldn't have her to go out with, to the newest restaurants serving the kind of food that my husband wouldn't dream of eating. She was very excited to be moving back East after graduation, to where I had started my life and although I understood her desire, I didn't want her to go.

Nonetheless, I continued to, enthusiastically, speak to her of all the new things that she would soon experience, never letting her know how much I wished that she would stay closer to home. I suddenly understand the depth of my mother's sorrow when I had moved away from home, so many years ago.

Yes, we would continue to see one another and speak on the phone all the time, but the relationship would change once she was no longer my little girl living at home, but was supporting herself and living on her own. When my daughter comes home, it will be as a guest. She will have a few personal belongings with her, in the same way as when she visits a hotel. Her base will no longer be the same as mine. We'll do fun things together, but there will be a sense of urgency about doing them, because we will know that we only have so much time to spend together.

When she comes home, I won't participate in any social diversions with my friends, because I'll be too busy trying to make sure that every moment of her day is fun and that she'll want to come home again. In the past, she would spend hours in her room just reading or watching television and this wouldn't bother me at all.

Now, I'll be jealous of any time she takes to be alone, because that time will take away from us being together. I long for the days when parents didn't have to check airline schedules to see their grown children. I remember Sunday afternoons at my parent's home, when there could be up to twenty relatives sitting around the table for lunch. There was laughter, yelling and a special feeling of belonging. Those days are now gone.

As I try to recall my feelings during my daily calls to my mother, I must be honest and admit that many times I made these calls out of a sense of obligation and guilt. But after my mother died, I realized that these calls were probably more important to me than to her. I don't want my daughter to have to wait until I am no longer with her to acknowledge the special connection between us, and yet I want her to have the freedom to enjoy her life without worrying about always trying to fit me into the picture.

I watch her as she goes through the same struggles that every woman experiences, and I'm proud that she possesses a certain ability to handle what life throws her with grace and strength. Unfortunately, I inherited a lot of my mother's "bad" traits. One of them is the ability to instill guilt in my children when they do something that displeases me. I selfishly hold my children very close to me. My sons decided to move wherever the wind blew them and worry later about my ensuing wrath, but my daughter always tried to stay near me, for as long as she could.

She was always drawn to helping others and chose to live in the special service dorm in college. A student living in this dorm had to pledge a certain number of volunteer hours each semester. Upon graduation from college, she was offered a job in a field that furthered her mission to serve others, and she jumped at this opportunity. This job was in Boston, many miles away from Texas. I had mixed emotions about her desire to live so far away from me, but in my heart, I knew that it was time.

She knew exactly how her life would play out and there was no stopping her. Upon graduation from college, she worked for four years as a teacher in a charter school for economically and socially disadvantaged high school students. Then, as she always said she would, she went to law school. I like to think that it was because I inspired her, but the truth was that she did what I never could; she made a life plan and strictly adhered to it, not letting anything or anyone stand in her way.

She married and became a mother, and, luckily, by then we were again living in the same state. Now our separation is not geographic, it is existential. We are two completely separate women, at different stages of life, trying to manifest our significance to the world. I finally understand that separation is a requisite state of being, which is essential for the development of a person's unique identity.

I often wondered why my husband didn't seem to mourn our children's departure from our home as deeply as I did. Is it possible that he had the same feelings that I had, but was conditioned, as a man, to conceal these feelings? Or was his acceptance of this loss because societal norms had declared that women had the sole responsibility for childrearing and thus the relationships with their children comprised a major facet of a woman's life that she didn't want to surrender?

The relationship that my daughter and I shared has changed, and this change was symbolic of the diminishing significance of a very important facet of my identity. In the past, my role as a mother had positioned me at center stage of my children's lives, but now I was demoted to being a supporting actor. My importance in life was shrinking, and I didn't like it.

CHAPTER 23
GOING NATURAL

As we grow older, we realize that we have very little control over most things in life. Our children grow up and do as they please, we get sick no matter how much we exercise or eat healthy and we're still afraid of flying in those death traps in the sky. For this reason, I say, "Go for it," whenever an opportunity presents itself for us to do something that gives us some freedom of choice and helps us to stand out from the crowd.

Although today, these words are a lighthearted example of a woman's right to make choices, in the Elizabethan Age my exhortation would be construed as heretical. Nannina de' Medicia expressed the sentiment of the day when she said, "Don't be born a woman if you want your own way" (UK Essays, p.1).

Today, it's up to each individual woman to decide what kind of appearance she wants to present to the world. But in Elizabethan times, there were rigid guidelines that women had to follow concerning their appearances, as society was the final judge of what was beautiful. Many of these practices caused great harm to a woman.

Pale complexions were considered particularly appealing, so women would lose blood to voluntarily become lighter skinned. Much of their makeup contained poisonous lead, which caused many women to get sick or die, and Sumptuary Laws dictated what was morally acceptable for women to wear in public.

Now that we agree on how lucky women are to live in the 21st century, let's think about one of the choices that women today spend a lot of time agonizing over. Compared to the old days, this choice is something that seems inconsequential, but for some reason, has a critical influence on a women's self-esteem. Let me tell you about my incredulity when I found out about the real meaning of my friend's choice to "Go Natural."

My friend, Sara, told me that she has decided to go natural. My imagination started to run wild. Did she mean that she'd decided to let her upper lip hair grow into a really distinguished moustache? Maybe she wanted to adopt the always-unique unibrow look in a bizarre attempt to imitate Frida Kahlo, the famous Mexican painter.

Or, had her childhood fascination with Tarzan movies motivated her to give up her suburban lifestyle and move to a hut in the Congo? Somehow, I couldn't picture Sara swinging through the trees with Tarzan to allow her inner self to live the natural life in the jungle.

If we consider what the word "natural" actually means, the scope of her transformation could be momentous. The definition of natural is that it is something that is inborn. It is not something artificial, or created by people. If Sara wanted to comply with the intent of this definition, she'd have to give up wearing clothes and would have to hunt for her own food. She'd have to learn to ride a horse, as there'd be no more riding in cars for her, and that would only be the beginning of her commitment to becoming natural.

The Journey of an "Invisible" Woman

My imagination going wild with the possibilities behind Sara's decision to go natural. But wait, it turned out that her decision just meant she was letting her hair go grey. Maybe she was finally tired of being asked the question contained in Clairol's 1956 "does she... or doesn't she" advertising campaign; but should her choice of hair color really be a topic of conversation? Clairol changed its message in 2001 to reflect the idea that beauty is not a specific size or look. Their new campaign slogan became, "Clairol, a beauty all your own."

How many of us can be honest with ourselves and choose to go grey—or not—just because, as Clairol said, "it makes us feel good?" Sara decided to proudly proclaim to the world that what made her feel good was to no longer color her hair. We shouldn't try to elevate the choice to the level of a platitude or a noble pursuit.

And yet, this very personal decision has engendered spirited conversation among people and, for many years, has become the focus of media advertisements. It's difficult to watch an advertisement on television or read a magazine ad without being shown products to get rid of grey hair or wrinkles. Unfortunately, the media successfully perpetuates gender norms to control a woman's decisions regarding her bodily image.

The decision of whether to go grey or not has become something that also impacts men's lives. In the past, men would grudgingly visit their local barber for a trim when their hair started to curl around their ears. Now, men religiously make their monthly hair salon appointments to not only get a haircut but also to maintain their grey-free hair color. Society has determined that a major guideline to identifying an older person is grey hair and wrinkles. People with grey hair are categorized as frumpy, cognitively impaired and asexual, and few of us aspire to embody this image.

Maybe Sara's choice was not a social statement, but just a decision to save some money and time by not having to keep her hair the perfect shade of blonde anymore. But can her decision really be that unaffected by societal influences, and are these standards the same for men and women? If we were talking about Sara's husband's grey hair, the word we would use to describe his look might be "distinguished," or that he is a "silver fox," a term used to imply charm and class.

Unfortunately, unless a woman is a young model, prized for her unique silver locks, grey hair on a woman is often associated with letting herself go or not caring about her appearance. In today's youth-oriented culture, people spend thousands of dollars yearly on products to look young. It's almost a given that women should dye their grey hair to appear younger and more vital for their careers and their social lives. But there are other reasons why people started dyeing their hair that date back thousands of years.

The use of hair dyes began with the ancient cultures. These cultures made their dyes from plants and metallic compounds or a mixture of the two. Occasionally, odd concoctions were developed, such as the Romans' blend of leeches and vinegar to produce black hair dye. Paintings show that, as early as 3400 BC, henna was used to conceal grey hair.

Back then, different hair colors were chosen to signify one's status. In Egypt, black hair symbolized vitality and wealth. Prostitutes during the early years of the Roman Empire were required to have yellow hair to indicate their profession. In the Middle Ages, red hair was the sign of a witch, werewolf or vampire. Medieval people thought that redheads were the offspring of parents who had sex during that "time of the month" and thus, maidens were hunted down and burned to wipe out the tint. That was certainly a severe form of birth control! If you were born a redhead, you definitely had a reason to change your hair color.

Although we no longer categorize people's station in life or other-worldly natures by their hair color, we've all heard the terms, "ditzy blonde", "fiery redhead", and "grey-haired old lady". As there is no standard of right or wrong concerning hair color, we should refrain from using derogatory language about a person's choice of hair color. Perhaps we can't change people's perceptions of the significance of certain hair colors, but underlying those perceptions is the truth that beauty is only skin-deep.

After returning home to New York after living in Dallas, Texas for many years, I was shocked to see that most women in Manhattan had very dark hair. This was directly the reverse of what I had experienced when I arrived in Dallas. I always thought that it was cool to have blond streaks put into my hair for drama. Somehow, after living several years in Dallas, these streaks had gradually morphed into overall platinum blonde hair. A visit to my family in New York for Thanksgiving resulted in a poll among my relatives about my new hair color.

The consensus was that I looked like my Aunt Mary, who was locked away in a mental institution; not the comparison that I was looking for. But this didn't dissuade me from keeping my new look, as part of my nature still made me revert to the rebellious teenager that I had been, many years ago. If my family didn't like my hair then I'd definitely keep the look, until one day, a glance in the mirror made me realize that perhaps this wasn't the best look for an olive skinned, Italian woman.

My hair definitely made me fit into a certain Dallas stereotype, and was the definition of an attractive Dallas woman, but that look didn't make me feel comfortable in my own skin. A stranger was staring at me when I looked in that mirror, and that stranger looked just like everyone else in my neighborhood. I knew that I'd never be happy being just like everyone else, so I dyed my hair RED. And I was happy.

However, some women are tremendously critical of their appearances and need more than a great hair color in order to be happy about themselves. They don't only question whether to go natural when it comes to their hair; they sometimes consider more permanent changes to their entire bodies. This consideration usually occurs if, with the passing of time, they notice a few winkles on their face or extra pounds on the scale.

There might be several reasons that prompt women to negatively react to these natural physical changes in their bodies. Most people know that they need to pay attention to their grooming if they want to attract a love interest. Interestingly, for millennia, stretching from 4000 BCE through the 18th century men also used makeup to enhance their appearance. This practice continued until the mid-1800s when religious values determined that the use of makeup contradicted the intent of the traditional definition of masculinity, and makeup was to be used only by women. However, today, if a woman is interested in engaging in a romantic relationship, she'll have to do a lot more than comb her hair, brush her teeth and dab on some lipstick in order to compete with the idealized images of women portrayed in the media.

Aside from possibly affecting a woman's love life, going natural is also shown to affect a woman's climb up the corporate ladder. Although good looks would seem to have no bearing on a person's ability to perform a job, more than "seven in ten hiring managers say that beauty is an asset to

The Journey of an "Invisible" Woman

women in the workforce," and they define beauty as 'tall, young, physically fit, and aesthetically symmetrical."

Does this mean that a woman with wrinkles and a potbelly is destined to lead a loveless life and is doomed to remain forever in the lower echelon of the corporate world? Women activists would cry out in outrage at this assumption and their advice to women would probably be to fight against these societal myths that claim that such superficial qualities are the determinant of a woman's success in life. Nevertheless, if a woman decides that, for whatever reason, she doesn't like the way she looks, it should be her choice and hers alone, to do something about it.

There's one thing that a woman can be certain about, and that is that she won't be alone if she chooses to go under the knife or suffer the prick of the needle.

Although a lot of women in America want to see change in society's factitious criteria for female beauty, they are tired of waiting and have decided to take things into their own hands, or more accurately put, to rely on their doctor to effect this change. In 2019, 18.1 million cosmetic procedures were done in the United States. The top five procedures in order were; breast augmentation, liposuction, eyelid surgery, nose reshaping and facelift. 92% of all cosmetic procedures were done on females. If surgery seemed a little extreme for some people looking for a change, there were always minimally invasive procedures, such as botulinum toxin injections, soft tissue fillers and chemical peels.

Women might choose to take advantage of these medical interventions instead of going natural, but whatever they do, it's up to them to make the choice.

Most people would, understandably, spend some time debating pros and cons before undertaking any kind of surgery. However, it seems incredible that my friends and I devoted so much time to discussing Sarah's choice of hair color; but the controversy about hair color focuses on more than just its significance to beauty.

As you'll see in the chapter "It's Only Hair", your hairstyle signals clues to the world about your overall femininity and professionalism.

Remember, when it comes to going natural, there's only one criterion: if it makes you happy, do it and then proudly strut around, asserting yourself as a very visible woman. Sara and I did just that.

CHAPTER 24
GIVING BACK

I quickly got over wondering about my friend Sara's decision to go natural when I was confronted with something that would change forever the comfortable life that I was living in Dallas. I finally had a network of friends who no longer laughed at my New Yawk accent, and all of my children were at the stage of life where they didn't need my constant attention. Things were going well and that's when the bomb exploded.

I was no longer working as a principal. While I was debating which career path I should next pursue on my rise to fortune and fame, I decided to keep myself busy by working as a part time realtor. I was headed home from a meeting at which I had unsuccessfully tried to close a deal on a house for a client. I was feeling a bit down and was looking for something to cheer me up. As I parked my car, I was a bit confused to see my husband's car parked outside the house. This was strange, as it was early afternoon. I went into the house to see my husband standing at the kitchen counter. He, mournfully, told me that his company had been sold and that his job was going to be given to an attorney from the acquiring company.

This was chilling news, as he was well past the desirable age for new employment, and we still had two children financially dependent on us. At this point in my life, I was floundering over what I wanted to do with myself. I had won my battle with the school district over the chlorine debacle, and although my legal victory resulted in a reasonable settlement, it also meant that my job at the school was finished.

Now, I no longer had a full time high-income job and neither did my husband. We'd have to pay a mortgage, taxes, two college tuitions and all living expenses on his severance pay, and the sporadic commissions that I earned as a realtor. Something had to give, and I was pretty sure I knew what it would be.

I had become pretty relaxed about finding my next job after I left the school in Dallas. I knew that my husband's salary was sufficient for our needs, never thinking that his job security would be threatened. Therefore, I'd decided, until I found my dream job, that I would temporarily get back into the real estate business. This profession had been a great fallback job for me when I lived in New York and needed something I could do while raising my young babies.

The hours were flexible and the atmosphere was so casual that I was able to take my children with me while showing houses to clients. I thought selling real estate in Dallas would have the same workability that it had in New York, but this was not the case. The Dallas real estate business was a cutthroat industry, where a person's success depended on connections.

Additionally, one out of every two women in Dallas was also a realtor, as this profession was considered a suitable one for women. However, because of the numerous realtors competing for the same clients, there wasn't enough business to go around. The little amount of commission money that I earned was thought of as fun money.

My husband's salary had paid all the bills. There were clearly major changes about to erupt in our lives, and one of them would be to get the burden of an expensive home off our backs. At least I was able to put my realtor license to good use when I became the agent to list our home.

After sixteen years in Texas, I thought that the end of my husband's job meant that we would finally return home to New York. However, I wasn't counting on the severe slump in the job market at that time, and eight months into my husband's unemployment things were still looking glum. It quickly became evident that there was no job for him in New York and that I had to forget my dream of going back home, for now. Even if I were magically to be offered a prominent position in a company offering me a great salary, I had to remind myself to look at the big picture before I made any employment decisions.

If I did a comparison of salaries for me and my husband, it was clear that, based on our last jobs, he made almost three times my salary and there was no way that I could make up this difference in income. It was indisputable that all of our energies now had to focus on getting him a new job as quickly as possible, and my ambitions had to be put on the back burner. My decision to temporarily opt out of a career was something that I assumed was my only choice, and yet this choice had an unfavorable impact on my career potential.

In the 21st century women are succeeding in high-powered jobs, but there is still an unstated principle in many marriages that the partners in a marriage are equal as long as the man's career is not disturbed by the wife's success. A study of Harvard Business School graduates shows that high achieving women are still not achieving their career goals, and it's not because of child rearing but "because they allow their partners' careers to take precedence over their own."

Apparently their self-sacrifice is taken for granted by their husbands, as "More than 70 percent of GenX and boomer men say their careers are more important than their wives." This attitude is just one of many barriers women must overcome in order to be successful. Do you think your partner would admit that, in his mind, his career is more important than yours?

When my husband first started looking for jobs in other states, I was very specific about where I would and wouldn't live, but, after eight months with no job offers, I was willing to go anywhere. Things were getting so dire that we were preparing to move into my parent's home in New York while my husband continued his job search. The moving truck was packed and the movers were preparing to start the long trip to New York when, miraculously, a job offer for my husband came in.

The movers thought we were deranged when we told them that there had been a slight change in plans and they would now be taking our things to Missouri. Yes, we were moving to St. Louis, Missouri. The only thing I knew about St. Louis was the song, "Meet me in St. Louis, Louis," but I was about to learn much more.

I knew that Texas was where cowboys lived with oil wells in their backyards and the popular show *Dallas* took place, but I was clueless about Missouri. I was surprised and happy to find out that it was a state with lush greenery, gentle hills and lakes, and a beautiful golden arch that was built as a monument to the westward expansion of the United States.

The people were hard working and honest but reserved. Things were definitely looking up. On the other hand, making friends turned out to be a little difficult. In the past, we had established our friendships through interaction with

The Journey of an "Invisible" Woman

the parents of our children's classmates, but now our children were adults and we'd have to reach out for friends in new ways.

My husband's new job required that he travel several days a week, which basically left me on my own. Having worked almost all of my life, I knew that I needed to find a job or activity that would contribute to my sense of accomplishment. At the same time, it was now up to me to develop some new friendships for my husband and me. I knew that I didn't want to become recertified as an educational administrator in Missouri, as I had gone through the process twice already, once in New York and then again in Texas. Therefore, I had to find a new way to establish myself.

Finally, I decided to become a volunteer, although volunteering never really appealed to me. As a volunteer, it was difficult to be a leader, since there was no real ladder to climb, but I decided to give it a shot. My first opportunity almost dissuaded me from this effort, as the nonprofit that I reached out to considered sorting paperclips—from a bag into paper cups—an appropriate activity for its volunteers. But you never know when an opportunity will arise. In this case, while mindlessly sorting paper clips, I started a conversation with a young girl seated next to me.

While commiserating over the mortification that we were both experiencing, she shared with me her excitement over an organization she had just joined, which promoted women's rights. As it turned out, this conversation resulted in a life changing experience for me.

A fire was ignited inside me, as I thought about this terrific opportunity to do something about the injustices experienced by women. I had been waging this battle alone for so many years, and now I could join thousands of other women in a common cause.

Sandy Camillo

I could hear my mother's voice ringing out to me as I read the marketing material for this nonprofit. The organization captured the essence of everything that my mother told me about overcoming the barriers that I would encounter in reaching for my dreams. I had finally found a place to focus my energy in righting the wrongs that not just I, but all women, faced in their daily lives.

I joined the local branch of this new women's advocacy organization and shortly after becoming actively involved in their activities, I was asked to serve on their local board. Our common purpose became the foundation for the development of many new friendships. My ambitions naturally led me to eye all potential opportunities to climb even higher up in the organization, but as I was already at the top of the local hierarchy, I knew that I'd have to look elsewhere. And I think I knew what I'd be zeroing in on.

This advocacy organization was a national women's non-profit headquartered in Washington, D.C. Its mission was to promote equity for women. The Board of Directors was elected by the membership, which were 130,000 plus members located all over the country. I identified this non-profit as my next chance for professional advancement, and I decided to run for election to the national board.

As this was an actual election, I'd have to convince the membership that I was the one that they should vote for. Since I had never been involved with politics, campaigning was a new challenge for me. Before I knew it, I was sending out Vote for Sandy rubber bracelets, and thousands of flyers imprinted with my slogan, "Listening to Your Voices."

I was listening to the member's voices and was hearing many stories of shattered dreams. I was elected and assumed what was to be a new role in my life. I soon began making frequent trips to Washington, D.C., and visiting branches around the nation to work for change.

The Journey of an "Invisible" Woman

On these trips around the country, I met women from all socio-economic backgrounds. They all had one thing in common, and that was that they were all angry. They were angry that women had been fighting for gender equity since the first demand in 1848 for women's suffrage and yet, women were still struggling for constitutional equality. They couldn't understand why there was still resistance to the passage of the Equal Rights Amendment or why women were paid less for doing the same work as men. The glass ceiling had been broken by women, and yet, "among the largest 3,000 U.S publicly traded companies, only about one in five board members are women and one in 10 boards have no women."

My visits to different branches enabled me to witness what women can do if they have the right motivation. Many of the branch members were retired, and they realized that any accomplishments that they achieved in promoting equity for women wouldn't personally benefit them. However, they were proud that their actions could make a difference in other women's lives and, in this way, they would be a presence in the world.

I spent four years as a member of the Board, two of which I served as Board Secretary. This volunteer service was followed by my assuming a paid position with the organization as an independent consultant in charge of compliance and governance. In my new capacity I was responsible for ensuring that the organization, and its over 900 affiliated branches remained compliant with all the laws and regulations affecting nonprofit organizations.

This was the type of achievement that I couldn't have envisioned growing up as a young Italian girl in Queens, New York. In my compliance position, I became the lady known as Ms. NO. Whenever an affiliate wasn't complying with the organization's requirements, I was on the scene to rectify the situation, and more often than not it was by saying, "NO, you can't do that."

I finally had found a job that fulfilled my aspirations. Perhaps the most important thing that I achieved throughout my years of service with this nonprofit was that I received affirmation that I was really capable of doing anything I set my sights on. I was an unknown person to almost all of the organization's 130,000 members when I ran as a candidate for the national board, and yet without anyone else's help, I was able to get elected.

The IRS code for nonprofits became as familiar to me as the words to "Row, Row, Row Your Boat," and even though I wasn't a lawyer, legal jargon became my modus operandi. The organization's members knew my name as well as they knew members of their own family, and they knew that I could be counted on to be there for them. There was no doubt that I was, definitely, visible—at least to 130,000 women.

CHAPTER 25
IT'S ONLY HAIR

The day finally came for me to move home to New York, and after being gone for over twenty years, I could understand if things might not be quite the same as in the past. But, strangely enough, this expectation didn't come to fruition. Apparently, New Yorkers cherished the past, as was evidenced in their housing and entertainment choices.

In Dallas, a home that was twenty-five years old was considered ancient and slated for demolition, while restaurants were lucky to survive ten years. Hundred-year-old homes in New York, however, were considered charming, and restaurants that I frequented when I was in college were still doing a thriving business.

The pulse of an East coast city beat to a conservative tune, when it came to changing its culture, delegating more avant-garde trends to cities on the West Coast. But it looked like New York had a rebellious side and bizarrely, the subject of its rebellion was hair. Specifically, New Yorkers' opinions were in complete contradiction to people in other parts of the country regarding appropriate hairstyles for women.

I noticed that the majority of women whom I met since coming home had long hair. Now, I'm not talking about just

Sandy Camillo

twenty or thirty-year-old women, but women of all ages. This was a contradiction of the adage that, when you got older, the long hair had to go—a dictum that women in many other parts of the country followed verbatim. Was this contradiction an anomaly that was only true in New York?

In the chapter "Going Natural," we declared our commitment to doing whatever makes us happy when deciding on the color of our hair. Yet, I find myself, again, addressing another issue focusing on hair, and the cultural, historical and provincial correlations between hair length and age. It's hard to believe that something as seemingly innocuous as hair could be so controversial. My friend Sarah would have been frustrated once she realized that that she wasn't done dealing with hair issues.

When I was a child, my father periodically reminded me that women were meant to have long hair, because his generation firmly adhered to certain distinctions between men and women. They believed that long hair was a feminine characteristic, along with a soft-spoken demeanor. I adored my father and hated to disappoint him, but the hippie culture of the 1960s that I grew up in guaranteed that I would rebel against this stereotype.

To add to the confusion, when the boys of my generation were teenagers, they all wore their hair long to emulate the latest rock star and attract the hottest girls, therefore the old rules on hair length seemed particularly irrelevant to me. Although, to be honest, some of my dad's Barbie doll perceptions about women did rub off on me and even exerted a subliminal influence on some of my behavior.

In the back of my mind, I must have believed that long hair would make me more glamorous, as I'd repeatedly tried to grow my hair. At one point, I even wore a ridiculously long wig. This wig caused many guys to recoil in shock when they attempted to run their fingers through my luxurious hair.

The Journey of an "Invisible" Woman

Unfortunately, my hair had other thoughts about my desire to grow it to ridiculous lengths. My hair was never my crowning glory. When it grew past a certain point it became stringy and the opposite of attractive. As a result, I guessed that I'd have to expand my wig collection if I wanted to fall in line with my father's concept of femininity.

There was only one problem with wigs and, to get the full picture, let me describe something that I experienced during my dating days. You have to envision a smoky bar, because back in the day, everyone smoked. I'm seductively leaning against the bar with a martini in one hand and a cigarette in the other. I'm surreptitiously casting an eye around the room, looking for a man that could become the man of my dreams, and I see Luke (remember the guy on the black horse).

He comes over to me, and after about an hour he nonchalantly puts his arm around my shoulder, only to have my wig catch on his watch and fall to the floor. Saying that I was mortified and that he was shocked would be a major understatement. I did learn something from my experience and that is, to never let a stranger put his arm around you in a bar, or just to never wear a wig again.

I thought back to when I lived in the Midwest and Texas. Older women religiously followed the exhortation that only young women should wear their hair long. If an occasional older woman had long hair, other women could be heard muttering behind her back that she should know better than to try to pass herself off as younger than she was. Strangely enough, other cosmetic attempts to remain younger-looking were acceptable.

It was ok to make a bi-yearly visit to the plastic surgeon to erase some telltale signs of aging. For some reason, Botox and fillers fell into the same category as mascara. In Dallas, women even had their eyelashes dyed so that they would be presentable while shopping at the supermarket, but it was still *de rigueur* for older women to have short hair.

Apparently, New York women didn't get the message about permitted hair length from their peers in the Midwest and Texas. Now that I was back in New York, I decided to do my own very limited statistical analysis of the number of women over forty in New York who had short hair. I attended an event for an organization whose membership was comprised of women, aged fifty plus. I noted that there were only two women out of one hundred fifty with short hair. My gym spin class had 40 participants. Thirty-seven of them were older women, and out of that number only one had short hair. It looked like there was a definite bias against short hair on women in New York.

I asked my hair stylist if my observations were accurate. He stated that only one out of fifty of his older customers asked for a short haircut. I began to closely scrutinize women's hairstyles in magazines and television news and shows. Here's where the discrepancy appeared between my real-life observations of women in New York and the media's portrayal of older women.

When older women were depicted, if they were noted at all, their hair was white and short. All the younger women had long hair. Does this mean that New Yorkers didn't watch television or read magazines? Or for some reason, were New York's older women desirous of looking "younger," and equated long hair with youth?

Obviously, the media plays a large role in swaying public opinion on many matters, and one of them is that long hair equates with youthfulness. The funny thing about this belief is that at one point in time, women in their 80s and older wore their hair past their waist. That was the accepted style for older women.

The Journey of an "Invisible" Woman

I remember my immigrant Italian grandmother letting her hair down, and it was really, really long. In the 1920s, it was scandalous when a woman cut her hair. The young modern flapper was a rebel and her short hair was a symbol of loose morals and independence.

I decided to do a little research on the historical significance of long hair. Maybe the idea that an older woman should have short hair derives from a tradition followed by the ancient Greeks. Widows would cut their hair and bury it with their husbands when they died. Perhaps, we're supposed to correlate the widows' sorrow with older women's sorrow over the loss of their youth and thus, "off with the hair?"

The short hair vs. long hair controversy has a long history. Slaves and defeated armies were required to shave their heads as a sign of subservience. The biblical figure Samson had immense strength until his long hair was cut and then he became weak. A symbol of the youth rebellion of the 60s was long hair.

In 1968, the show *Hair* opened on Broadway, where it ran for 1,742 performances. The main character's hair became the symbol of rebellion, the personification of personal freedom and the right to follow our destiny. It was the dawning of the Age of Aquarius.

It's difficult to believe that something that is mostly dead can have such an influence on a woman's life. Nonetheless, if women want to take prominent roles in society, they need to understand the significance of hair.

Fast-forward to modern-day, and you'll see that hair length is considered an important topic on job-hunting websites. Articles with titles such as, "Work Appropriate Hairstyles" and "Professional Hairstyles for Women" convey very specific directives regarding appropriate hair length in the workplace, and the recommendation is always that short hair for women is the executive look. In *Today.com*, women are advised that, "Short hair in contemporary American culture is typically seen as less sexy, but more professional".

Rose Weitz, author of *Rapunzel's Daughters: What Women's Hair Tells Us About Women's Lives*, recalls a conversation with a women executive who said, "you could look at the company's organizational chart-the chart that shows who's in charge of whom and you could draw a line; Above that line, no woman's hair touched her shoulders". So, it came down to whether you went to work groomed to catch the eye of a potential husband or to advance your career. I wanted both.

Choice of hair length may also be associated with a person's sexuality. The offensive slang term "dyke" has been used to describe the macho, masculine, butch partner in a lesbian relationship. Some lesbians have reclaimed the use of this term, as they consider it politically empowering. The old adage, "You know her when you see her. She wears men's clothing, *short hair,* no makeup," has been used for many years to describe someone who is called a dyke. Perhaps, a patriarchal society thinks that you can change someone's sexual predilections and make them adopt what they consider an acceptable sexual persona by forcing them to have long hair.

Women of all sexual persuasions will maintain their own perspectives regarding long vs. short hair on a woman's head. However, women are not quite so easy going about accepting hair on other parts of their bodies. In the scholarly *Psychology of Women Quarterly*, a paper was published attempting to quantify the disgust women feel about their body hair, their own and that of other women.

The consensus of the participants in the study was that hair on any part of the body other than your head was filthy and disgusting, particularly if there was hair in the armpit.

The Journey of an "Invisible" Woman

The author of the study suggested that this deep-seated revulsion, arising from the neglect of such a mundane habit as shaving, is the result of "omnipresent sexism directed towards those who violate practices to maintain the female body." Or more simply put, score one point for the proponents of patriarchal ideas of femininity.

It's clear that this crazy obsession with hair length is nothing new, as there has been substantial significance associated with hair throughout history. Short hair has been viewed as analogous with someone who exhibits weakness, subservience, and loss of vitality.

These characteristics are sometimes attributed to older women and, thus, some people think short hair is meant only for older women. But on the other hand, there is a large consensus that short hair will give you the edge, regardless of your age, if you aspire to achieve an executive position in a traditional organization. So, I guess a pair of scissors can determine your destiny.

CHAPTER 26
AND THEN I WAS AN ORPHAN

There are many hindrances that women face in their struggle to remain visible in the world. The many things that threaten to overwhelm us, such as inequities in our professional lives and strife in our family interactions, become almost meaningless in comparison to the devastating heartbreak we experience when someone we love dies. After spending many years fighting to become powerful women in charge of our own destiny, we can't cope with our feelings of helplessness and the reality that death cannot be controlled.

We rarely contemplate death unless its actuality is forced upon our consciousness. Until that moment we keep its presence buried in the dark recesses of our minds. Like many children, I worried about my mommy and daddy dying, but it was an almost surreal thought because I couldn't imagine life without them. However, once I was an adult, I understood that the specter of death was definitely going to visit each of us, whether to take a loved one or ourselves. It was inevitable. We just wouldn't know when it would happen and no matter how young or old we were, it would always be a surprise. My surprise was soon to come.

The Journey of an "Invisible" Woman

My mother wouldn't use a bedpan. We didn't do things like that in our family. She was now living on a hospital cot in the living room. This is the same room that we were never allowed to sit in, and that had all its furniture covered with plastic until my siblings and I were out of our teenage years.

The house she had spent a lifetime scrubbing and redecorating was now worn and tired-looking, but her nearly blind eyes couldn't see the changes. Her memories were full of images of herself as a young bride, stepping into one of the prettiest houses in Bayside, New York.

She was going to be 96 years old, and yet I never thought of her as old. She still went into Manhattan to get her hair colored and could hold her own in any conversation. I expected her to always be there for me. Her decline started with a single cut.

It was Mother's Day and my mother was going to my sister's house for a special celebration. This was something that she had been looking forward to for the past week because it meant that she would be able to socialize with her oldest daughter and grandsons. Although she still loved to talk and share a meal with people, her opportunity for doing these things had dwindled, as most of her friends and siblings had already died.

Therefore, she was very excited as her grandson hurried her out the door of her home and down the patio steps leading to his car. As she went down the last step her ankle got nicked by a protruding piece of brick. She didn't think it was a big deal at the time so she didn't mention the injury to anyone.

The next day, my mom complained to me that her ankle had started bothering her. At the time, I was still living in Texas, so the telephone was my only lifeline with my mother. It was a lifeline that I used to call her several times a day, but it was no substitute for seeing her in the flesh. Hearing her acknowledge her discomfort concerned me, as she would rather have open-heart surgery with a local anesthetic than admit to being in pain.

The only time she had ever been sick was when, at the age of 88, she had a mild heart attack caused by two blocked arteries, but even with this event, her reaction had been that she simply wasn't quite feeling herself for a few days. My mom's uncharacteristic complaint about her ankle indicated to me that something was going on, and it wasn't good.

My mother's live-in aide called me a few days later to say that, while my mother was eating, her head suddenly slumped to her chest; she started to drool and seemed out of it for a few moments. She then continued eating as if nothing had happened. I immediately got on the telephone with my brother, and we both agreed that my mother had to be seen by a doctor.

My daily calls to my mom now consisted of my ranting on and on to her about the importance of her visiting the doctor. She'd hang up the phone on me, as she generally did when I spoke to her about something she didn't like. If I was a strong woman, she was superwoman.

You didn't make an Italian mother do something she didn't want to do, and my mom didn't want to see a doctor. The pain in her ankle increased until she reluctantly agreed to the visit. The doctor took one look at her and ordered her hospitalized.

It took only one night in the hospital to have my mother screaming to go home. At this point, an entirely new array of symptoms had appeared. Her knee and stomach were now swollen. She was no longer urinating and her pulse was alarmingly low. She would allow only noninvasive tests to be administered.

They set up IVs for hydration and infection and said nothing else could be done if she didn't want any invasive

The Journey of an "Invisible" Woman

procedures. She was still begging to go home and, against her children's better judgment, she was released. I jumped on the next plane to New York to see firsthand what was going on.

Now, my mother was home with all her children. This was all she ever wanted. Her condition quickly escalated from bad to worse, and it was apparent that she wasn't going to recover from her illness. We gathered together to wait for the end. It came two days after her 96th birthday.

The responsibility of daily phone calls and visits was over. It suddenly occurred to me that she might have found our conversations less than scintillating, as recitations of my daily activities might not have been that entertaining. Looking back, I think our conversations were mainly egotistically centered on me.

She had accomplished her goal of raising me to be an accomplished, independent woman, but now one of the things that I did best was no longer happening. I knew how to be a daughter, but that role no longer existed. I was an orphan and the last person who really knew me, was gone.

Our husbands or wives love us for certain qualities. Our mothers however, love us just because we exist. In their eyes we will always be their adorable children, even if the world sees us as a barely visible human being. Although society may begin to minimize our importance as we get older, our mothers are always there to bolster our confidence. My mother's words of encouragement still ring in my ears, as she exhorts me to never give up my climb up the ladder to achieve personal fulfillment. Those words, "You're never too old or too plain for greatness and you'll only fail if you stop trying," still drive me to, tenaciously, cling to my dreams.

But now she was gone, and it was my turn to be called and visited, and the thought was frightening. I had spent all my life being the daughter, asking for advice and seeking approval. No matter how much more educated I was than my Mom, I still relied on her wisdom. Many times, it was a comfort just to know that I could ramble on to her without making sense or being judged. Will I be as selfless with my children?

Can I smile when my son plans his vacation to Hawaii when I really wish he would visit me? My mom encouraged me to travel and enjoy myself. I now understand the adage that you can't know how someone feels until you walk a mile in his or her shoes. My mother's shoes were always a little tight on me.

When my mother died, the anchor to my identity was severed. This was a transformative event for me because I was now missing a part of myself. To add to my grief at the loss of my mother was the outrage that I felt about the attitude of people who inferred that, since she was 96 years old, her death wasn't such a big deal. As many women know, society declares that a woman's self-worth diminishes as she ages.

Now I understood that ageism affects women even after they are dead. Although this concept is new to me, researchers who study the impact of parental death apparently have recognized it. Senior research assistant at the School of Public Health at Drexel University, Miriam Moss states, "Old people are not valued in this culture. In society, the loss of an elderly parent is not seen as particularly important."

The term "Disenfranchised Grief" is the term used to define grief that is ignored by society. Because society thinks it's normative to die after a certain age, the loss of an older parent doesn't elicit the same sympathy as if the person was struck down in the prime of life. Nonetheless, love is love, and its loss doesn't become any easier because the person you love has become older.

The Journey of an "Invisible" Woman

There is no ranking system to judge levels of grief. Each loss affects us differently depending on our relationship with the deceased. Past hurts and resentments can affect how we react to a death. However, one thing is certain, and that is that when death taps someone near to us on the shoulder, it serves as a reminder of our own mortality. We are still someone's child, even if we are in our sixties and still have a living parent.

When that last parent dies, we instantly become the older generation and with the death of my mother, I was now the next generation. I recall a conversation that I had with my brother after one of his close friends died. He remarked to me that you knew that you were old when your friends started dying. I've not had that experience yet, but the death of my parents pointed out to me that I was now on the" front line of mortality."

I didn't think that I'd ever stop crying over the death of my mother, but I did, because I knew that she would be proud that I was following her instructions to be a strong woman. Whenever something happens in my life, the desire to pick up the telephone and call my mother is still overpowering. I look at her photo and realize she will always hear me calling her. I'll just have to listen a little bit harder to hear her answer.

CHAPTER 27
I'LL TAKE THE TOASTER

I've been told that I talk about death a lot and perhaps this is true. This seeming fixation on death may be because, when death commands our attention by calling our loved ones into its arms, we have no choice but to give it the attention that it demands. Before we bow to this command for attention, we need to look at the gender differences surrounding the subject of death, and also consider how the circumstances surrounding the end of life can impact your self-image and your perception of life.

An Icelandic research article, "Death Talk: Gender Differences in Talking About One's Own Impending Death", indicates that the majority of women who participated in the study-initiated talk during interviews about their own impending deaths, but men were reticent to share their thoughts. Studies also indicate that widowed men have higher mortality rates than non-widowed men while, on the other hand, widowhood is actually a protective health factor for women. Death is an instance where women finally get the upper hand.

I recall my mom constantly telling me that she wanted to be cremated. I was a bit confused at her adamant request, because many old time Catholics were against this practice. She finally explained her reasoning to me. If she was traditionally buried, she was concerned that she wouldn't look her best as she lay in her coffin. Her sister would then gaze at her body and make vicious comments about her appearance.

I'm not kidding about this. She had high standards regarding a women's appearance and would have loved participating in that Icelandic study in order to regal others with directives for her death. No matter how or when we die, the real drama begins after death, as we will learn in the following stories.

It was 1:30 a.m. We woke up to the telephone ringing and immediately wondered which of our four children were sick or in trouble. However, this time the news was almost expected. My father-in-law had been begging God to let him die for the past week and tonight, his wish had been granted.

Patrick was ninety-three years old, and living independently until the past month, when he'd finally agreed to hire a part time caretaker. His home was in the Bronx, a dilapidated suburb of New York City. The neighborhood was dramatically referred to as, "Fort Apache, the Bronx," in the 1981 blockbuster movie by the same name.

As a young man, he proudly purchased a three-family home in this neighborhood filled with hard working Italian, Irish and Jewish immigrants, and took in tenants to make ends meet. He spent many happy nights on his stoop singing, placing bets with the local bookie and slinging down shots of rye.

Now, he entertained himself by sitting on that stoop and thinking back on the good times. But memories of things like his son's first service as altar server (which, back then, was referred to as "altar boy") were often pushed aside by strange new sounds. A constant sound in this new reality was of a chicken screaming as its neck was snapped.

His new neighbors used the blood of this bird as an important ingredient in their religious ceremonies. The chicken's screams competed for attention with the sounds of warfare among the gangs, fighting in the street. These sounds drummed out the tinny melodies squeaking out of Patrick's old record player, as he sat alone on his porch listening to music.

Patrick wanted to be everyone's friend. If you asked him about his neighbors, he would never refer to their race or religion. He felt happy that he was sharing his home with people who were as dear to him as his own family, and he offered his tenants the same amenities that he enjoyed in his own living quarters. An old man living with strangers sometimes gets taken advantage of, but nonetheless, they will often overlook these mistreatments rather than be alone.

Patrick's tenants understood this, and became heartless in their actions towards him. One of his tenants hadn't paid rent in months and the other no longer paid utilities. They would throw their garbage out their windows because they were too lazy to bring it to the outside trash pails.

Maybe his old eyes could no longer see the peeling paint and unhygienic conditions in his house, but he never lost his pride of ownership. The day Patrick died, both tenants decided that now they would live for free, for as long as possible. My husband, as the executor of his father's estate, had to deal with these tenants, and the interaction was a living nightmare.

After two years of lawsuits and eviction proceedings, the house was finally sold, and we were happy to think that things would settle down. Little did we know that the fun had just begun. Suddenly, relatives and friends came out of nowhere, claiming that Patrick had promised them various possessions. The will couldn't be probated until these claims were resolved.

My husband was emotionally involved, so as a result, I had to assume a new role as an impartial mediator between all the warring parties, a leadership position that I wasn't expecting or anticipating.

All of our nightly conversations now centered on who should get what. One neighbor even maintained that Patrick told him that he would get his house when he died. Relationships ended and enemies were made. Patrick was a proud member of the old school of Italian men, and this meant that the men in the family were kings. This could present many problems, especially if you were Patrick's wife or daughter.

As Patrick's wife was deceased, that only left the daughter. She had always resented her father's conviction that her brother was the chosen one because he was a boy. It seemed almost natural to him that the son should be encouraged to do great things in life, while the daughter shouldn't be encouraged to reach too high. Now that Patrick was no longer around, his daughter decided to direct her long held wrath to her brother.

My sister-in-law would be particularly irritated to know that gender inequity persists, even after death. Thanks to the computer-generated rebirth of some dead celebrities, these celebrities can still earn after they've left the earth. Because, as Patrick might have understood, marketing shows that dead celebrity men are worth more than women. The BBC quotes Forbes magazine's 'highest paid dead celebrities of 2018' chart to show that, "of 52 top-earning dead celebrities, only five have been women, since 2001."

My husband was aware of his sister's feelings and tried to commiserate with her. In his role as estate executor, he also tried to be as fair as the biblical judge Solomon but, as often happens in family disputes, no one walked away happy. The fascinating thing about Patrick's death was that most of his possessions, aside from his meager house, held little monetary value, and yet people were fighting among themselves, as if items from the Louvre were being distributed.

My husband tried to do his job as executor as best he could, but each side demanded that he should only satisfy their individual desires. All my efforts at mediating among family members couldn't prevent the split between my husband and his family. There was obviously more at stake here than monetary considerations.

On the other hand, unlike my father-in-law's situation, when my mother died there were substantial assets to be distributed. The house itself was deeded in my mother's will to me, but the items in the house were not designated for anyone in particular, and as you will see, this act led to a free-for-all among the family.

I was still living in Texas at the time of my mother's death, therefore; I relied on the wise counsel of my brother to get things done. As he, too, was living out of state, he engaged a local realtor to facilitate the sale of my mother's house. Late one day, I received a call from the realtor, who was exasperated over the condition of the house. She said that there were broken beer bottles, cigarette butts, leftover food, and trash everywhere you looked.

During our telephone conversation, the realtor also cryptically made a reference to missing objects. I realized that it was time for me to fly to New York, to see in person what was going on.

Even when my mother's health was failing, she always maintained the cleanliness of her home, so I wasn't prepared for what I was about to see when I walked into her house. The realtor had understated the house's condition, as filth was everywhere. It looked like house parties were going on 24/7, but the greatest shock was when I realized what the agent meant by missing objects. The dishwasher, clothes washer, wall clock and even the glass doorknobs were missing.

Also, all my mother's clothes, furniture, jewelry, and basically anything that could be removed from the house had been removed. It looked like a bunch of marauding vandals had raided the house. My friends recommended that I call the police but I couldn't do that because unfortunately, I knew who was responsible; and that person was a close relative.

The knowledge that I had been betrayed by one of my own relatives saddened me more than any lost possessions. It was understandable that someone might want a memento of my mom, but the motivation for these acts wasn't sentimentality. Instead, it was leaked to me that these items had been sold for cash. Needless to say, family relationships were irrevocably changed because of what had happened. Like in so many families, my mother was the glue that held the family together. Now that she was gone, it was every man/woman for him- or-herself.

As a result of these events, family members started to scurry around like a bunch of ants that had recently lost their queen. This was the moment I realized that, although I might have been a sparkling diamond in my mom's eyes, I'd have to prove to the rest of the world that I wasn't just a cubic zirconia. I had to make others see that I really was that rare diamond, so I decided to become the new glue in the family and try to pull everyone together.

A friend of mine once remarked to me that one of the benefits of growing up in an extremely poor family is that when parents die, there are no fights, because there are no material assets to fight over. However, I don't know if this reasoning is always true. If Patrick's case is used as an example, most of his possessions wouldn't command more than ten cents on the dollar and yet, there was almost bloodshed over the division of his spoils.

Death brings out hidden emotions in all of us. To some people, the reading of a will confirms their long-held belief that their parents loved them less than their siblings, or they believe that their parents shouldn't have left anything to the ne'er do well sibling or wealthy child. These people see their siblings as rivals for their parents' affection and attention, and the parent's death intensifies these insecurities.

When these feelings are combined with envy, because of feelings that, "I want what you have," a combustible situation results. Money is not the only thing at stake.

I recall an article that I read in the Washington Post that reported about a method to help reduce these after death battles. Parents would gather their adult children together and hold a pseudo auction for their possessions. Monopoly money was used and the children bid for the different objects.

A record of the results is kept with the parent's will for future reference and hopefully a peaceful distribution of assets. This might seem silly or even macabre at the time of the auction, but it might help preserve family relationships once a death actually occurs.

My inheritance of my mother's house was an unexpected windfall, but to the baby of the family, it was also validation that I wasn't just an afterthought in her eyes. Someone else might have grabbed my mom's toaster, but my bequest didn't just have monetary value; it was proof of my mom's love, and that I was someone important and visible in this world.

CHAPTER 28
CHANGES

After 26 years living away from our home state, we were finally back. My excitement was tempered with guilty memories of my mother begging me each day to come home, and now that it had happened, she was no longer alive to welcome me. Many momentous events had happened during the years that we were away from New York. Perhaps, one of the most horrifying was 9/11.

This terrorist attack took not only lives, but also engendered overwhelming feelings of anxiety in the state's citizens. I remember bragging to people in other states that I always felt safe wherever I went into New York City because I was a native New Yorker. 9/11 changed that sense of security in even the most hardened New Yorker.

New Yorkers became very vigilant wherever they went. It was now *de rigueur* to identify the location of all exits in a venue before attending any event. Looking back to when I was a little girl, I remember my mom taking me to the gigantic Macy's department store in Herald Square. At the time, I thought it was so silly that she would remind me every time we were in the store what we needed to do to escape the store in the event of a fire.

Sandy Camillo

I had never experienced such a dramatic event in my life and therefore thought she was being neurotic. If you had suggested the possibility of a 9/11 scenario to friends and family back then, they would have committed you to a mental hospital.

Now, common sense demands alertness to your surroundings with exhortations everywhere that, "If you see something, say something." Sighting an abandoned suitcase at a train station is justification enough for notifying the police. There is even a national awareness day on September 25th each year to remind us of lurking dangers, as if it would ever be possible to forget them. We may not be able to prevent another catastrophe but we are definitely always aware of the possibility of its occurrence.

It wasn't just my personal life back home that was changing. In recent years; the world had undergone major social and economic changes. Church attendance dropped in the previous 15 years, as people turned to other forms of spirituality. Marijuana was legalized in many states for both medicinal and recreational use. Interracial and same-sex marriage gained acceptance, so couples were able to lead their lives without harassment.

A 2018 Gallup poll revealed that a majority of Americans thought that first trimester abortions should be legal, and that 94% of Americans would support a woman president. The first black president, Barack Obama, was elected, and a major step forward for women was taken when Kamala Harris, the first African American, Asian American woman was elected as Vice President. The majority of women preferred to work outside the home and the idea family was small, with 0-2 children.

The world became hyper-connected because of advances in technology. In 1998, cell phones were a rarity and self-

The Journey of an "Invisible" Woman

driving cars existed only in sci-fi movies. Now, as of February 2019, 81% of U.S adults own a smartphone.

The changes continued at a rapid pace. The Internet and social media provide education and communications to people worldwide. Twitter and Facebook are the new forums for social interaction. 9/11 made terrorism a focal point of the news, and this awareness changed the way people lived. Social responsibility became a rallying cry, with Occupy Wall Street symbolizing a lack of trust in financial institutions.

People demanded that the government address the issues of income inequality and climate change. And the "ME Too" movement represented women crying out against sexual harassment and discrimination.

Team building was the rage in corporate America. This resulted in new business structures that involved major change. The book *Who Moved My Cheese?* was a motivational business fable on how to deal with change that became a hot best seller. So much had changed in the 25 years since I had moved away from home, but these changes were easy for me to accept, since they were happening to everyone. The changes that nearly did me in were the ones that affected only me.

The pain inflicted on those left behind from the death of a loved one is staggering in its intensity. My mother's death is a recurrent theme in much of my writings perhaps because of the unresolved guilt that I harbored when I left her to move cross-country. She continually beseeched me to return to New York, but my husband's job made that impossible. Now I was back and there was no mom to visit, take out to lunch or just to hug. I had returned too late. This change could never be reversed and my memories would always remind me of my loss.

In the back of my mind, I thought that when I returned to New York, I could surround myself with friends and relatives to fill the void left by my mother's death, but my old friends had moved away, and I soon realized that establishing new friends wouldn't be easy. My children were now adults, so new friendships could no longer be made based on the commonality of parenthood.

Our attempts to reconnect with our relatives were superficially successful, but these interactions were not on the intimate level that they had been. During the years that we were living out of our home state, our relatives had gone on with their lives and developed long-standing friendships that had little room for outsiders.

I also have to admit that during my years in Dallas and St. Louis, I didn't make much effort to stay in contact with these relatives, and now I was sorry for that neglect. Families in Dallas would brag that their children went away to college but always came back to the neighborhood, and in St. Louis, you were identified by which high school you attended.

I smugly laughed at how provincial all of this sounded and yet, underneath my smugness there was envy. I had felt like a nomad when I lived in Texas and Missouri. My roots were far away, and I longed to feel connected again.

There's some truth in the saying, "Be careful what you wish for." My husband and I were finally back home, but we were alone. Our children were scattered all over the country and we couldn't complain, because we had set the stage, by leaving our families so many years ago. It was apparent that a major part of how we had defined ourselves had been through our parental responsibilities. For many years, our children's health, education and happiness had taken priority in our lives, competing with our personal priorities. We would now have to fill the void left in our lives, because of our new status as adults without dependent children. It was time to remind ourselves that, once again, we needed to focus on our own fulfillment.

The Journey of an "Invisible" Woman

Despite my excitement at moving back to New York, the move itself was a shock to my system. I thought that it would be as easy and rewarding as all of our other moves, but boy was I wrong.

We still, gleefully, remembered our successful real estate transaction when we moved from New York to Dallas, Texas. The New York real estate market had been booming, and foreign investors and dot-com guys were carrying pots of gold to real estate closings. We never even had to list our home. My husband was approached on the bus to the train station by one such investor. The investor asked my husband to say a $ number and, sight unseen, the deed was done. We left for Dallas with our pockets overflowing with the money that we had made from that sale.

We bought a stunning mini-mansion in Dallas in the most desirable section of town. When we later moved again from Dallas to St. Louis, the real estate possibilities were even more amazing. The house in St. Louis was not only sprawling, modern and in the best neighborhood, but it also had a park like backyard. We quickly forgot that the Dallas and St. Louis real estate markets were in a different universe from the real estate market in New York.

We had a real surprise to look forward to when we began our search in New York. To make matters even more discouraging, this wasn't a relocation move and therefore all expenses came out of our own pockets, and our pockets were no longer overflowing with cash.

Pouring over real estate listings on Zillow and Realtor.com quickly deflated our expectations of living in a house similar to the ones we'd left in Dallas and St. Louis. I had become very sentimental about moving back to my native state, and was determined to move back to the neighborhood where our first house was located when we were newlyweds.

Sandy Camillo

I didn't get attached to houses, because we never stayed in one longer than seven years and I liked the excitement of moving. We had owned seven homes in three states by the time we planned our return to New York, and I was determined that our eighth home was going to be a winner.

Maybe my heart sensed that this might be our final house, so it became an especially important purchase. Because we were still living out of state, finding a house wasn't a simple task; it meant arranging airline flights, hotels, and pet sitters. After several trips and visits to ninety houses, I decided that I needed advance reconnaissance, and I enlisted my sister, who lived in New York, to attend open houses for us.

After attending several disappointing open houses, she finally called to say that she saw the perfect house, but the price was double what we wanted to pay. At this point, our house in St. Louis had sold and we would soon be out in the street. We jumped on the plane and went to see the house.

It looked like a wedding cake, and seemed to be calling out my name. When my husband looked at potential homes, all he wanted to know was where the television would be mounted. When I looked at houses it was to find a house that had that special indefinable something that made it a home. This house had that "special something."

Without hesitation we bought the house, and just the two of us moved into a 5-bedroom home in the middle of a neighborhood filled with young families. Its price also meant that we would be watching our wallets for a long time. Most of the people our age were selling their homes in New York and moving to sunny Florida, but I knew that this was where I was meant to be. Perhaps living in my wedding cake house wouldn't make me the belle of the ball, but every time that I went into the city and saw my old stomping grounds from college days or passed by the house that I grew up in, I felt

The Journey of an "Invisible" Woman

good inside. I was connected with my past. The familiarity was as comforting to me as slipping on an old sweater that had been worn by my mom.

However, it was time to acknowledge that my struggle, as a woman, to remain visible was different than it had been when I was younger. The big change came about, because now I was an older woman. The gender inequity that I confronted in my personal and professional life in the past now incorporated ageism into its fold, to present additional challenges to my success.

This reality inspired me to emphasize the plight of older women's rights in my advocacy efforts. I quickly found out that, not only did most people cast a blind eye to ageism against women, but also even the victims themselves accepted this discrimination. I started to get deeply involved in ageism, particularly its effect on women. Before too long, I was writing a daily twitter blog on ageism and had attracted followers from all over the world.

In order to spread awareness of the danger of ageism for women, I started presenting workshops on ageism to nonprofit women's groups. During one of these presentations, I was astonished to hear a woman tell me that she had never been the subject of ageism. Several weeks later, I received an email from this same woman.

She told me that, recently, she'd recognized that she was being discriminated against, because of her age. She and her group of "older" women friends had rented a beach house. Everything that could go wrong in a rental went wrong in this house.

As a result, the renter left a scathing review on the rental website, followed by a response from the landlord. The landlord commented that the ladies' complaints should be ignored because they were, "a bunch of *old* ladies who were disgruntled because they weren't attractive anymore and they should just stay home, knit and make cookies." This landlord managed to bundle together, in just a few words, several derogatory sexist ideations.

My guess is that this man's words represented issues usually hidden from polite society and I had a big job in front of me. In the past I was looking to even the playing field for myself, but now I was determined to level the playing field for all women.

I was finally home again, but this time it was without a mother or children. I had adapted to many changes and would now focus on enhancing my visibility through helping other women. Little did I know what was coming down the road.

CHAPTER 29
"OLD" AND FEMALE, FUHGEDDABOUDIT!

Remember the woman in my first chapter who couldn't get the bartender's attention? Maybe she was invisible to the bartender, because she had several characteristics that he considered unappealing, such as being ugly, obese, or inordinately shy. Anything is possible, but my bet is that the predominant reason she was ignored was because she was "old."

I was raised to believe that intelligence was a prized quality in a woman. However, society has prioritized certain superficial traits to use when determining a woman's value other than her intelligence. Gender stereotypes define the perfect woman as one that possesses at least three specific traits.

Beauty and sexuality are two of the qualities that are fairly obvious to judge. On the other hand, the third criterion is a little more difficult to appraise, since most men are hesitant to admit that this is what they secretly desire in a woman. Hopefully, you're now breathless with anticipation to learn about this third characteristic of the perfect woman.

Let me tell you how I learned about the mysterious skills I'd need to become a perfect woman. Shortly after my

Sandy Camillo

engagement to Blue Eyes, we decided to meet with my soon to be father-in-law at his home, to tell him about our engagement. To the casual observer, Patrick was a great guy to be around but, unknown to me, that niceness was reserved only for his interactions with men. He was lively and always had a good tale to tell.

My fiancé and I had gotten engaged after the third date, so I hardly knew my future father-in-law when we went to meet him. Actually, I didn't even know Blue Eyes very well. Therefore, it came as a surprise when Patrick asked to speak privately with me.

We sat down together and within moments, he told me that the most important thing that I should remember if I wanted to be a good wife, was that women were good for only three things; cooking, cleaning and f...king. He then added that I'd better perfect my cooking and cleaning skills, as my sexual desirability was almost at an end, because I'd be 30 years old in two years.

I couldn't decide whether to run out of the house or give Patrick a slap across his face. I knew that his son was a good guy, so I decided to consider his words the ranting of an ignorant misogynist. Suddenly my mother's words rushed back at me. She too had implied that my value as a wife would diminish as I got older. That's when it really hit me that I better hurry up and reach for the stars, before I'd be too "old" to reach them.

Society's obsession with youth creates a spiraling effect that impacts older women in all aspects of our lives. My friends and I all used to joke about dreading our thirtieth birthdays. Even though we were only in our twenties, we were aware that women were marginalized based on their looks and we thought beauty was reserved only for the young.

The Journey of an "Invisible" Woman

This marginalization becomes a much more serious issue when a woman becomes older, and the visible markers of aging become correlated with specific social implications. Pretty women get their pick of men and are hired for plum jobs. A woman's psychological well–being, body image and ability to succeed at her career can all be adversely affected by gendered ageism.

For instance, women are constantly bombarded with negative images of aging in the media. They're told that having wrinkles and grey hair is the same thing as waving a flag that is imprinted with the words, "Expired, no longer desirable."

Marketing companies often take advantage of an older women's fear of becoming invisible and hype numerous anti-aging products to us with the promise that these products can change our lives. Advertisements for "anti-aging" beauty products sustain the belief that aging is something to be feared and avoided at all costs.

The American Academy of Dermatology sponsored a Facebook ad that stated that a board-certified dermatologist could help a woman with her anti-aging goals. The ad perpetuates the idea that aging is a sickness that a doctor can cure. However, from the time we're born until we die, we're aging. Products that claim to stop aging would, therefore, stop life.

As women become more aware of the ageist inferences behind some advertisements, some companies try to be socially correct in their use of product terminology. The end result is often confusing and ridiculous. Color the World Lipsticks has an ad that states their lipsticks are made for the Pro-Age Woman. Well I guess it's good to know that some women are "for" Age although I'm not quite sure of the meaning of those words.

Women are often "brainwashed" to purchase products that can be harmful and/or dangerous, in a desperate effort to look younger. Kylie Jenner is an American media personality, socialite and model who has been criticized for her walnut face scrub because it is very abrasive to the skin.

If you really want to get that radiant complexion and "renew" your skin (hint—make it younger), as noted on Kylie's website, a cheaper alternative might be to run outside and rub your face on the bark of a tree. Keep this image in your head if you get tempted to shell out $22 for a 3 oz. tube of this magic elixir.

The beauty industry has declared war on wrinkles and has promoted the idea that a woman will only feel good in her own skin if she looks good and you can't possibly look good if you have wrinkles. Older women only appear in cosmetic ads if they are the "before" image in a "before "and "after" depiction of women.

Women want to look like the "after" photo and will waste money and sometimes safety to attain a youthful image. Many of these problems result from a significant lack of regulation of the U.S. beauty industry. As of 2013, the U.S. FDA has only banned or restricted 11 chemicals from cosmetics, while EU law bans 1,328.

Cosmetic companies rarely deserve an award for best comedic advertisements, but the *Huffington Post* published an article that did give an award for the worst ad of 2014 for Boomers, and it was hysterical. Perricone MD won the second-place award for its ad for its neck firming cream that declared, "Don't let your neck reveal your age." The author satirically recounted a conversation between a woman and her neck. The woman begged her neck not to reveal her age and the neck responded by blackmailing her. Wow, what a high price we pay for beauty!

The Journey of an "Invisible" Woman

Age also goes hand in hand with beauty as an important determinant of employment. When researching how employment is affected by age. The *Independent*, a British online newspaper, reports that "Researchers found that 'unattractive' women only had a seven per cent callback rate, whilst 'attractive' women were called back fifty-four per cent of the time."

A 2015 study by three economists similarly concluded that age discrimination in hiring is particularly bad for older women. These economists sent out fictional resumes in response to 40,000 job ads, with the result that older women had the fewest callbacks. Therefore, it is no surprise that from 2007 to 2013, the unemployment rate for older women (over sixty-five) spiked from 14% to 50%.

Women who were once overlooked because of their child rearing duties now found themselves scorned again. It's assumed that, although they are no longer caretakers for children, they have now become caretakers for parents and therefore, their ambitions are waning. Yet a man can be the father of six children while simultaneously supporting his parents, and still be considered an asset to a company.

A specific example of ageism in the workplace against women can be found in a Glassdoor blog that told the story of an older woman's job interview. She recounted how she met with a recruiter and had to watch the look of disappointment on the recruiter's face when the recruiter saw how old she was. The recruiter told her that many of their requests were for recent college graduates because they haven't developed bad habits yet.

There have been some attempts made to correct this type of hiring discrimination. Companies like Microsoft and Unilever in Mexico are testing holding the first three minutes of interviews with applicants behind screens so that first impressions were based only on what was heard. I was actually somewhat encouraged when I read about this on a Glassdoor blog because I was impressed that this meant that perhaps women would actually make it as far as the live interview. Most recruiters simply Google an applicant's name and up pops their age. If the older woman is past the acceptable age, she never gets a second glance, even though she may be the best fit for the job.

I realize, though, that we shouldn't just blame recruiters for perpetrating gender ageism, as many times they are simply complying with a client's request. Tejal Wagadia, a technical recruiter based in Phoenix, Arizona, told Jobscan that the client specifically asked for "young pretty people." "They said, "I don't care how many years of experience they have; I need young pretty people." Since a man is rarely described as "pretty" it's obvious that this client is looking for a young woman.

At this point, you might be thinking that ageism must also affect older men and you'd be correct. However, extensive research studies, such as the one conducted by the National Bureau of Economic Research (NBER), have shown that older women are more likely to experience age discrimination than older men because of both physical appearance and weak legal protections.

The study confirms why the phrases, "older men are silver foxes" and "older women are hags" are some of my favorite analogies. Society often colorfully uses these terms when describing an older man or older woman. You don't need to be a Rhodes Scholar to see the implied bias against older women in these descriptions.

The NBER study concludes that "Evidence suggests that physical appearance matters more for women, and that age detracts more from physical appearance for women than for men. "If older women suffer from discrimination because of

The Journey of an "Invisible" Woman

both age and sex, anti-discrimination laws may be less effective than thought...."

Although throughout their careers women have become accustomed to being overshadowed by men because of gender inequity, it's clear that older women have even more reason to feel marginalized and invisible because of age discrimination. It's difficult enough to maintain good self-esteem if ageism hurts your career, but it's even worse if you are constantly being told how old and dreadful you look.

Perhaps the saddest part of all of this is that gender ageism is insidious and is accepted by even its victims. Ageism is rampant in the music industry. You don't know whether to laugh or cry when you hear that musician Bebe Rexha, at 29, was told by a male music executive that she was getting too old for her image.

Television shows and movies also portray older women as doddering, unfashionable characters. We all know that in Hollywood everyone is eternally youthful. Meryl Streep, Jane Fonda, Jennifer Aniston and Maggie Gyllenhaal are just a few women leading actresses who say that they have all been discriminated against because of their age. Ms. Gyllenhaal recalls being told that, at thirty-seven, she was too old to play the lover of a fifty-five-year-old man.

Magazines also publish many articles that demean older women. For example, *Vogue* published an article that states that Retirement Wear is having a moment with the under 35s. It purports that soon, young women will be opting for the same elasticated, easy to wear pieces that their grandma is wearing and the article reminds them not to forget the ribbed aerobic socks and New Balance 608 trainers.

An even more depressing news blog recently revealed that older women would even belittle themselves with ageist language if it gave them notoriety. The author of this blog, an influencer on social media, called attention to her blog by naming it "style crone" and flaunting its ageist connotations.

We can see that gender ageism destroys self-esteem, careers and relationships, and this is something that I've, personally, experienced. Surprisingly, one of those experiences occurred at a woman's advocacy nonprofit organization. At this organization, it was common to hear the younger employees and members talk about the reasons for the undesirable attitudes of certain women in the association.

According to them, these poor attitudes were attributable to the fact that these women were older. As I was a party to some of these discussions, I am sad to say that I cowardly became silent.

As I got older, I became very aware of how ageism could damage my professional aspirations, and therefore I did everything to make sure that my younger associates never knew that I was one of the older women. I'm ashamed to say that I even remove myself from Facebook each year on my birthday so I won't have to respond to the question of how old I was.

I had another brush with gender ageism when I was participating on a Zoom call. One of the men on the call was asked to describe a female acquaintance's appearance and he responded that it was difficult to judge, as she was a woman in her sixties. I guess he felt that her age said it all, and perhaps it did. In a few simple words this 54-year-old man had proven that in the eyes of the world older women are sometimes invisible to others because of their age.

Oh, and yes, if you haven't guessed by now, the third characteristic of a perfect women is YOUTH.

CHAPTER 30
THE TALE OF A MODERN-DAY CREPEHANGER

What can you do if you are tired of working at a run-of-the-mill job, crave attention and don't mind being around people who are sad and crying all the time? Let's throw into the mix the fact that you are a woman and perhaps getting on in years. My family had provided me with the answer to these questions, by grooming me to assume an unusual role in life. But before I give you your answer, I need to brief you on an Italian custom.

There's one thing that we can say about death and that is it plays no favorites. It doesn't distinguish among age, gender and wealth. It's an example of a true equal opportunity employer, and it's also a popular topic in the conversations of Italian families. There are all the elements of an archetypal melodrama in everything surrounding the demise of someone and, as everyone knows, Italians love melodrama.

Just think about the exaggerated emotions, family tensions and depressing environs of the funeral parlor. I knew what it was like to participate in the gamut of these experiences when my mother and father died. I was no stranger to this macabre fascination with the tragedy surrounding death. But I bet you didn't realize that there was, and in some places still is, a designation for someone who attains a certain type of bizarre notoriety from mourning the dead.

These people are called Crepehangers or Crapehangers. This is the job that fills all the requirements of your search, so let me tell you a little more about this unique opportunity and some of the responsibilities that you'll have as a Crepehanger.

Although the term crepehanger is rarely used today, it was a common term in the early 1900s. Undertakers' assistants were hired to drape black crepe across the windows and mirrors of a house in which a person had died. Sometimes family members and friends would take over this responsibility.

The grieving widow was supposed to wear black crepe clothing for at least eighteen months after the death of a loved one. As Italian people tend to be melodramatic and a bit depressive, my great-grandparents' generation wholeheartedly adopted this visible representation of grieving into their lives, and a family tradition was born.

The Crepehanger had to be well versed in Italian funeral traditions. There are many superstitious beliefs in the Italian culture about death. A major one is that the dead person always wants to come back to the land of the living. They must be buried with enticements to make their trip to the next world successful and, above all, you must never, ever speak of the dead or they may think that you are summoning them back to earth. My mother carried this bizarre belief to an extreme, as she wouldn't even watch old movies if the actors were now deceased.

It was common in Italian neighborhoods to see women garbed in black walking with their heads hung from the weight of their sorrow. These women had attained a special status in the community and were granted respect as befitted someone who has experienced great suffering. Although, without doubt, they were suffering, it was also undeniable that these widows appreciated the attention their attire and demeanor attracted.

The Italian tradition of hanging black crepe paper in the home of a deceased person to signify mourning was considered the epitome of deference, for not only the dead person but also their family. The sight of windows festooned with this crepe paper alerted the entire neighborhood that a tragedy had occurred in a specific home and the inhabitants would be the recipients of special treatment.

Although the term crepehanger was the actual title of the person doing the crepe hanging after a death, my Italian family also used the word, "crepehanger" to generally describe a person who exalts in misery and creates melodramatic situations out of innocuous events. A crepehanger's voice always is tinged with hints of impending doom. Strangely enough, these bearers of bad news were usually surrounded with devotees eager to hear their next tale of woe.

A crepehanger must be gifted with the ability to transform even the most mundane experiences into something worthy of a Shakespearean tragedy. Every mole becomes skin cancer and not just basal cell carcinoma, but melanoma. The slightest cough is not just the aftermath of a cold but is a symptom of emphysema or cancer.

Competition is fierce in the world of crepehangers, and it is not a job for the faint of heart. The most accomplished are ruthless in their quest to discover tragedy and to enthrall the largest audience with their depiction of the dire misfortunes of themselves and others.

Modern day crepe hanging is not confined to just those of Italian heritage. Anyone with a little imagination and desire for attention can develop the requisite skills to become a crepehanger. However, some basic rules must be followed before you can be guaranteed that you will stand out in any crowd.

Black clothing preferably, a bit worn looking, must be worn at all times. No hanging out with anyone under fifty years old; they don't have enough gruesome stories to share yet. Keep all windows covered in your home. Don't use light bulbs with more than 25 watts illumination and never use bright colors in your décor.

Always remember when decorating that your goal is to create a truly depressing atmosphere in your home. Music should be able to elicit tears in even the most jaded listener. It's always safe to have music playing in the background from the death scenes of operas such as *La Traviata, La Bohème* or *Madame Butterfly*. Practice your deep breathing so you are able to engage in long durations of loud crying. And, above all, if you inadvertently find yourself in an outrageously funny situation, remember to keep your mouth tightly closed so the result is more of a grimace than a smile.

Now you are prepared to begin your journey as a novice crepehanger, properly equipped to spread some melancholy into the world. Remember, you need to maintain your role as if you're a method actor, and don't ever think of breaking out of your crepehanger persona. Save the merriment and laughter for when no one is looking.

Some families take great pride in handing down the role of crepehanger from one generation to another and my family was one of those families. Unfortunately, not all crepehangers are really comfortable in their inherited role, and do everything possible to resist the lure of being the bearer of bad news. I must confess that I am one of those ingrates who, at first, was not overjoyed with assuming my ordained role.

The Journey of an "Invisible" Woman

However, I found myself reverting back to my heritage when I realized that embracing my role as a crepehanger gave me the freedom to entertain all my neuroses, and most importantly, to guarantee that I would be the center of attention. It was a new way for me to enhance my standing in the neighborhood.

So I worked on sharpening my skills of hand wringing and sorrowful keening. Finally, I was ready to serve. I realized that a priority in my work would always be to make sure that I stood out as an important person in my new role.

A good crepehanger must be ready to act, no matter the circumstances. This can be particularly challenging when the crepehanger is personally involved in the tragedy. I recall an incident a few years ago when I was standing at the sink washing a dish and suddenly, WHAM! Lights started flashing in my eyes.

Since I hadn't been drinking anything stronger that orange juice that day, I naturally jumped to the conclusion that I was either going blind or had an inoperable brain tumor. Although I was numb with fear, my inherited duty as a crepehanger was calling out for me to take action.

After consulting with everyone in my family and all my friends and lesser-known acquaintances, I called my doctor for an appointment. Now, every Italian knows that a call to the doctor is the first step on your way to the morgue. My apprehensiveness magnified when, after hearing my symptoms, the nurse uttered those rarely heard words, "come in immediately."

As I sat in the waiting room, my crepehanger responsibilities prompted me to check my body signals to make sure that anyone looking at me would see a tragic figure. I immediately slumped over in my chair, held my head between my hands and intermittently exhaled loud sighs. The nurse called my name and I slowly made my way into the examination room. My doctor's serious countenance and surreptitious mutterings during the exam were a confirmation that my worst fears had come true.

Suddenly I wanted to be anywhere else but in his office. My fervid imagination filled with images of operating rooms and solemn faced doctors huddled over my unmoving body. My heart was racing and my ears were filled with white noise when I finally heard my doctor say, "You have ocular migraines; nothing more serious than a headache in your eyes." A budding catastrophe was cut short with the discovery that I had an over-the-counter malady that could be resolved with a few Tylenol.

I was filled with exhilaration at the good news. Then, in alignment with my new role as a crepehanger, I fleetingly considered the neurotic, yet very dramatic thought, that the doctor was mistaken in his diagnosis or that he wasn't telling me the truth. I knew in my heart that the doctor was now making a call to my husband, to break the news to him that my time on earth was limited.

Although this scenario would have been a sensational treasure trove of misery for a crepehanger, I wisely pushed these insane thoughts aside and I decided to be content that I now had a somewhat less dramatic tale to recount. I could celebrate escaping the grim reaper until the next calamity occurred in my life.

Until then, I could be proud that I had performed admirably as a modern-day crepehanger and had found a unique way to maximize my visibility. I had an important role to play that would continue until I had no more tears to shed and until I could milk every minute of my hard-earned notoriety.

What if you've decided that you're not cut out for being a crepehanger, because you don't cry well or you're just basically a deliriously happy person? You shouldn't despair that you'll never be the center of attention because there are a variety of jobs that will make people take notice of you.

People will definitely admire your courage when you tell them that you're an alligator hunter. This annual hunt lasts 30 days each year in Louisiana. It used to be a job just for men but women have recently joined the men in keeping the waterways safe for humans. Maybe you could become an OTR (Over the Road) 18-wheeler rig driver, like Nancy Scott and Deborah Davis.

Scott was one of the first women drivers in the Frito-Lay Corporation. Imagine the "thanks" you'll get from people for transporting their Frito–Lay products to stores to satisfy their munchies. Don't worry if you're not excited about these jobs, because you think they don't give you enough exposure. I've found the perfect job for you. It's guaranteed to have everyone look at you. The only skill that you need is the ability to stand perfectly still. Oh, and yes, you'll need nerves of steel. You can become a knife thrower's assistant.

Obviously, not all jobs are as exciting as the ones that I just mentioned, nonetheless, there are many opportunities for a woman to enhance her visibility. Although we've just been focusing on the workplace, keep in mind that opportunities to express yourself exist in everyday situations.

Perhaps, the greatest challenges that I faced as a leader was during my service as a director in a women's advocacy nonprofit, and although there was no financial remuneration involved in my role, I received immense personal satisfaction from this volunteer position. During the few years that I was unemployed I also was able to establish myself as a leader by putting my energies to work in the PTA and various community service organizations.

Of course, even today I continue to perform my job as a crepehanger when called upon. Does anyone need a professional crier?

CHAPTER 31
BIG BROTHER

Sometimes visibility isn't all it's cracked up to be, especially when it means that Big Brother is watching you and that you'll be squeezed into a generic class for marketing purposes based on age, gender, or socio-economic status. There are many labels used to name this type of advertising, the most popular ones being personalized or targeted advertising. Personalized advertising is an Internet based system that uses software to track user traits and online behaviors to generate marketing strategies.

My antenna was raised when I started delving into the research about the use of data mining of consumers, to classify them for marketing purposes. This research led me to question my grand plan to establish myself in the world as a woman of unique talents. How unique could I be, if I could be categorized by an algorithm? To try and answer this question, I decided to learn about all the ways that businesses promote and sell products or services by using advertising directed towards audiences with certain uniformly assumed traits.

I knew that the best way to resist being manipulated by these marketing techniques was to follow the aphorism to

The Journey of an "Invisible" Woman

"know your enemy." I began my research by looking around me and noting examples of this forced conformity. It didn't take me long to decide that I would do everything necessary to defeat this marketing onslaught.

Do you ever get the feeling that your television knows you a little bit too well? When my husband and I sit down to watch television, we always have our trusty remote in hand to jump over the annoying commercials. But sometimes, if we're slow on the trigger, or are watching an unrecorded show, some commercials pop up.

I've noticed over the past few months that many of these commercials are about medicine for some diseases that particularly affect older people. How do these commercials know things about our medical conditions? A few months back I had to use eye drops for an eye condition and all of our sudden, every other commercial on television was advertising the latest eye drops.

Perhaps, there is a tip line in our local drugstore that is linked to major pharmaceutical advertisers, to let them know that someone in our home has a condition that requires medication.

Conceivably, it may be that advertisers think that people breathlessly anticipate receiving information about constipation during their dinner hour and that they are diligently taking notes on these anti-constipation drugs to impress their doctors with their newfound wisdom, at their next checkup. How come older people never see commercials for new hiking boots or contraceptives? I finally couldn't take it anymore.

Although I rarely watch live television, the thought of anyone trying to control and/or influence my buying habits was infuriating to me. As I wanted to keep streaming, the one solution that I couldn't use was to disconnect my television from the internet. However, I was able to do the next best thing, and that was to turn off my television's automatic content recognition. I thought that I had beat the television tracking demon at its own game, but this didn't stop all the snooping.

Television is not the only spy in our midst. Many of our homes have a little gadget innocently sitting on our counters and shelves, and it has a name. The gadget's name is feminine. Perhaps, the inventor remembered that the famous spy Mata Hari was a woman and tongue-in-cheek decided to give the gadget a feminine name, and so Alexa was born. Alexa listens, and based on what she hears, can collect all types of data.

Many friends and family members refuse to have Alexa in their homes because they insist that she is listening to them without their knowledge. How crazy is that thought, although maybe not as crazy as people may think. I read about an incident involving Alexa's notification to the police that a person was hurt and that they needed to respond to a certain address. It turned out that Alexa somehow picked up a trigger word in a conversation that was a signal for her to take action.

Now, having Alexa around could be great if someone was actually in danger. However, let's picture the following scenario: Paul has his VR headset on and is engrossed in some fantasy world. He's oblivious to all real world sounds around him. Meanwhile, a SWAT team has mistakenly identified Paul's home as the residence of a terrorist and is getting ready to make an arrest. Paul doesn't hear the SWAT team banging on his door. The team rushes in with guns raised and yell for Paul to lift up his hands, but of course he can't hear them. Shots ring out and a frightening event has occurred because Big Brother couldn't distinguish between a real and imagined emergency.

The Journey of an "Invisible" Woman

Alexa also eavesdrops on marital communications. Many of my conversations with my husband are about political candidates. Observing the behavior of today's politicians is similar to watching a reenactment of a sexed-up version of *The Godfather*. There's greed, fraud, conspiracy and adultery. In short, you have everything in one package.

Things can get quickly heated, as we verbally eviscerate a controversial politician, sometimes with one or both of us shouting, "He should be shot!" Of course, this is just rhetoric, but recently I noticed that our Alexa would turn on without being summoned, whenever we had these heated conversations. As a result, I now try to keep Alexa unplugged during these verbal interactions to abate my growing paranoia of becoming a new episode on *The Twilight Zone*. So, the next time you see Alexa's light flashing when you haven't called her name, think about what she's hearing and if it might make for a great headline in the news.

You might think that print and online advertising are not as invasive as Alexa. But just because these media sources can't hear our words, it doesn't mean that there aren't other intrusive ways for them to interject themselves into our lives through use of personalized advertising. We've been living in the era of personalized ads for many years, despite the fact that this type of advertising categorizes people's needs and desires by erroneous age and gender norms.

Algorithm-based personalized ads epitomize age and gender discrimination by assuming that households with older people are only interested in anti-wrinkle products, sexual dysfunction, incontinence or life-threatening diseases. If tracking shows that a woman resides in a home, then advertisements for cosmetics and weight loss products become the focus of the marketing. Advocates against ageism and sexism feel tremendous revulsion when they're confronted with these instances of age and gender discrimination.

There's no denying that, for SOME older people, certain medical conditions are problems, but these people have doctors and not the media to help them resolve these issues.

Woman can choose to ignore these aggressive assaults on their sexuality and health as inconsequential. On the other hand, personalized ads regarding employment can seriously affect a women's professional advancement. The American Civil Liberties Union filed charges with the Equal Opportunity Commission against Facebook and ten other companies, claiming these companies' personalized ads prevented women from viewing job ads in male dominated fields by targeting these listings towards men only. Advertisers on Facebook were permitted to choose the gender of the user that it wanted to reach.

ACLU lawyer Galen Sherwin said that gender discrimination is evident in these ads for professions usually dominated by men, and that the discrimination "is insidious because it perpetuates the exclusion of women from those jobs." It seems that Big Brother isn't satisfied with controlling women's buying habits. It looks like he also wants their careers.

However, don't think that personalized ads just offend older woman. Although younger women may not be seeing ads for laxatives or wrinkle creams, they're still being targeted for product marketing as if they're clones of one another. Millennials or Gen Ys were born between 1981 and 1995.

They're one of the largest generations in history and have very different priorities from generations before them. They're the first digital natives, and yet it would be marketing suicide to target ads to Millennials as if they're all airheads hooked intravenously to their computers, interested only in themselves and having little disposable income.

Unlike some of the other generations, Millennials are unlikely to buy a product just because it's pitched to them. Instead, they consult social media, read online reviews and research products and then, contrary to the myth that they only shop online, they walk into retail stores to shop.

They are a source to be tapped, as they spend $600 billion on consumer products per year and are slated to spend over $1.4 trillion as of 2020. Millennials, Boomer, Generation Z and the Silent Generation are all different from one another and unique within themselves.

If companies want to successfully market their products, they need to understand that people resent being grouped together like a bunch of sheep just because they are the same gender, race, religion or in the same generation. Big Brother needs to take some sensitivity training to learn how to avoid discrimination in marketing to each of these different groups.

Being bombarded with depressing commercials is no fun for anyone and results in a hard workout for the remote, to quickly skip over these offensive ads. Discrimination takes all forms and personalized marketing subliminally contains many prejudices that perpetuate the myth that a woman's worth depends on her adherence to mistaken social norms.

In many households these homogeneous advertisements fall on deaf ears, because no two older people or women are alike. It would be more productive for advertisers to stop dehumanizing people and realize that there are no universal interests for members of a particular age or gender group So, if you just can't take it anymore, you might decide to watch only recorded, ad-free television.

But what about the Internet? Unfortunately, this is not a safe haven if you want to escape Big Brother. We all love to browse shopping sites, even if we don't immediately need anything. No harm, right? Think again. Remember how you are intermittently asked, while browsing, if you will accept cookies, and no, I don't mean the delicious chocolate chip kind.

These cookies are small pieces of code that advertisers use to follow you as you browse the web. Once your shopping habits are identified you will be inundated with certain items again and again on different web sites, until you give in and make that impulse purchase for something that you probably didn't want or need.

During the 2020 pandemic quarantine in New York, I was going stir-crazy after being locked in the house for two months. I knew that, either I had to find something with which to occupy myself, or the enforced closeness between my husband and me would result in tragedy. My solution to this dilemma was to buy a digital keyboard, so I could learn to play the piano. After spending a little time on Google searching for the perfect keyboard, I decided to spend a little more time thinking about this potential purchase.

Little did I know that I was about to be targeted with a marketing blitz from every keyboard store in America. True to the perversity of my nature and desire to be an independent thinker, I refused to let the avalanche of ads affect my decision, and instead, methodically began my own research to find the keyboard that would actually suit my needs.

Maybe advertisers should realize that we no longer exist in the Mad Men era, in which men are hard drinking, insensitive chauvinists, and women are stay at home moms watching soaps all day or sexy babes out to catch a husband. Seventy-year-olds run the country; women have broken through the glass ceiling and are CEOs of large corporations, and young people in their 20s are making a fortune in Silicon Valley.

In addition to the negative attention that advertising firms have attracted because of perpetrating discrimination in their segregated use of digital data, an individual's right to privacy is also a growing concern. For example, the retail giant Target was able to find out that a teenage girl was pregnant before even her father knew by utilizing personalized advertising.

Target statistician Andre Pole correlated their customer's buying history and demographic information with historical buying data for all the ladies who had signed up for baby registries. He then used this data to establish patterns that resulted in a pregnancy prediction score. Target thereafter would send coupons for baby items to the women with high pregnancy scores.

This personal marketing system backfired when an irate father went into a store in Minneapolis to complain about his high school age daughter receiving the coupons, as it might encourage her to become pregnant. As it turned out, the algorithms that Target used were accurate, as confirmed when the daughter finally confessed to her father that she was pregnant.

When this story was reported in the New York Times, many consumers were outraged and Target received much unfavorable publicity. People were creeped out by this invasion of privacy and yet the retailer's revenue growth, $44 billion in 2002 to $67 billion in 2010 was partially attributable to Target's personalized marketing to the pregnancy market.

Aside from the privacy issue, you also have to ask yourself if you're comfortable having intimate parts of your life be the subject of a conversation among a bunch of programmers as they sit munching on donuts. No one likes being talked about behind their back, unless the talk is praiseworthy. The use of data mining to produce personalized ads sometimes gives people the same unpleasant feeling as being gossiped about.

It's time for advertisers to stop spying on sample consumers in order to stereotype people's interests based on perceived characteristics. Women and men, both, feel the sting of dehumanization when they are bunched together as a faceless mass. People in their twenties are not all beautiful, nor do they all like to party nonstop.

Older people aren't necessarily frail, technologically inept or forgetful. Some of them still enjoy fine food, good sex and having fun. Maybe that 80-year-old woman is shopping for her next motorcycle, but targeted advertisers wouldn't notice her because she has deviated from the software norm.

The rock band The Police anticipated data mining along the lines of George Orwell's *1984* with their lyrics, "Every breath you take and every move you make, I'll be watching you." I've spent the greater part of my life promoting my visibility as a woman, but this type of visibility wasn't what I had in mind!

CHAPTER 32
RETHINKING PLAYTIME

I never played with my children. I was trying to balance the responsibilities of motherhood with my aspirations for becoming a "somebody" in my professional life. The end result was that I might have been invisible to my children.

There was a nineteen-year age difference between my first and fourth child, so my no-play zone not only existed over a span of many years but it also covered a lot of territory as they grew up in New York, Texas and Missouri. I took my children to museums, plays, puppet shows, movies, bowling, and I read to them, but I never just sat down and played with them.

My energy level fell to zero after putting in a long day's work in the office. Then I was faced with handling the everyday tasks of raising four kids. I just couldn't motivate myself to get down on the floor at night to make forts with them out of Legos.

As my children got older, I was an enthusiastic spectator at all their wrestling matches, baseball and football games and swimming meets. I clapped so vigorously at their school performances that the palms of my hands stayed pink for days. But that was the thing; I was always an observer, not a participant, in their playing.

I guess the truth is that, even when I was a child, I never, really, just played. I was always going somewhere or doing something with a "purpose." I made potholders so my family and neighbors would ante up a few pennies for one of my creations, not because I had fun making them. My friends and I produced and acted in little vignettes in my garage in the hope of receiving praise from an audience. And even when I was at my most favorite place on earth, the beach, I had my head buried in a book.

It was summer and my husband and I, as part of our yearly tradition, had rented a house in the Hamptons. My oldest son and his family lived in California and our opportunities to babysit his daughter were virtually nonexistent. This particular summer, they were visiting us for two weeks, and he and his wife had jumped at the chance to visit friends in Manhattan and have us babysit.

Unfortunately, there would be only me babysitting, as my husband had been called back to work for an emergency and I was left alone at the house with my granddaughter. It had been many years since I was responsible for entertaining a small child, therefore, I was extremely nervous when my son asked me to watch my granddaughter for 24 hours. Would this mean that I had to play with her?

My son was as big a beach freak as I was and took his daughter to the beach every day. My granddaughter had ridden the waves with him for six days, so now the beach had lost its allure for her. I feverishly racked my brain for things that a 7-year-old would enjoy in a beachside town.

Then I started praying that it wouldn't rain, because then I'd really be stumped for things to do. We started the day by playing miniature golf, followed by a visit to a toy store and then lunch at a Chinese restaurant. My heart clenched as I realized it was only 12:30 in the afternoon. Half a day hadn't even passed.

Luckily, two children's movies were playing back-to-back in the theater in town. Happy that more than four hours could be passed, we nestled into our seats to watch talking animals and wizards. This was a particularly severe form of penance for me, as I hated children's movies. We emerged from the theater bleary eyed from staring at the screen for hours.

Although we were bloated from all the junk food we had consumed, we didn't let it prevent us from visiting the local pizzeria to wolf down some slices of pizza. Our next stop was the supermarket, to buy things that would give us a sugar rush later that night. Finally, we headed for the video store to finish our day with a mind-numbing rental movie. I figured we were set for the night.

After trying several times to unsuccessfully start the DVD player, the realization hit me that I wasn't behaving like the grandmothers idealized in storybooks. I always said I would teach my grandchildren the proper foods to eat and entertain them with scintillating interactions. The fact was that I was selfish, and bored with the idea of building sandcastles and drawing buildings.

I had my first child at the age of 19 and I still had one child at home. I had been a school principal and spent my entire life, either with my children or other people's children. Is it possible to be burned out on all things relating to children? I was feeling guilty, and finally decided to do something about it.

Since it was still too early to sleep, I virtuously asked my granddaughter if she wanted to do a puzzle or read together. Unfortunately, I had picked the two things that she least liked doing. Memories flooded into my mind of my mom baby-sitting for my children, and then chastising me about the "bad" things she had discovered about me from my kids. Not wishing to repeat my mom's mistakes, I resisted the temptation to spend the evening interrogating her about her mom and dad.

Suddenly, a strange idea popped into my head. We could talk, but not about anything bad. She could tell me about all the things she loved or disliked, and maybe there were some things in my life that she might find interesting to hear about. She told me about when she went clamming with her father and how icky it was to put her feet into the water to dig up the clams. Apparently, she wasn't too overjoyed with this experience. She also told me that her father then took her on an ocean fishing expedition and she didn't like that experience, either. She recounted to me how all the other people on the boat kept throwing up as the boat rocked back and forth in the rough sea.

I told her how amazed I was that she didn't throw up too. I admitted to her that I had never gone on a fishing boat, as I couldn't swim and was deathly afraid of the water. If nothing else, she would certainly have vivid memories of this summer.

And now it was my turn to share with her. I told her about significant milestones and traditions in my own children's lives such as when they went fishing and clamming with their father and grandfather. I knew that to a 7-year-old the word "tradition' is fairly meaningless and yet, I hoped that she could relate these events to her own experience with her dad. I also asked her to think about how, every Christmas, she puts out milk and a cookie for Santa Claus, because I knew that it is something that her family does at Christmas. I then said that milk and cookies for Santa is her family's tradition. She nodded in understanding. I held her close as I told her how at first her daddy was terrified when he went on the fishing boat with his father, but then after a few years he became an avid fisherman.

As we continued talking, I recalled another tradition that would help her understand the importance of clamming to our family. Every summer, even when we lived in Texas or Missouri, we would return to the Hamptons. We knew that summer had begun when the smell of linguini with clam sauce filled our house. I was in charge of cooking the fresh clams that my husband and son had dug up.

Summer wasn't real until we were eating that pasta and clams. Someday, she would have a child and someone special would take him or her on a fishing boat or clamming. She would tell her child about the first time that she went fishing or clamming with her own dad, and a new family tradition would be born.

I was happy that it seemed that my granddaughter accepted my attempt to explain why our family insisted on doing such yucky things. However, it looked like she had more to say to me about some unpleasant experiences in her life. She took a deep breath and asked if we could talk about something that was going on in school.

My granddaughter then confided in me that the children in her class at school often made fun of her because she liked to play with blocks and do number puzzles instead of staying in the doll corner with the other girls. She said that she didn't care about dolls but loved making intricate buildings and figuring out math problems, but was embarrassed because she wasn't like the other girls in her class.

For a moment I wasn't sure how to answer her, as I always sensed that my sons only halfheartedly supported my feminist leanings. It was tempting for me to start lecturing her on gender equity, but I didn't want to step on my son's toes by forcing my values on his child. On the other hand, I felt an obligation to help my granddaughter deal with her feelings of shame because her classmates had labeled her as odd.

I wished that she was old enough to understand that a Carnegie Mellon neuro-imaging study had proven that there are no biological differences between girls and boys that effect math aptitude, and that it's not unfeminine or odd for her to love math. Hopefully, as she matures, she'll be cognizant of the gender prejudices existing around women in STEM careers and become determined to let her skills empower her to overcome this type of discrimination.

It's difficult for a child to understand that being different is sometimes a sign of leadership. A leader must often stand alone in making decisions and no child wants to be alone. I tried to explain to my granddaughter that one day her abilities would be recognized as a gift, and that people will clamor to know and be friends with her. In the meantime, I'd be sure to alert my son that he needs to inform my granddaughter's teachers to encourage her interests in math and spatial cognition skills. I reminded her that she could be anything that she wanted to be. She just needed a little help.

As she listened to me talk, she became very quiet and snuggled even closer to me. We kept telling each other stories until I looked at the clock and realized that it was way past her bedtime and I hadn't actually played with my granddaughter once. As I was tucking her into bed, she looked at me and said, "Nana, I had so much fun with you today."

In my frantic pursuit of recognition in my life, I had forgotten that the most important recognition comes from the people who love you. Strangers may pat you on the back over your achievements, but they quickly forget your successes. Instead, it is memories of shared moments with our loved ones that are long remembered and that make us unique.

The Journey of an "Invisible" Woman

On that summer day, I realized that, not only did I have fun with my granddaughter, but I had also unknowingly engaged in Lev Vygotsky's theory of cognitive development with her. Mr. Vygotsky was a Russian psychologist who developed what has become known as sociocultural theory. He established that children acquire their cultural values through collaborative dialogues with more knowledgeable members of society.

After spending the day together with my granddaughter, I hoped that she would think that one of those knowledgeable members of society was me, and I also hoped that when my granddaughter plays, she will capture the essence of Mr. Vygotsky words, "In play a child is always above his average age, above his daily behavior; in play, it's as though he were a head taller than himself."

Maybe my idea of playing was too limited in scope. If it simply means having fun, then I guess that I've been playing for most of my life, but I just didn't know it. At least I know that in my granddaughter's eyes, I'm very visible.

CHAPTER 33
THE ENEMY WITHIN

We've spent a lot of time talking about barriers women face in their battle to remain visible in the world. Often, these barriers stem from societal acceptance of long-standing myths about gender norms. However, many women not only deal with institutional sexism but also must confront obstacles arising from their personal, physical, mental or emotional infirmities. These women can choose to live the way others expect them to, or reach for the lives they know they deserve.

We've come a long way with treatments available to deaf-blind people since those that were used in the 19th century. The supposed cures then ranged from being slowly poisoned by ingesting mercury to having dead animal parts and artificial metal eardrums inserted into your ear. A deaf-blind person was being asked to play a game of Russian roulette that ended with a player either suffering excruciating pain or dying, and there was no actual winner because no one ever got better. It was a challenge for even a healthy woman during that era to assert her autonomy in the world and almost impossible for someone who was deaf-blind.

The Journey of an "Invisible" Woman

However, there was a woman who beat the odds and achieved success despite her condition. We're all familiar with the name of this great woman, who overcame adversity to achieve greatness. This woman is Helen Keller: Swedenborgian, humanitarian, and co-founder of the ACLU. She lost both her sight and hearing at 18 months of age and yet toiled for 25 years to learn to speak, so that she could communicate and work on behalf of others living with disabilities. She worked tirelessly to promote attention to social issues, including women's suffrage, pacifism and birth control, never letting her disability interfere with her purpose.

Helen is not alone in being an inspiration to women. There are numerous other women whom we admire for their great achievements, many with hidden disabilities. Many of us have read and enjoyed the moving poetry of Maya Angelou, but few of us know that, after being sexually assaulted by her mother's boyfriend, she developed selective mutism and didn't speak for five years. She had no voice and yet, she went on to become the voice of many unheard women.

Finally, we can't discuss women who tackled physical limitations and went on to make their mark on the world without mentioning Senator Tammy Duckworth. She's made a name for herself with a number of firsts. She was the first female helicopter pilot to lead a combat mission, the first double amputee of the Iraq war and the first woman with a disability elected to Congress. Her disability might have hampered her mobility, but it certainly had no effect on her determination to achieve her life goals.

There are many examples of physically disabled women who have made outstanding contributions to the world. However, some disabilities, in and of themselves make it difficult for a woman to function, because they are of a cognitive/mental nature. Woman with these types of disabilities are often victims of the most grievous offenses against a woman's rights. A woman's access to legal recourse is often hampered due to assumptions that her credibility is flawed because of her mental disability.

There was a case that landed in the Ontario Court of Appeals that perfectly describes the legal barriers that sometimes exist in situations involving mental impairment. In this case, an adult woman reported that her stepfather sexually assaulted her. The woman gave evidence of the incident and yet, the case collapsed when the trial judge declared that the woman didn't understand the duty to speak the truth. Does this mean that a woman can lose the rights over her own body if her competency is questioned? Hopefully, we won't revert back to treating mental illness as portrayed in the 1948 movie, *The Snake Pit*.

The movie's memorable scene was the gruesome image of mentally ill patients being thrown into a pit of snakes, in the hopes of snapping them back to normalcy. In the real world, our medical communities would never allow such an aberration, although there are atrocities occurring all the time against women at psychiatric hospitals. For example, at least five female patients at Timberlawn psychiatric hospital in Dallas, Texas, including a 13-year-old, have reported unwanted sexual contacts, since 2014.

A woman has a right to protection from sexual assault, regardless of her cognitive state. We need to understand that a disability is not a hindrance and that it's a part of who a person is. Defining a woman by her disability prevents her from realizing her true self.

Perhaps the most overlooked barrier to a woman's quest for recognition is something that almost every woman has experienced. The issue isn't new and it can be traced back as far as 1900 BC, in Egypt, and the use, back then, of the term "hysteria" to describe any women's health issue that deviates from expected gender roles. Although there is an actual mental disorder that was once called hysteria and is now called conversion disorder, the more common understanding of the definition of the term today is simply, someone who is guilty of showing emotional excess.

This excess can involve numerous emotions such as sadness, anger, happiness, love and shame. Although at one time it was thought that an excessive expression of any of these emotions was a physical illness, now we understand that it is simply a sign of deep passions.

Most women have experienced this depth of emotion when they become involved in romantic relationships; and therein lies the potential problem. As long as a woman is secure in her relationship, her professional and personal life remains on a success track. However, if a breakup occurs, everything comes tumbling down and this includes her focus on her ambitions. Men are taught, when bad things happen to just suck it up and move on, and that's what they do. Women however, are encouraged to show their soft side and go with their emotions.

These women then spend tons of time analyzing what went wrong in the relationship and talking endlessly to friends about the breakup. They never think that maybe the guy was just a skunk. Occasionally, real depression sets in, as the woman's self-esteem plummets and her plans for working on her visibility in the world are put on hold.

I remember being so wrapped up in the drama surrounding several of my romantic relationships that I, too, momentarily forgot about my vision for myself. Thankfully, I was able to quickly get myself back on track.

Every now and then, my high school Latin training returns to me and I put into practice what I learned so many years ago. One handy thing that I was taught was to always look at the root of a word to ascertain its true meaning. The root of the word disability is "disable" and one of its meanings is to debilitate or impair.

This root search helped me grasp the fact that some people may not have an officially designated disability, but nonetheless have a condition that aversely impairs certain aspects of their life and debilitates their ability to actualize their objectives. Although I am fully mobile, able to see and hear and possess full mental capacities (although my husband might disagree), my life's ambitions have been altered by a disabling condition.

Since childhood I have suffered with an autoimmune disorder that makes me extremely vulnerable to infections. Generally, I'm in good health, but that can change the moment that I'm exposed to someone who is sick. This vulnerability might make me sometimes appear a little odd, as I do my best to avoid people who are obviously ill. On one occasion I recall fleeing from the room during a board meeting, because I was seated between two board members who were coughing so loudly that it sounded like they had tuberculosis.

Needless to say, I looked like I was a little deranged, leaving an important business meeting so abruptly, but the only other solution was to walk around like a leper with a label on my chest revealing my condition. Regardless of the eccentric behavior that my condition sometimes caused, I was determined to not let myself be dissuaded from fulfilling my ambitions.

The lesson to be learned here is quite simple. Our disabilities, whether they are physical, mental or emotional can exist as the enemy within us, or we can accept them as an intrinsic part of who we are, and vow to let the world know that every part of ourselves is valuable.

CHAPTER 34
THE ROTTEN RAIN

I had my first taste of what it felt like to be on center stage and gazing out at an adoring audience when I performed in my kindergarten musical. I'll always associate that magic moment with rain, as the song that I sung was "April Showers". Although I knew that I was just one of twenty children, in my dream world I also knew that I stood out from the group when I stood on my chubby little legs, twirling my umbrella and singing my heart out.

Rain would always have a prominent place in many important events in my life. Maybe these events didn't directly add to my visibility as a woman, but experiencing them helped form who I was to become as a person.

My husband and I were finally back home in New York and everything seemed new to us again after living out of the state for twenty-six years, but there was one thing that was the same. In all the places that we'd lived, there was the rain. You always read about fire and brimstone in descriptions of hell, but rain is supposed to be life giving, but not at my house.

My plants were always dying and I had mold growing on everything as if they had been fertilized with a special mold growth hormone. Is it possible that two weeks of heavy rain had transformed my lawn from a carpet of green into a brown field of mushrooms that thrived in these wet conditions?

The chant "Rain, rain go away, come again some other day," repeats and repeats in my head like some magical incantation. But it doesn't work any magic. After living with grey skies for days on end, the rain finally stops and the tiniest ray of sunshine now has me shielding my eyes like a vampire in a horror movie.

I thought back to the last time that my family and I had spent a summer like this, with so much rain. I was a young mother, and my husband and I had just scraped together enough money to rent our first summer house, actually a shack, in Westhampton Beach, New York.

We spent every weekend huddled together in our damp and tiny living room, listening to the never-ending rain and playing so much monopoly that before long we were almost convinced that we really were real estate magnates. It was only on each Sunday night, as we began our drive back to the city on the traffic-clogged Long Island Expressway, that the sun finally beamed through our windshield, taunting us with promises of beautiful days on the beach if we would only return.

After all, this was the swinging Hamptons, where we would transform our images from that of a young suburban married couple into club hopping, disco maniacs. Therefore, to quell our Disco Fever, we were able to put up with the rain, as long as our boogie nights continued.

I had it all, a great husband, adorable children, and was hobnobbing with the rich and famous, if only vicariously, by reading about them dining in some of the restaurants that we, too, occasionally frequented. This was the visible lifestyle that I had envisioned for myself.

The Journey of an "Invisible" Woman

I'd be the bon vivant of my neighborhood, regaling everyone with tales of my fabulous weekends in the Hamptons, omitting, of course, the real story. It wouldn't contribute much to my image to admit that most hours during those summer weekends were spent in the house, with my children crying for the sun to come out so they could go out to the beach. But, oh, those nights!

Bolstered by the innocent gullibility of our youth, we returned again and again each weekend, always believing this would be our lucky weekend to perfect our tans at the beach. We ate and drank ourselves into a stupor during those many rainy weekends. We began to think that this eternal quest for the sun would wind up with us having lifelong memberships to Weight Watchers and AA.

As the years passed, we got much older, but apparently no less naïve, and maybe even a little stupider. We had moved from New York to Dallas and were now living in St. Louis, Missouri, but we still harbored dreams of one day owning our own home in the Hamptons. Our minds, conveniently, had forgotten those days when we sat in a cramped rental house with nothing to do but pray for the sun.

So, as now we had apparently developed amnesia, we decided to follow our dreams and finally buy a summer house in East Hampton, New York. We made this purchase before we had permanently moved back home to New York and were still living in St. Louis, Missouri.

Missouri had lakes, a wine country, and plenty of pastoral countryside, but it was missing something that was very important to me, and that was the ocean. Since the rain gods knew how much I loved the water, they made it their business to make it keep raining, so I'd not only have an abundance of water in the nearby ocean, but also in the basement of our very own summer house.

Sandy Camillo

We spent many happy weekends bailing water out of our basement and telling ourselves how lucky we were because, in our minds, as native New Yorkers, we had attained a major milestone in our life and that was to live in the Hamptons. I also learned something important from attaining this milestone. I realized that where you live is inconsequential, and the real reason that my summers were always amazing was because I was sharing them with the people I most loved.

The first week at our new summer house it rained. However, it was sort of cozy staying in and just being lazy. By the second week, during which it continued to rain, I had cruised the local shops so often that I either had to start spending some serious money or risk being suspected of being the reconnaissance person for a heist. I had seen all the adult movies in the theaters between Montauk and Hampton Bays, and was now facing the prospect of going to the children's shows without any of my children in tow.

I woke up each morning fearful of peeking out the window and seeing more rain. However, I realized that if the weather had been sunny every day, I would never have visited some of the local art galleries and unique shops in the Hamptons. I suppose you could say that even the rain had a sunny side.

I guess now it is time to be honest and acknowledge that our rain curse didn't begin with our summer vacation rentals in the Hamptons. Our curse actually began with the sale of the first home that we ever owned, which was in Manhasset, New York. It was raining hard the day of our open house.

Despite the installation of a sump pump and French drain, my husband and I wound up scurrying between our basement and kitchen, alternately holding back the raging waters rushing through our basement walls, and running upstairs to put pails under the leaks in our kitchen ceiling. Needless to say, the open house had to be cancelled.

As time went by, we realized that wherever we decided to live, we could pretty much guarantee days of rain. We couldn't even escape our rain curse when we moved to sunny Dallas, Texas. The only difference from dealing with the rain in Dallas was that there are no basements there.

The Texans aren't foolish enough to consider a subterranean space suitable for human habitation, so the rain had to find a different path to destruction. Its wrath was even more upsetting, as it was often accompanied by tornados.

You checked the weather multiple times before venturing out in your car, as your mind was filled with television images of cars floating away in past storms. Unfortunately, my husband and daughter got to experience this firsthand, in one of these monster storms.

They went to the music hall in Dallas to see Tommy Tune in *My One and Only.* I was supposed to take my daughter, but there were reports that a storm was on the way. Having an over-the-top fear of tornados, I asked my husband to go with her instead. As it turned out there were no tornados in the storm, but the rain was so heavy that, in the middle of the play, Mr. Tune noticed that water was rushing down the main aisle and everyone was asked to leave the theater.

When my husband and daughter got outside, they were greeted with the surreal sight of cars floating in the parking lot. Luckily, they were parked on high ground and they were able cautiously to drive home. How could something as seemingly ho hum as rain result in such destruction? Tornados, hurricanes, tsunamis, earthquakes, wildfires, mudflows, and blizzards were acknowledged as natural disasters, but the gentle rain was always associated with romantic allusions as pictured in the old movie *Singing in the Rain.* I was beginning to understand that real life wasn't always as idyllic and enchanting as depicted in the movies. When had the rain become so rotten?

The day finally came when I had to face certain truths, as I had entered a new stage of my life. My children were now out of the home, my husband was no longer a high-powered attorney, my parents had died, and I would never be a socialite or own a mansion on the ocean. I was on my way to having only an ephemeral presence in the world. However, the one thing that would always be there is the rain, with each raindrop representing a memory of the triumphs and sadnesses of my life.

Looking back on those rainy days, vignettes of family interactions filled with laughter pop into my mind. Long gone family members live again. The clock keeps ticking, and those days of dancing all night and participating in marathon monopoly games would now be supplanted by grandchildren and finding new purposes in life.

Nature is an elemental force, but my perception of its vagaries depends on which generational lens I'm viewing it through. When I was a young child, I was thrilled with the prospect of a blizzard and having a school vacation day. However, as an adult, the idea of a blizzard horrifies me as I contemplate the extra hours I would spend shoveling snow and commuting to and from work. Nature hasn't changed. I have changed. The rain isn't rotten or good; it is just rain, so perhaps those rainy days weren't so bad after all.

We all have times in our lives when metaphorically it seems like it's always raining. I'm reminded that, just like the flowers that bloom after April's rain, our time in the sun will eventually come.

CHAPTER 35
SHELL SHOCKED

My mother lied to me but, at the time, she didn't know it. She told me that I could do anything, but I found out that wasn't true. Although I dedicated my life to keeping my loved ones safe, the day came when my efforts were wasted.

I wake up at 2:00 a.m. to check his neck for a pulse. His snoring, that used to transform me into a wild woman, now sounds like angels singing. Several years ago, my husband suffered an aortic dissection and almost died.

My husband had always been the original energizer bunny, so I knew something was wrong when I saw him sitting quietly on the sofa at 3:30 on a Saturday afternoon. He had been taking down a picket fence at the front of our house in St. Louis, Missouri. He told me that he felt a little strange and therefore had decided to sit a bit. When he explained that "strange" meant chest pain, I decided to rush him to the hospital. This meant my driving, as he refused to have me call an ambulance. In his mind, because of his stubborn Italian nature, riding in an ambulance equated to showing his vulnerability to the world. In my panic, I didn't give him the aspirin that you're always advised to give when someone complains of chest pain, and this negligence on my part saved his life, since aspirin would have sped up the bleeding.

As I sat with him in intensive care, I couldn't conceive of what I would do without my main cheerleader. My husband kept me going whenever I wavered in my determination to make something of myself, and now it was my turn to see that he survived this nightmare.

My husband was released after a week in the hospital, but everyday things would never be the same. He was told not to lift his grand-babies and to be very careful to minimize his stress. The days of wine and roses were over, as I now had to take over many of his responsibilities. I learned to keep many of life's trials to myself, as I didn't want to cause him any anxiety. My focus on my own development was diverted to convincing my husband that his life would eventually get back to a new normal.

Unbeknown to my husband, I'd end each day by hiding out in my bathroom with the shower running so he couldn't hear me crying. I recalled another time when I'd hid, crying in a bathroom in a Dallas hotel room. I now realized that my reaction to relocating was ludicrous and self-indulgent when measured against the frightening realities engendered by what was now a life and death issue.

All our arguments are now one sided, as I swallow my Italian volatility and give in to my husband's often authoritarian edicts. If I don't, his blood pressure can shoot up into the danger zone with disastrous results. We attract incredulous stares as we walk together through airports with me grunting as I struggle to carry suitcases almost heavier than I am. He can't lift anything heavier than twenty pounds, hardly anything at all.

This was a hard nut to swallow for a guy who was raised by a tough Italian dad who taught him that male-female relationships were centered on the "me Tarzan, you Jane" philosophy. Although he is a brilliant attorney, he still erroneously equates masculinity with strength.

He becomes embarrassed when he encounters some jerk that gets arrogant with us and is forced to back off, because his pressure might elevate if he gets into a shouting match with the idiot. The images of vacations to exotic places suddenly are fraught with dread at the thought that a medical incident could occur that the local hospital would be unable to handle.

My children constantly remind me not to let my husband see that I am frightened of what the future holds. They tell me to remain strong for him, but I want to yell "What about me"? I have now started taking blood pressure medication to combat my over-the-top blood pressure readings and also added Advil to soothe a chronic backache from the unaccustomed lifting. Our life has changed, and sometimes I want to run, and run and run.

How do you live a normal life with the thought that any minute the sky could fall in on you? We've all participated in hypothetical conversations that begin with "If you only had so many days to live what would you do"? That hypothesis has now become a reality for my husband. He has seen his mortality and has decided to live each minute to the fullest while I, on the other hand, am terrified at what will remain, if he is no longer here.

He's heard all the doctor's admonitions, and yet, he prefers to throw caution to the wind and do things that, for even a minute in the past, he wouldn't have contemplated doing. His excitement at taking up skydiving throws me into fits of panic. Every time I tell him that he needs to take it easy, I'm reminding him of the possible nightmare to come.

We all know that death is inevitable for everyone, and yet something changes when someone you love has a time bomb ticking inside them. Everything has a bittersweet tinge to it.

Sandy Camillo

You and your husband go out with friends and you wonder if these couples' outings would still be available to you if you were alone.

During the weeks that he was home on disability, the issue of finances kept popping up. We became anxious when we realized that his disability check would never cover our living expenses. The reality had also sunk in that a big reason that I was able to pursue my professional goals without worrying about compensation was that, for many years, my husband had been carrying the heavy financial burden of supporting our family.

It was easy for me to get on my soapbox and say that money wasn't that important since I never had to worry about not having it. His hard work provided me with the freedom that I needed to pursue my dreams. I couldn't imagine becoming the primary breadwinner.

Even watching television became tainted because of my husband's brush with death. You decide that a medical show on television that you once loved to watch together is now too morbid, as it seems to portend future events in your lives. Now that the children are gone, it can feel very lonely in the house. It's wonderful to have someone to sit with in the evening, to simply discuss the day's events and it's inconceivable that this joy could one day end.

There isn't anyone who looks at me in the same loving way that my husband does, regardless of whether my hair is a mess or if I have put on ten pounds. I think back to a time that I had broken my finger during a playful bedroom tussle with my husband. It was late at night and I couldn't get to sleep because of the pain. Every time I drifted off and then opened my eyes, there he was staring at me to make sure I was ok. My husband's job required him to travel quite a bit and those evenings alone portended the lost feeling I would have, if spending evenings alone became a permanent reality in my life. As I write about these feelings, I recognize that he is my best friend and the true sunshine of my life.

And so, I become a nag. I remind him to drink water with a glass of wine because of a certain drug's requirements. I spend hours poring over medical articles on his condition to be sure that we are pursuing every path to recovery. A nutrition tip notes the importance of a banana a day to maintain the correct potassium level. I nag a little more each day, to remind my husband to eat his banana, until we're both totally frustrated and he reminds me that he's a grown man, not a monkey.

He asks me to eliminate the words, "Is something wrong?" from my vocabulary, as these words are driving him crazy. I call him at work to see how he feels and remind him that he is working long hours. He tells me that he always has worked these hours and I respond that now it is different. He says I'm not his mother and I excuse myself to go up to my room and cry. Obviously, during this time of my life, I do quite a bit of crying. He lives in denial, and I live in constant anxiety.

Passion in the bedroom provides the foundation for my most frightening vision of my husband lying on top of me dead. His moans are now monitored for sounds of distress, because they can be indicative of something other than passion. How can I get carried away in the throes of passion when I can't stop thinking of how this one act could kill him, even though my husband tells me that he can't think of a better way to go?

The term post-traumatic stress disorder is used to describe trauma that can develop after exposure to a life-threatening event. Almost seeing your husband die can certainly qualify as such an event, and yet, those who have yet to have life punch them in the face consider the resulting feelings of fear abnormal. Is it normal to go on with life as if nothing ever happened, after experiencing such a horrendous event? Women spend a good part of their lives fighting against sexism and establishing their identities, and yet once they become caretakers, they must prioritize their lives to put the needs of their partner first.

It does sometimes cross my mind to wonder if my husband would so carefully tend to me if the tables were turned and he became the healthy caregiver and I was the ill spouse. I'm a little nervous at this thought, as I remember past instances when his attention to my needs left a lot to be desired.

For example, if I was sick in bed with a virus, instead of demonstrating his concern for my health, he would become petulant and act annoyed, as if I had done something wrong. I have concluded that the thought of my incapacitation was so frightening to my husband that he decided to just deny the entire situation.

Apparently, my husband isn't the only man who reacts poorly to the illness of his spouse. At least he doesn't abandon ship and find caring for an ill spouse so stressful that divorce becomes the preferred solution. Clinical studies have found a larger risk of divorce when wives become ill than when husbands do, or, in particular, when wives are diagnosed with cancer.

Do these findings imply that since established gender roles designate caregiving as a women's responsibility it's unreasonable to expect men to competently care for their spouse; or conversely are some men just selfish cads who are only there while the going's good?

Sometimes the caregiver needs as much care as the patient, but it's often considered selfish to ask for this care. Modern medicine has pills to even out our emotions, but there must be other paths to help the caregiver, short of having them become a stoned-out zombie. Yet, I remember

The Journey of an "Invisible" Woman

being grateful for the modern world of pharmaceuticals when I took Valium for the first time, as I sat next to my husband when he was in intensive care. After watching his bedside monitor nonstop as it beeped and screeched up and down with the rhythm of his heart, I realized that everything was hazy, and I was shaking so hard that my teeth hurt.

The doctor was talking to me but I didn't know what he was saying, because I was having a full-blown panic attack. I knew it was time to admit that I wasn't as strong as I thought I was, and that if I wanted to help my husband, it was time to swallow my pride and ask for a tranquilizer. Although, to many people, taking a tranquilizer is a common routine, I equated it to fulfilling a gender misconception about women and their pills.

The film industry has successfully exploited woman with substance use disorders in films such as *Gia* and *Valley of the Dolls*. Both films show sexualized portrayals of women too weak to face life's challenges without the help of happy pills. I was determined that I would never be one of those women.

Although the loss of my husband would mean I would experience great sorrow, I am confident that my identity doesn't depend on my marital status. I might be exiled from the realm of couples, but at least I wouldn't be subjected to dehumanizing practices, as happens to widows in some countries. In Kenya and Tanzania widows must undertake a ritual cleansing that entails the widow having sex with her husband's brother or other relative and then she must marry that brother or relative.

A former practice in India is called sati or widow burning, in which the widow would throw herself onto the husband's funeral pyre. My research doesn't come up with any equally frightening traditions for widows in the United States.

Instead, women only lose their standing in society with the death of a mate.

All of the years that I spent planning my rise to prominence didn't prepare me for the most important role that I'd have, that of caregiver. Each of us will encounter sickness and death in our lives, and yet we're uncomfortable discussing it. It's almost as if we don't want to tempt fate by reminding it of our existence. Instead, we think it would be easier to hide in the shadows.

We all need to be educated about the skills we'll need to deal with the very real possibility that we may become caretakers at some point in our lives. If that happens, let's not forget that a woman can learn and grow from undergoing these horrific parts of her life. She can choose just to survive or she can choose to become wiser.

The decision is hers to make. However, if she chooses to become wiser, she will get over being shell shocked and will be able to continue working on establishing her identity in the world.

CHAPTER 36
A TABLE FOR TWO

Sighing deeply while gazing at your spouse across a table in a restaurant can mean one of two things. Either you are contemplating how lucky you are to be married to this incredible person, or you are bored out of your mind and thinking about taking a solo trip to Tahiti.

Combine this sigh with one of the spouses staring off into the distance at nothing more interesting than a crack in the wall, and you have a description of the way many long-married couples share the experience of a restaurant dinner.

Unfortunately, many times this behavior is the result of them having nothing to say to each other, but perhaps there are other, more uplifting, motivations for their silence. After spending most of my youth clamoring to be seen and heard, my observations of these older couples terrified me with the thought that one-day, maybe even my husband would cease to see me.

When I was a young girl, I would go out to dinner with my boyfriend and observe, with horror, older couples sitting like zombies waiting for their dinners to be served so they could end the ordeal of having to spend another "fun" night out with each other. I was sure that this would never happen to me.

All my relationships were still at that flirtatious stage where every word that was uttered held romantic and exciting connotations and subtle meanings that were meant to measure whether this date could be the beginning of an enduring relationship. My mind was bursting with ideas of what I should say next, to engage my partner and make him want to see me again.

The quality of the food wasn't important; rather it was a question of whether the conversation was witty, intellectually stimulating, and sexy. It was comparable to a one-on-one job interview where a call back depended on your presentation. These dinners only had the possibility of ending in one of three ways; either I had to fabricate a sudden illness to escape what was obviously a bad date, my companion and I would suffer through the meal and he would never call me again, or we would hit it off and plans for the wedding would soon be on the horizon.

One of those dinner dates had turned out to be the one leading to my marriage to my second husband. I was now a newly married woman with expectations of experiencing the excitement of many "firsts." When we went out to dinner, my husband and I tripped over our words with exhilaration, as we interrupted each other to share the latest news of our experiences.

We talked about buying our first home and selecting its furnishings. We had never-ending conversations about having children together, vacationing in places we had never been before, moving to far away states, and looking forward to job promotions and all the accompanying benefits that came with them. It took us forever to decide what we would buy on our weekly excursions into the city. Would it be a painting or a new lamp?

The Journey of an "Invisible" Woman

We confided to each other our worries over how we would pay for all our dreams. These dinners became private forums where we could focus on our lives with the intensity usually reserved for earthshaking world events. We were totally engaged with one another, and were shocked when we realized that, while we were so engrossed, the restaurant was shutting and it was time to go home to let the babysitter leave.

Memories of all the years that I'd seen older couples sitting silently in restaurants came flooding back into my mind. I couldn't imagine how they could sit together without speaking. Their silence was puzzling, as they certainly had a shared history that could be the basis for a conversation. Instead, they would dig into their food without once glancing up at one another, as if this was their last meal on death row. I was confused by their aloof attitude towards one another, as I couldn't imagine my husband and me in that situation.

As we got older our discussions at restaurants became more serious. Now, when we spoke of our children it wasn't to giggle about their cute rendition of "the itsy bitty spider," but instead to wonder if we smelled alcohol on their breaths when they came home from a party.

The plans for trips to see our parents were now tinged with sadness, as we debated whether it would be best to relocate them to a nursing home or hire an in-home caretaker. The anticipation of the celebratory feast that my mom would prepare in the past for our homecoming when we went to visit her was now just a memory.

Instead, this heart-warming memory of my mom was replaced with the reality of worrying about whether she was getting enough nourishment and taking her medication. We still spoke of the thrill of climbing the corporate ladder in our professional lives, but this excitement was dampened by the news of layoffs. And yet, these experiences still engendered deep conversations over dinner. We were in the middle of everything.

We shared our children's triumphs and failures as they stood on the brink of adulthood, and were increasingly called upon to help our aging parents as their lives became burdensome. The minutes were flying by, but we didn't notice, as we were running as fast as we could just to keep up with our responsibilities.

During one of our dinners at a neighborhood restaurant my husband pointed out to me that there was a third party at our table. I was horrified at the thought that he was either seeing ghosts or had tiptoed over the edge of sanity one too many times and was now certifiable. I cautiously asked him to explain to me what he was referencing and he responded that he was tired of being snubbed.

Now I really was concerned that his next home would need padded walls to confine him. I decided this time that I'd ask him a direct question, "Who is snubbing you" and that's when he explained that I was guilty of phone snubbing or what is more accurately called, "phubbing" him. Apparently, this term is used to describe someone who snubs the person they are talking with in person in favor of their phone.

My phone was in its place of honor on the table and I immediately sheepishly covered it with my napkin. I knew that I was guilty as charged, as I couldn't control my eyes' tendency to glance every few moments at my phone instead of focusing on my husband.

My husband and I could be in the middle of an earth-shaking conversation and I would use any excuse to grab my phone to fact check some trivial point that was brought up. My fingers itched to check my latest emails and messages, and even checking the weather gave me a special thrill. It was time to admit that I was hooked, and this addiction was disrupting my personal relationship with my husband.

The Journey of an "Invisible" Woman

Many research studies have compared excessive cellphone use to cocaine addiction and have said that its lure is so strong that the "urge to check social media is stronger that the urge to have sex." I had a friend who eventually broke up with her partner because his relationship with his cellphone took precedence over her.

I suppose that my cellphone had become a refuge that I could always hide behind in order to compensate for any lulls in the conversation with my husband. My memories of being forced to be silent at the dinner table as a child made me feel uncomfortable with these moments.

Since my relationship with my husband was a priority, I decided to break the spell cast on me by social media and from then on, I'd leave my phone in the car.

All too soon, it was just the two of us again. We were comfortable with each other and no longer had to work hard to impress one another. We knew each other well, perhaps too well. As our friends and family died, our world was becoming smaller, and we were forced to face our own mortality.

Our calendars were no longer filled with our children's dance recitals, soccer games and school plays. Instead, Dr. Stephens and Associates were penciled in all too often. Suddenly, we no longer looked forward to exotic vacations because we were faced with the specter of having to scale down our lifestyles to save money, in acknowledgement that retirement was not too far off.

Our incomes would be much less, and although it is said you need less in retirement, you still need money to let you do the things you want to do.

The thrill of consumerism was gone because we had everything we needed. We were no longer looked upon as rising stars at our jobs and our professional goals no longer seemed as relevant. Many times, the topics of our restaurant conversations were so depressing that we chose not to speak.

When my husband looked into my eyes, it might have been difficult for him to see the vivacious, adventurous person he married. Life's adversities had planted seeds of doubt in my determination to distinguish myself, and perhaps this was reflected in my countenance.

But I still refused to have my light extinguished. Instead, I'd let any silence be a time for reflection, as I outlined in my mind, the next steps in mastering my destiny.

Perhaps the older couple who seemingly ignore each other as they sit across the restaurant table, have reached the point in their lives where silence is comforting. They might understand that some things are better left unsaid.

Often people believe that unpleasant thoughts will come true if they're said aloud, and others believe it is bad enough living through hard times without having to make them a topic of conversation. Or, they might be deep in contemplation, devising plans to take over the world.

Sometimes, the realization that we're no longer the center of the universe needs to be acknowledged; when we see an elderly couple sitting and not speaking in a restaurant, it might not be boredom that we are observing, but wisdom.

CHAPTER 37
LOOKING IN THE MIRROR

As we learned in our last chapter, that older couple sitting quietly in the restaurant would probably prove the hypothesis that sometimes things we observe only show the surface reality of a situation. There may be many underlying circumstances and societal expectations that determine the way the world looks at us. Likewise, these norms also influence the way we look at ourselves.

I was visiting a young woman for background information about the attitudes of Millennial women concerning aging. As I came into the room, she was just putting on the finishing touches to her makeup and smiling at her reflection in the mirror. She clearly liked the image that she saw. She confided in me that today was her thirty-fifth birthday, but she said that she didn't feel that she looked any different than she did when she was a teenager. She also said that she still socialized with her friends from high school.

As we continued talking, I asked her if she thought that these friends appeared older. She looked surprised and replied, "Yes, they have changed." I pointed out to her that perhaps her friends also saw their younger selves when they looked in their mirrors. Sometimes we only see what we want to see.

Sometimes a piece of glass doesn't always reflect everything about a person. At some point in our lives, we've all asked ourselves the question, "Who am I?" and have tried to piece together the answer from studying our reflection, as seen from the perspective of others.

I had a conversation with my mom shortly before she died at the age of ninety-six and she said that she knew that realistically, her body was wrinkled, sagging and way past the stage that anyone would call attractive by society's standards. But she explained that her essence was still the same as it was when she was a young girl. She was still Katherine, dreaming her dreams of what happy things tomorrow could bring. It got her angry when all people saw, when they looked at her, was a little old lady.

The comments of people who told my mom that she looked good for her age infuriated her even more than when people totally ignored her because of her age. She felt that she was being reduced to an age-based statistic, instead of being considered as an individual with unique qualities. My mom doubted that these same people would tell someone who was gay that they looked straight because they understood that would be discriminatory.

She knew that she couldn't run a marathon or play a fast game of tennis, but that didn't mean that she didn't want to have fun anymore, or love and be loved. It's sad to think that the appearance of our bodies defines to the world who we are and, to the world, the last thing that you want to be is an older woman.

Our culture has accepted attitudes that often promote the degradation of a woman's worth because she has "lost" her looks. Scientific polls, such as those taken by the Pew Research Center, confirm that desirable traits are judged quite differently for men and women. Not surprisingly, a man's honesty is lauded as his finest trait, while physical attractiveness is judged to determine a women's value.

Yann Moix, a well-known French writer and director, was quoted as saying that older women are "invisible" to him and "I prefer younger women's bodies, that's all. End of. The body of a 25-year-old woman is extraordinary. The body of a woman of 50 is not extraordinary at all."

He apparently didn't have a clue that what he'd said was incredibly insulting to women, but thankfully, he did spark international outrage at his remarks. I have a feeling that his dating life might have taken a downward spiral as a result of his despicably sexist comments.

If we see an adult skipping down the street singing, we steer a wide path around them and think, "Wow, what a nut." And yet, a smile comes to our face if we watch a child doing the same thing. The CEO of a Fortune 500 company sees himself or herself as a dynamic leader wielding unlimited power. This same leader, hospitalized with a stroke, is now perceived as little more than an infant, reliant on others for all of his or her needs.

An elderly couple walks into a hot new dance club and receives incredulous stares from the young partiers. If they dare to get up and dance, these stares now are accompanied with giggles and outright laughter. They've done nothing inappropriate or funny, but they're not meeting the world's expectations of who they should be.

Even the medical community uses preconceived gender stereotypes in their treatment of woman patients. Many times, this treatment reflects gender bias. For example, there is evidence of doctors treating men and women differently for the same health problems, as well as inflicting moral judgments on a woman's reproductive choices. Female patients are twice as likely as men to be diagnosed with depression.

The medical community admits that the reason is that women are more likely than men to present their psychosomatic problems to their doctors. At the same time, women are seen as emotional. Clearly doctors are sometimes seeing their women patients through slivered mirrors.

The image we convey though our behavior is also often a reflection of society's bias. Young women debate for hours what they will wear to that same hot new dance club, and once there, unabashedly, dance as if auditioning for a music video. No one laughs, although many people stare at this jubilant display of exhibitionism. Dancing, as an activity, only requires that you have feet and can move.

There are no age requirements; you just need to enjoy yourself. And yet, elderly couples and young women receive very different reactions from their audiences, although they may both be experiencing the same feelings of exhilaration. Apparently, the audience sees very different things, as they look at these dancers.

Similarly, a trip to the gym confirms the fact that people's image of themselves sometimes doesn't necessarily reflect reality. Many of us have seen the lady who believes she is a *femme fatale*, and accordingly exercises with her face heavily made up, never breaking a sweat. For her, the gym is an opportunity to receive the admiration of other gym members, never thinking that these members might not consider her worth noticing.

Or what about the man who entertains the other men in the locker room by exposing parts of his body that only should be seen by his doctor or loved one. But maybe our impression of these people doesn't mirror the reality of who they are.

The Journey of an "Invisible" Woman

Let's consider some other possibilities for this eccentric behavior. Perhaps the overly made-up woman is actually insecure, and is slathering on makeup so she can hide her anxieties about her looks. In the same way, the man might not be an exhibitionist, but was raised in a household where everyone walked around naked. Now he thinks that his nudity is natural and should be accepted by everyone.

I also remember a woman who was strutting around the locker room totally naked until a little child asked her why she was so fat. She appeared shocked by the question, as if she had never noticed her extra fifty pounds of weight. In her mind, she was as lithe and trim as a gazelle. That was her image of herself.

What genetic traits are some people born with that enable them to have such an inflated sense of self-esteem and how can the rest of us emulate those traits? Women generally bemoan even a slight weight gain or new wrinkle. Is there a magic spell to help us to not denigrate ourselves because of slight imperfections?

Remember when you were a teenager and a song would come on the radio that reminded you of a special moment with your latest love? A special song can still trigger memories of important times in our lives. We don't stop remembering as we get older; there are just more things to remember, so it might take us a little more time to find a specific memory.

Our hearts still ache to feel the magic of a first kiss. The knight on the white horse still rides in our dreams, only now he has some grey hair, and a little paunch around his middle.

What we see when we look at someone is rarely a true depiction of who that person really is. On the surface, my friend Matt had everything going for him. He was handsome, smart and had a family who supported and loved him. Although he was a college graduate, he couldn't seem to hold onto a job without getting into confrontations with his boss or another employee. He refused to believe that perhaps, the person he saw in the mirror might be different from what other people saw. Eventually, people pulled away from him.

Matt had no empathy for others and apparently had never learned to read social clues. His relationships with women were short lived because he kept looking for the perfect woman, not realizing that it was his imperfections that doomed any lasting connection with another person. Matt will continue to change jobs, friends, and girlfriends. He can keep running, but things will never change for him because he's not able to escape from himself, and the person he sees in the mirror.

We have all had those "if only" moments. If only I didn't have children, then I could have been a brilliant scientist. Or, if only I didn't have to work ten-hour days, I could have written the great American novel. But if we're honest with ourselves, we'll admit that our "if only" moments are just pretexts not to face up to the truth, namely, we didn't want these things enough to make the effort to get them.

Giving up one hour of television a night would give us seven hours a week to write that important book, and nothing except lack of motivation keeps someone from going back to school after their children are grown. It is so much easier to see ourselves in a positive light if we hide behind our excuses rather than admitting our true nature.

For me this meant that blaming motherhood or my parent's directives for my failure to become a lawyer or journalist was a fallacy. I was actually attacking the straw man. The truth was, that I simply didn't want my dream badly enough. Just like the young girl on her 35th birthday, when I looked in the mirror, I only saw what I wanted to see.

When that thirty-five-year-old young woman celebrates her fifty-fifth birthday will she be able to look in the mirror and see the woman that she has really become, or will her vision be clouded by false conceits and the expectations of others?

And, if the woman whom she sees in the mirror is someone who is vibrant and purposeful, will this be the same person whom others see in the mirror or will they cease to see her at all, because as an older woman she is no longer relevant.

CHAPTER 38
~~EQUAL~~ OPPORTUNITY

Much of what we see when we look in the mirror is influenced by things beyond our control, as part of our fate has already been shaped by gender norms established while we are still in utero. I don't know how many of you have ever attended a "reveal" party, as this event wasn't around until the late 2000s.

The process is a simple one. The gender of the baby is revealed to family and friends by using a variety of methods such as presenting cakes, balloons, colored smoke or other items in the respective gender associated colors of pink or blue. This practice has generated much controversy because of complaints that a gender reveal party reinforces gender stereotypes, particularly for the LGBTG community. The spectacular celebration of a child's gender declares that gender is of utmost importance and should determine how that child will be raised and whether that child will be visible or invisible in the world. In addition, it assumes that gender is binary.

A well-known experiment known as "Baby X" conducted in 1975 affirmed the conclusion referenced above that a person's gender greatly influences how they are treated by society. The study dressed the same baby alternately in blue and pink and varied calling it by girl and boy names.

An adult was then told to take care of the baby. The same baby got very different treatment depending on the color of its clothes and name. The perceived girl was treated gently and considered upset if she cried, while the boy was treated more roughly, given trucks to play with and judged to be angry if he cried.

How sad that a balloon's color is a predicator of a child's interests. If your friend's reveal party is filled with pink balloons does that mean that her daughter will love dolls, have long hair and wear pink bows? I'll tell you a little secret; I always hated the color pink.

Once a woman reaches adulthood, playing with trucks and rejecting a wardrobe consisting of pastel colors might not be the only gender taboos that she faces, in fighting against the pressure to conform to rigid gender stereotypes. Unfortunately, these stereotypes may seriously affect a woman's ability to get the life that she wants.

The education system in America continues to cast a blind eye on the inequities that exist in the education of women, from the time that they are little girls excluded from the block corner to their being coerced into specializing in "female" professions or modifying their leadership aspirations in male-dominated professions. For example, if a woman decides to enter the medical field, the likelihood of her performing brain surgery is slim. As of 2019 there were only 1,424 female residents in neurosurgery nationwide.

It appears that women have been discouraged from entering certain surgical specialties. According to 2017 data from the AAMC, women make up less than one quarter of 10 surgical specialties, and are the least represented in orthopedic surgery at 5.3%. A 2019 study in JAMA confirms that even the surgeons themselves agree that women belong in family medicine, not surgery.

Women who wish to practice law must confront even more roadblocks to success than women entering the medical profession. Although, in 2020, women made up 54.09 % of students in ABA-approved law schools, this majority status becomes irrelevant if women aspire to leadership positions in major law firms.

Hollywood has convincingly portrayed the iconic Wall Street lawyer as a preppy frat brother type, and this image is not far from the truth. A survey by the National Association of Women Lawyers reports that in 2018, women comprised only 19.5 % of equity partners.

What do these numbers tell us? It's great that women are going to law school and getting jobs in law firms, but they still have a long way to go if the power leadership roles are off limits to them.

They might have been sufficiently taught the academics in school needed to gain entry into their chosen careers, but persistent confining gender norms hurt their chances for advancement. The top leadership positions in law firms require that an attorney possess the qualities of assertiveness and self-promotion.

However, these same qualities in a woman become a double-edged sword. If she's too assertive, then she's not ladylike. On the other hand, if she's not assertive enough then she lacks the confidence to be a leader. This dilemma exists even at the highest levels of the law.

Although women have gotten greater representation on the United States Supreme Court, as of 2018, 65.9% of all interruptions are directed against the women jurists. Woman lawyers have turned to working in corporate settings, where there is more flexibility in hours worked, so that they can juggle their lives as mothers and lawyers.

The Journey of an "Invisible" Woman

A dear friend of mine in Dallas left a lucrative job at a prominent law firm to work at a corporation, because she'd be able to attend her three daughters' swim meets. If she wanted to succeed in a big-name law firm, she'd need a wife to carry on what she wanted done for her family.

In 1829 Supreme Court Justice Joseph Story said it best when he described the law as "a jealous mistress that required long and constant courtship." Apparently, this is still true today.

Needless to say, perceived misconceptions about women's' math ineptitude also contribute to their small numbers in the fields of finance and engineering. There are many other nonprofessional careers that underrepresent women in management positions.

The restaurant and service industries have been guilty of delegating lower-level entry positions to women and only advancing men into leadership roles. It becomes clear that a woman's education needs to provide her with not only the core of academic knowledge to meet the skill requirements of her chosen career but, more importantly, to equip her with the tools she needs to combat sexism in the workplace.

Gender bias in the education system must be resolved for women to be able to open doors that have been shut to them. Not only does the system as it stands reinforce a women's lack of confidence in herself, but it also leads to academic mediocrity. This can be noted in observing the typical coed high school classroom.

In a coed school environment, we can immediately sense an undercurrent of sexual tension between the boys and girls. Obviously, in single gender classrooms, most of this tension is absent. Students in a coed classroom often accept gender norms that dictate that the male is always the top dog.

This dismal fact portends poorly for a girl who hopes to develop her leadership skills in the classroom, but it does reflect the real-life workplace example reported in "Business Insider," that as of 2020, roughly 8% of all Fortune 500 companies are led by women.

Advocates of single sex schools hypothesize several theories on coed schools that may be accurate or not. They assume that girl students in coed high schools are easily distracted from their studies because of their interest in boy classmates.

They don't want to raise their hands too much and appear like a brainy nerd. As a result, girls are left with many unanswered questions that minimize their knowledge development.

These young girls would see the world end before they'd admit in front of their classmates that they are better at math than some of the boys. The advocates suggest that girl students have decided to pretend to acquiesce to the gender stereotype that girls would rather sit around quoting poetry than solve complicated math problems or gaze at a molecule through a microscope.

Girls learn at an early age to subvert their own feelings, including their need to get the approval of others. They wind up with self-esteem issues if they can't get this approval from their boy classmates and teachers. Boys, on the other hand, will be boys and don't hesitate to speak out and demand attention.

This translates to girls generally being less assertive in class, and teachers having to adapt their teaching to control the boys. Consequently the girls are ignored. It's all too obvious that girls and boys learn differently, and that girls are negatively affected if these gender differences are not addressed in the classroom. Maybe, as some would argue, the solution is to have single sex classrooms and schools.

The Journey of an "Invisible" Woman

My daughter and I, both, attended all-girls' high schools. I remember sitting in a classroom and looking down at a giant spot on my uniform skirt that I hadn't noticed when I got dressed earlier that morning. My hair hadn't been combed for over 24 hours, but I didn't care because there were no boys for me to impress in my class.

I was there for one thing, and one thing only, and that was to beat out every other girl in the class with the highest grades that I could possibly get. Like me, my daughter admitted to being distracted from her studies by boys when she attended a coed school, but when she was in her all-girls' school she, too, excelled at her subjects.

I'm sure by now your mind is spinning with all sorts of objections to what looks like my support of single gender schools. Perhaps you think that women will never learn to work with men later on in life if they can't interact with them in school. Maybe you would assert that women have fought hard to get equal rights, so single gender schools would simply reinforce entrenched gender stereotypes. You might also ask why a boy's focus in school isn't similarly affected by being in a classroom with the opposite sex?

These are all valid considerations. However, we need to remember that girls have barriers to overcome, because of discriminatory gender norms that don't affect boys and therefore extraordinary resources must be offered to girls to make up for these biases. Girls are irreparably harmed if their education is not structured in a way that enables them to meet their unique needs.

Now, let's go back and look at the spiral that's created if a girl is embarrassed to simply raise her hand in the classroom for whatever reason. By failing to raise her hand, she won't have her questions answered, and will now have a hole in her knowledge base.

This hole might prevent her from getting the foundation she needs as a base for additional learning. Her grades will, invariably, suffer. Because her grades are not great, she likely won't get into the college of her choice. Her career choices might also become limited. She might not have the qualifications to meet certain professional schools' strict admittance policies or she'll be lacking in the skills required to obtain the job she wants. And ultimately, although she may obtain a position in her desired profession, she might never attain a leadership role. Her ambitions might be crushed, all because she was unwilling to raise her hand.

When a girl is very young, she might not yet know if some day she'd like to be a leader. However, we should make available to her everything that she will need, if she decides to make that choice in the future.

Perhaps the answer is not found in the establishment of single gender classrooms or schools. Teacher education courses should be redesigned to emphasize gender equity, so boys and girls are taught that brainy, outspoken, visible women are the new norm. Girls are not genetically deficient in math and science or soft voiced.

Gender bias change must come from the top down, as studies, such as Trautner, indicate that teachers' gender-specific expectations may be important facilitators in the widening of gender gaps. Other studies like, Hinnant, O'Brien and Ghazarian (2009), and Ready and Wright (2011) indicate that teachers overestimate the linguistic skills of girls, while they credit more skill in mathematics to boys, as shown by Jussim and Eccles (1996)

These biased gender norms that influence a teacher's expectations of a child can jeopardize a child's education and future. Girls should remember the words of the Canadian philosopher, Matshona Dhliwayoa: "In a world full of pebbles, dare to be a diamond."

CHAPTER 39
THE MEN IN MY LIFE

I've spent a lot of time telling you about my husband Blue Eyes, my ex-husband and some assorted boyfriends, and now it's time to share with you some things about the other men in my life.

My father was the biggest influence on the development of my identity. Aside from his beliefs about certain superficial gender characteristics, such as the importance of long hair on women, he truly could be considered a male feminist when it came to gender equality. He didn't just talk the talk; he also walked the walk.

He was a devoted father and an avid deep-sea fisherman, who included all of his children and grandchildren, regardless of gender, in his weekly fishing excursions. My sister was a tough cookie, who gladly accompanied him on these smelly fishing boats, which were filled with veteran fisherman who could be heard muttering to themselves about the idiocy of having women on a fishing trip.

My father didn't let this dissuade him from treating the females in his family the same way that he treated the males. I, on the other hand, am a big sissy and I'm terrified of the deep blue sea, so I remained on dry ground while my dad and sister were busy catching that night's dinner.

There are many theories that say women look to replicate their father in the choice of a mate. In the case of my father, replication would be impossible, because he was one of a kind. As a young man, he worked three jobs in order to support himself and to save enough to open his own business.

During the week he drove a truck, delivering Wise potato chips, did part time bookkeeping for Macys and also performed on the weekends in a Vaudeville show, playing the accordion. My siblings and I learned at a young age that you had to work hard to get what you want in life. Although my father worked extraordinarily hard, he always found the time for his family, and to indulge his passions for music and the dog that he took to work with him each day.

Regardless of his hectic schedule, he would show his unconditional love for his children by always dropping everything to help us whenever he was needed. I loved to sleep, and many days this resulted in my missing the bus that would take me on the half hour trip to my high school. I never worried, because I knew that my dad would jump in his car and drive me to school.

After my marriage to Blue Eyes, my mother initiated a bizarre ritual involving my father and his daughters. At the time, I lived a block from my sister and although we were both in great financial shape, my mother decided that she would send meat weekly, from her expensive butcher, to her daughters, and the delivery man was always my dad. Every Saturday I'd hear his car horn alerting me that my delivery had arrived. If all this wasn't example enough that my dad should have been canonized as a saint, my dad made the ultimate gesture when I had my fateful encounter with Luke in Indiana.

The Journey of an "Invisible" Woman

As you already know, Luke had dumped me again. I was stranded with my son in Indiana until superman dad came to the rescue. Although he was in his seventies, he gamely rented a U-Haul truck and drove from New York to Indiana to pick up me and my son, along with all of our possessions.

He never made me feel like a foolish young girl. Instead, he showed me what pure love looked like. The best compliment that I ever received was when my mom told me that I was just like my dad, because both of us worked and partied hard.

My dad became a giant in the gourmet food industry. He demonstrated his belief that women and men deserved the same opportunities when he designated my sister as the person to take over his business when he retired. At the time, there were no women running a business in this industry. This was a major achievement for my sister.

When asked if he had children, my father would say he had three children, never distinguishing them as a son and two daughters. To him, they were the same. I was inspired by my father's conviction that gender shouldn't be a determinant in his daughters' attainment of their life goals.

My dad was the first male influence in my life, but in short order, three other men would be exerting their presence into my existence. But the gods were laughing at me every time I gave birth. I always wanted a daughter, whom I could use to inadvertently challenge all the feminist guidelines about female attire by dressing her in frilly dresses and bows.

I assumed my wish would quickly come to fruition, since my mom always told me, "if you try hard enough, you can get whatever you want." But this time, it didn't matter what I did, as my husband, or in my case husbands, called the shots when it came to the gender of my children.

Sandy Camillo

As everyone knows, it's the man's chromosomes that determine a child's sex. This is one of those times when a man truly has control over everything. So, I gave birth three times and optimistically picked out the name Jennifer each time, for the baby who I was sure would be a girl.

But for me it was lucky number four that proved to be the charm. I finally had my Jennifer, but I also had three boys, who would make my life something special. And one of the side benefits was that my boys' boisterous natures guaranteed that we would attract attention whenever I went out with them, and I loved getting attention, whether it was good or bad.

It wouldn't be a major understatement to say that having a child at the age of twenty is a major life-changing event. I didn't know who I was or what I wanted from life when I gave birth to my first son at that age. He became a part of everything that I experienced in life, and because of him these experiences were totally different from those of other people my age who didn't have a child. We were both growing up together.

Early in my career, I was a director of a pre-school. I was younger than most of my teachers and the parents of the students. I still had much to learn, as I hadn't experienced all the trials of parenthood yet. The teachers and students became best friends with my son, who accompanied me to school each day. They loved being around this adorable little boy. He was always at my side.

When I moved to Indiana, he became my companion as I sat idly all day, waiting for my lover's visit. After I returned home to New York and temporarily moved in with my parents, my son would wait for me to come home from my job in Manhattan to put him to sleep. And then I got married again. He latched on to my second husband with all his heart and whole-heartedly accepted him into his life.

293

The Journey of an "Invisible" Woman

We were now a family unit. However, although my first husband had abandoned my son, my new husband had to formally adopt him. The image is still fresh in my mind of my child standing in family court as Blue Eyes petitioned to adopt him. That day brings back sad memories, as I remember my son forlornly watching my first husband sign him away.

As the years passed, I saw my son grow into an accomplished man, and yet he was still almost my peer as we were only twenty years apart in age. His mind astonished me, as he could do complex mathematical calculations at warp speed in his head, and his intellectual prowess quickly catapulted him into becoming the president of a Park Ave brokerage firm. However, the thing that meant the most to him was family.

My son's relationship with my parents was deep and unbreakable. My mother was almost a second mom to him, as she had helped raise him while I was in school. He shared the same passion for deep-sea fishing as my father, who took him to fish several times a month each summer.

When my father lay dying, in the bedroom that he and my mother had shared for so many years, my son lay down on the bed with him to talk about the good times. My son's presence helped fill my father's last days with solace.

Some people might think that my son was a hindrance that made it more difficult to achieve my career goals, but the reverse was actually true. His birth gave me an added incentive to do great things, so that he could be proud of me. He showed me the meaning of independence when, as a child, he bravely went to summer camp and ate bugs in the Canadian wilderness. I had much to learn about resilience from him.

I remarried a half-Italian man whose Italian side engendered in him a desire for a large family, so shortly after we married, my second son was born. There were eight years between him and his older brother. Therefore, I was careful not to do anything that would create jealously between the two boys, and my second son made it an easy task. From the very beginning he was quiet and undemanding, and he would have been a ringer for goldilocks, if goldilocks were a boy.

When he attended kindergarten, his placid nature was misunderstood as possibly something more sinister. His teacher complained that when he was told to sit quietly, he would do just that.

How screwed up is the educational system when an obedient child is viewed suspiciously. After a slew of psychological tests, we were told what we already knew and that was that this son was a sweet, smart child. We didn't know how smart until, at the age of fifteen, he started detailing cars in our driveway to make some extra money. And boy did he make money.

On a single weekend he could earn $300 or more, and we soon became the envy of all the neighbors who took note of the procession of Ferraris and Porsches that lined our driveway. He had a disconcerting trait that was evident upon our move to Texas, and that was stubbornness. In resistance to our move, he refused to set his watch from eastern to central time.

He maintained this symbol of his defiance for over a year, until he gradually accepted his new home. He was always there for his friends and family, although he might work hard to keep his emotions hidden. People flocked to be close to him, because of his kind nature.

Knowing my extreme fear of surgery, my son showed his deep love for me by flying from Texas to New York to be with me for a major operation. If anything good could be attributed to that moment, it was my surgeon's comment to

The Journey of an "Invisible" Woman

me as I lay in the recovery room. He said that he was touched by the display of emotion that he saw in my son, who was waiting with tears in his eyes when the doctor told him the good news that I was going to be okay. The empathy to other people and determination to succeed that he exhibited as a young boy detailing cars translated in later life to him becoming a successful entrepreneur and author.

And that silent persona that he'd had as a young child was gone. He could now talk for hours and made a point of having the requisite data that he needed to back up his opinions. When he talked, people listened. There were many times when I faltered in my determination to reach a certain objective.

He would encourage me not to give up, by reminding me of all the great things that people have accomplished regardless of age or gender. He was always my personal advocate.

There is a seventeen-year age difference between my first and third son. Needless to say, people thought I was insane when I said I was pregnant again. I had a great job in a law firm, my older sons were at the developmental stage at which they were no longer demanding every moment of my free time, and my parents were available to babysit, so my husband and I could travel and enjoy the good life. But something inside of me wanted to try one more time to have a daughter.

I worked, up to the week before the birth of my third son and had every intention of returning to work after his birth, but that thought went on the back burner when my son, at one year of age, developed a mystery disease. A rash appeared all over and inside his body.

After dragging him from one infectious disease specialist to another, the diagnosis was a possible penicillin allergy. This baby had almost died, so I was no longer in any rush to leave him to the care of others. He was the image of the Gerber baby with the most startling eyes. His eyes were so beautiful that my mom nicknamed them, "Diamond Eyes." Because his sister was born eighteen months later, he became, either by nature or circumstance, a fantastic caregiver.

After the birth of my daughter, the nurturing side of my son's personality really came out. His sister would barely put her finger up to point at something she wanted before he would race to have it in front of her. He was pure love. He was filled with a zest for life and was curious about the contributions that technology could present for future generations.

Like his oldest brother, the wanderlust in his blood eventually carried him to many exotic places in the world. Upon graduation from college, he decided to fulfill his love for Japanese culture by moving to Japan to teach English. I was startled by the thought of him going to the other side of the globe to live alone. He was a fearless adventurer, and unlike me, he was willing to live in a hut if he thought it was exciting. My idea of exploring was to arrange luxury excursions from my room in a five-star hotel. However, I was able to live vicariously through his many exploits.

The day finally came when he returned home from Japan, and he was able to fulfill his dream of using technology to venture into new worlds. He was hired by a startup company to help pioneer the emergence of virtual reality. He was doing what he loved, but his family still came first. As an adult, he was still the same nurturer that he had been when he took care of his baby sister.

My major surgery had laid me low for months. During that time, I couldn't move from my bed and required tons of help. My youngest son took a sabbatical from work to care for me and never revealed this act of kindness to me until

The Journey of an "Invisible" Woman

many years later. Although he could decipher all the mysteries of technology, to me he was still that little boy with the diamond eyes, and when his eyes shone on me, I was illuminated.

Prominence, accomplishments and adoration are things that I have searched for all my life, in order to maximize my self-image. All the men in my life have greatly contributed to the fulfillment of those goals, as they are the living embodiment of all my aspirations and each of them has played a role in helping me to become the woman that I am.

CHAPTER 40
YOU CAN'T GO HOME AGAIN

The car rental clerk asks me if I want to rent a GPS for an additional $29.95. I explain to him that my body could instinctively find its way to my destination even with my eyes closed.

It is six years after the death of my mother and I am going back to visit my childhood home. This is where I became the woman that I am today. It's the place where I was taught never to give up my dreams, because anything was possible. I had my whole life in front of me and it was guaranteed to be wonderful.

I hadn't yet faced broken hearts, hostile work environments, traitorous friends, sickness, death, or the specter of fading into obscurity. The word "invisible" had no meaning to me other than triggering a memory of the 1933 movie titled, "The Invisible Man." It would be many years later that I would unwillingly associate myself with the concept of invisibility, a concept that became a reality of my existence.

As I drive my car down the familiar streets in the neighborhood where I grew up, my mind is like a camera operating in reverse. When I pull up in front of my childhood

The Journey of an "Invisible" Woman

home, snapshots of my life appear in my mind, revealing memories of my past that I rarely contemplate. These snapshots race through my consciousness with a frightening rapidity. Many are heartwarming, but there are ones that I'd rather not mull over.

Snap! I am eight years old and my friend Janie and I are setting up a makeshift stage inside my garage to regale our neighbors with our dramatic abilities, in our own version of the latest Broadway play. Neither one of us could act or sing, but that didn't stop us. We were great and we knew it.

Snap! Another image flashes of me flying down the street on my bike at daredevil speed to prove to the neighborhood boys than girls were no wimps. Unfortunately, I didn't see the rock that caused me to fall off my bike and run crying home to my mom.

Snap! I can feel the heat coming from the flames that were licking at my mother's apron as she lay writhing on the kitchen floor after her potholder caught on fire. I listen to the sound of my big sister crying as she tries to suffocate the flames with a towel.

Snap! I smile at the picture of my dad recapturing his vaudeville days, by captivating us all with his performances on the house organ. He was so proud of his musical ability and we were so proud of him.

Snap! I witness my older sister's first kiss, while I hide behind a sofa in our living room, dreaming of the day when it would be me in a young prince charming's arms.

Snap! I remember my mom and me peeking out my bedroom window late at night to see if my first boyfriend's car would circle my block one more time. And he did, three more times.

Snap! The next image is of New Year's Eve festivities in the basement. Today it would be unthinkable to have a party in a basement, but back then it was the perfect place. Over one hundred relatives and friends would pack their bodies into a small room for hours, to listen to my father play his accordion.

At the stroke of midnight my mother's brother would dance into the room dressed in a diaper, to capture the essence of the baby new year. After the witching hour, my father would be joined by his brother and his brother's band, to happily jam together into the next day. And I would sneak off to share those magic moments with whomever was then the love of my life.

Snap! I'm in a car on the street outside my home. There is a tug of war game going on between my mother and a man I loved, and I am the rope between the two of them. The man, whom I thought loved me, was pushing me out of the car, while my mother was trying to pull me into the protection of her loving arms.

Snap! The years go by, and I see my future husband innocently telling my parents that he wants to marry me, never suspecting my mother's angry outburst at the news. She was afraid that I would make the same mistakes again that I had in other relationships. She was also an old-fashioned Catholic who didn't believe in divorce. She couldn't understand how I could marry again, as in God's eyes, I was still married to my first husband.

Snap! My heart is heavy at the next images that I usually keep pushed the furthest back in my consciousness. I'm suddenly back, sitting next to my Dad as he lies silent in his deathbed, no longer surrounded by music. I'll always see him, either playing the piano or his accordion, with a smile on his face. Each of our family members took up their own private vigil in our house and waited for the end. My brother sat in the easy chair at the bottom of the stairs, not speaking a word. My mother retreated to the comfort of her kitchen refusing to accept what was happening in the upstairs

The Journey of an "Invisible" Woman

bedroom. And I lay across the end of my daddy's bed, hoping by my presence to forestall the inevitable.

Snap! My mother sits in the living room. She has decided that this is where she will spend her last days. She wants to remain close to what had been the gathering place for so many happy family events. Even at the very last moment, she is concerned about her children's needs.

She worries that they need to get home to their own families and shouldn't spend so much time with her. This house is the place where my mother and father took their last breaths.

Snap! I get out of the car to get closer to my old home, so I can read the sign posted on the door. The sign reads, "This house has been condemned." To me, the word 'condemn' signifies something unfit for use. How can something that was once the place where so many people loved, hated, cried, and laughed, now be unfit for use? But maybe this condemnation is not a bad thing?

My parents were the lifeblood of our family and now that they are gone, our home is just a pile of bricks. Would it have been any easier if, instead of seeing the condemnation sign, I'd seen a light on in the living room, with a family watching television? Their stories would form a new history for the house. Instead, the condemnation guarantees that the story of our home ends with our family.

None of my children understand the sentimentality that I attach to my childhood home. When they were growing up, my husband and I moved our family from house to house and even to different states. As one of my sons told me one day, "there is no house that I'm attached to." I think to myself that it's sad that he will never understand this warm feeling that I still get in my heart whenever I drive past my old home. At the same time, I realize that it's easier for my children to follow the money in their search for fame and fortune, because they have no nostalgic memories tied to where they live.

When I lived in Texas and Missouri, I felt like a vagabond untethered from my true roots. I thought that when I was finally back home in New York, all the pieces of the puzzle that comprised my life would neatly fit together as they had in the past, but this was a baseless fantasy.

Now, my husband and I are alone in a large five-bedroom colonial that we call home. In the six years that we've lived in this house, we've yet to accumulate many family memories because most of our family lives in other parts of the country. A house without memories is just an empty shell. Who I am and who I can become have nothing to do with where I live. Nonetheless, I take one more snapshot of my old childhood home.

Snap! The sign says, "You no longer live here and you can't go home again."

CHAPTER 41
DO NO HARM

I knew that I could never go home again and recapture my childhood experiences. My life has taught me that all of our drive, determination and schooling doesn't always prepare us for the sometimes-unpleasant surprises that life brings to our door. Our lives can be drastically changed when either a loved one or we, ourselves, become stricken with illness.

Suddenly, our feverish quest for fame and fortune seems misplaced, and we find ourselves in the position of either adjusting our expectations of what our lives should be like, or falling into a web of self-pity. I once was faced with a situation that challenged my illusion that I had total control of my life. Since I couldn't escape the situation, I knew that I had to figure out a way to have it make me stronger.

I am terrified of doctors. This fear is right up there with my fear of bugs, although I'm lucky that I'm not in the 3% of the population that has iatrophobia, the medical name for this phobic fear of doctors. For over thirty years, I had suffered with stomach problems, but always failed to mention this during my yearly physical.

Although I was smart enough to know I needed these checkups, my stupidity made me withhold crucial information from my doctor. An Old Italian superstition was that if you mentioned something, you could be sure that it would occur. In this case, I was sure that every pain and ache that I had was cancer, so I didn't want to mention these pains.

Crazy to the tenth degree, but I couldn't help it. I gave up dairy, gluten and just about anything else that I thought might be the cause of my bad stomach. Eventually, the stomach pain became so bad that I couldn't even leave the house. I could only find relief for short periods of time by getting onto the floor on my hands and knees. I sometimes stayed that way for hours.

Since I couldn't get much done in my life on the floor, I knew that there was nothing left for me to do, except to go to the doctor and tell him the truth. If I was leery of doctors in the past, I became desensitized to them after this experience. I was subjected to every test you can imagine by multiple specialists, ultimately to hear that I needed surgery, and that there was a chance that cancer would be discovered.

Fortunately, my fear of dying took precedence over my suspicion of the medical establishment's treatment of women. As I noted in a previous chapter, gender bias towards women doctors is evident in the determination of a physician's medical specialization. This bias is even more egregious when practiced against women patients, as it becomes a matter of life or death. As a result of this bias, many women discover that patriarchy is alive and well in medicine.

Although it might seem that a straight path led me from my visit to the doctor to the operating room, the actual process was extremely circuitous. My original doctor had the mindset that women were too emotional to handle their own health matters, and not bright enough to understand medical lingo. Therefore, when he called me with my test results, he asked me if I had a family member nearby. I quickly brushed off his condescending question, and asked him for my test results.

He then proceeded to tell me that I needed to have immediate surgery and that he had already called the surgeon for me. When I told him that I wanted a second opinion he disdainfully responded that it wasn't necessary. I don't know if this guy was just the most patronizing doctor in America, had a God complex or was just an idiot.

As it turned out, I did need surgery, but his diagnosis had identified the wrong organ to be removed. Thankfully, since I didn't like taking orders from any man, I went and got a second opinion that probably saved my life.

I was lucky, but things don't work out as well for all women. For some women, gender bias then becomes a life-or-death issue. Numerous studies, such as those done by Aggarwal, Patel and Nehta, et al.,(2018) have indicated that, although a heart attack is perceived as a man's disease, cardiovascular disease is also the leading cause of death in women, globally and in the USA; it leads to a similar number of deaths in men and women.

Many of the studies in the past have been male-focused and have not recognized heart risk factors unique to women. A woman's complaints are often misdiagnosed as anxiety or "hysteria," and often, she ends up paying with her life, because "only 22% of primary care doctors and 42% of cardiologists feel well prepared to assess a woman's cardiovascular risk" (Pawlowski, 2019, p.4).

Some physicians base their diagnoses, or should I say misdiagnoses on their personal beliefs in certain biased gender stereotypes. These stereotypes could be tremendously misleading when determining the correct method to diagnose and treat mental disorders.

If a physician assumes that women are predisposed to be emotional and capricious, he, or she, might forgo the use of evidence-based assessments. Such gender bias might mean that a woman never receives treatment for her attention deficit disorder or depression, because her doctor is attributing her ailment to what he assumes is a condition common to women, instead of judging her simply as a person.

I knew that I'd have to give up some of my control and put myself into the hands of a surgeon. However, the physician that I chose treated me as an individual not a gender, and so I chose to have the surgery. I placated my craving for recognition by reminding myself that this was a moment in my life when I was truly the center of everyone's attention. The doctors, nurses, and family members were all there for me.

However, if given the chance, this one time in my life, I would have taken a back seat to someone else if that person could have climbed onto that operating table for me. I wasn't as tough as I pretended to be. I was scared and I didn't care who knew it.

The surgery itself was a surreal experience that I underwent in a trance-like state. The good news was that there was no cancer, but I woke up from the operation minus ten inches of my colon. After three months of bed rest, I started to gradually get back into my life, with the knowledge that I wasn't superwoman, and that the world didn't have to recognize my worth for me to be happy. I was happy just to be alive.

Before too long, I finally got back to plodding through the everyday business of living. I had a new grand-baby, whom I would actually get to see grow up. My other grandchildren lived cross-country, so I wasn't able to be a part of their lives when they were young.

This new grand-baby lived only forty-five minutes away, and I was excited at the thought of being there for all the milestones. Things were rolling along nicely. I was involved, professionally, in a new endeavor, helping abuse victims, and was falling more in love with this new grand-baby every day. And then the world crashed!

COVID19 attacked the entire world, and it soon became apparent that this new virus was going to change everyone's lives forever. New York became the epicenter for the slaughter, with more victims than anywhere else, globally. Schools, businesses, stores, parks, and even beaches were closed. Social distancing was practiced everywhere; people wore masks, and everyone looked like the lone ranger.

The stock market tottered and shaking hands was now equated with wishing someone dead. Older people and people with underlying conditions were told to self-quarantine in their homes. I had to self-quarantine in my home with my husband, because I am considered immune compromised from a condition that I've had since birth.

Initially, everyone thought that this was just like the flu, until people started dying by the thousands. After the seventh week of quarantine, I had washed and polished every square inch of my house and was running out of things to do.

Doctors and family gather around you when you are sick, but now those same people can be the carriers of your death sentence. For many years, I tortured myself on the weekends over finding the right restaurant to dine at in Manhattan, or seeing the "in" play. I'd bitch at my husband if we didn't have every minute of the weekend filled with unique adventures. Now, my greatest wish would be to touch my children and grandchildren.

Sandy Camillo

Although my surgery had taught me that I wasn't bulletproof, nature now taught me the valuable lesson that no one is invincible. It's inevitable that eventually we all have to deal with unpleasant things happening in our lives. However, we can't let the fear of life's dangers paralyze us, so that we can't reach for the stars.

CHAPTER 42
THE END?

By the time this book is published, one of several of the following scenarios may have occurred in the world. Human contact is now akin to playing a game of Russian roulette. People are walking around wearing medical masks, while trying to maintain a minimum distance of six feet between one another.

Walking the dog is analogous to dodging land mines in a field, but now the mines are people themselves. Half the world's population has died, and only healthy people under the age of fifty populate the earth. World economies have crashed, and millions of people are jobless, and spend their days waiting on breadlines to get their meager share of free food.

But perhaps, this dystopian nightmare will not happen, and everything will magically return to the way it was before the most horrific catastrophe in history happened. I'm talking about COVID19, an itsy, bitsy little virus that turned the world upside down, and with its merciless potential annihilation of the human race, ended all my plans for ascendancy to world prominence.

Sandy Camillo

My many years of worrying about becoming an Invisible Woman became as insignificant as a drop of rain in the ocean. My new goal in life was simply to stay alive. Covid19 didn't discriminate on the basis of gender, race, religion, or economic status. It was an equal opportunity employer that was insatiable in its quest to find new victims.

"Taking pause" became new buzzwords for the nationwide quarantine. Everyone, except essential workers, huddled in their homes to wait for the signal that it was safe to go outside again. Couples learned new things about each other, and some of those things would later be the grounds for divorce. Families home schooled, and began to read and play games with each other. And everyone contemplated their past lives, and re-evaluated the things that, in the past, had made life worthwhile.

But the one thing that didn't benefit from this time of introspection was politics. The virus became the focal point for bitter fighting between America's two major political parties. The national pastime became watching daily virus briefings on the various news stations, and reading Twitter to learn whether it was worth getting out of bed in the morning. Polarization between people intensified, depending on which side of the line they stood on social distancing and mask requirements.

Friends and family members became estranged from one another because of their ideological allegiances. The media was exploding with rallying cries of, "give me my freedom" or, "you're killing others by not taking action to mitigate the spread of the virus."

People were dying by the thousands, and yet underlying the gravity of this national tragedy were the silent maneuverings of politicians, determined to use the pain of the nation to their own advantage. People were afraid, and this fear sometimes caused irrational behavior.

The Journey of an "Invisible" Woman

At this point, I began to realize that the mundane aspects of my existence were an important part of what made my life count. Many, many months of home quarantine alone with my husband made it clear to me that the world wasn't missing me.

The cheering crowds idolizing me for my outstanding accomplishments were gone. The world didn't know if I still existed, and if the virus got me, I'd just be another number in the tally of the dead. It looked like I'd never be on television or lauded with a national award for my achievements, but maybe all this time, I had overlooked the fact that, in the end, the only meaningful accolades are those given by family and friends.

My family believed that I was the cornerstone that tethered the family together. So, I prepared for the weekly family zoom call as if I had been granted an audience with the Queen of England. I tried to look my best after months without a haircut or color, and gathered humorous stories and anecdotes to share with my family.

This was my chance to dazzle the people who really counted, and I had, for most of my life, stupidly pushed to the back of the line in my quest for recognition. I had learned my lesson; hopefully it wasn't too late.

Looking back on that bartender in the fictitious bar noted in my first chapter, I acknowledged that he might still ignore me when I ordered my martini, but now it was of little consequence. The Covid19 virus had made me focus on the existential meaning of life, and prioritize the steps that would lead me to self-actualization; social status ranked low on this list.

All my life I had, tenaciously, fought against becoming an invisible woman. The fight was long and hard, but once the world was put on pause, there was no more first prize to win in society's game. No one knew when or if the game would again begin. In the meantime, it was just my family and me, living in a surreal universe; but in that world I would never be an Invisible Woman.

EPILOGUE.
THE ACCUSED (HIDING BEHIND A CURTAIN OF GUILT)

Throughout this book we've talked about the many seemingly insurmountable barriers that women must knock down in order for them to achieve their ambitions in life. Now it's time for each of you to think about those impediments that have personally threatened or might yet threaten your successes in life and pledge that you'll never be an Invisible Women.

But before you take that pledge, we need to look at one more thing that is not normally construed to be a result of gender bias against women, and yet many gender bias taskforces have shown, "that victims of rape and sexual assault were judged harshly on their appearance, demeanor, lifestyle and reputation," because they broke the gender norm that defined the appearance and behavior of a "good" woman. This chapter is written as an epilogue because I won't be supplying its conclusion. The ending will depend on what you, the reader, believe is true.

Any discussion of sexual harassment elicits passionate emotions from women and must be a part of any conversation about gender bias and gender norms. I'm a card-carrying feminist and am proud to have raised a feminist daughter, but I am also an unabashed lover of men, as I've had two husbands, a father, a brother, three sons and, without sounding a little loose, quite a few boyfriends.

Because of these two facets of my identity, I sometimes appear schizophrenic in my reaction to current events that involve sexual harassment. I will always stand up to defend women who have been destroyed by sexual abuse, but I simultaneously struggle with judging a man's guilt or innocence based on an assumption that all women are saints, and all men are evil predators. Perhaps, therefore a look should be taken at the possibility that innocent men are sometimes automatically thrown into the same barrel with slimy guys who abuse women.

My reflections aren't meant to excuse the behavior of the type of man that the "Me Too" movement targets. There's no punishment ghastly enough to punish a man who abuses a woman, although, if given a moment, I can think of several pretty gruesome ones. But similarly, there's nothing worse than suffering for something that you didn't do.

This internal conflict has prompted me to question whether, as a good feminist, I will automatically align my loyalties on the woman's side of a sexual abuse accusation or if I'll be able to follow the legal dictates of innocent until proven guilty.

We all know that men, as well as women, are victims of sexual harassment. My goal is to impartially explore the intricate nature of sexual harassment, as it affects men, as well as women. The difficulty of maintaining my impartiality while also speaking candidly is predicated on my ability to abandon personal prejudices and stereotypical assumptions about the innate natures of men and women.

Conversations on the topic of sexual harassment are always controversial. When sexual harassment issues arise, tempers flare and people sometimes rigidly align themselves with either the alleged victim or the alleged perpetrator.

Victims of sexual harassment often erroneously believe they are responsible for the abuse, because they've been told that their behavior or appearance tempted the perpetrator. These victims not only endure unwanted sexual attention but also experience a loss of self-esteem and purpose, sometimes causing them to hide the alleged abuse for many years.

When a woman is the victim of sexual harassment, she sometimes feels that her value in the world has become subverted to her unwilling role in fulfilling a sexual abuser's fantasies. Her sense of power often is diminished, as she doubts certain facets of her identity.

She wonders if she could have resisted the unwanted actions of the abuser. The victim is no longer a woman ready to take her place in the world as a leader. Instead, the mere disclosure of the alleged sexual harassment may now elicit some negative connotations associated with her being a victim.

Invariably, some people question the truth of a woman's accusations, citing instances of women seeking vengeance for unrequited love. Apparently, they are remembering the words from the 1697 play *The Mourning Bride* by William Congreve: "Heaven has no rage like love to hatred turned, nor hell a fury like a woman scorned" (Book Brow, ¶1).

A woman may also be subjected to personal humiliation and professional damage if there is any speculation that her accusation is falsely based. Even if her veracity isn't questionable, society might still demand that a woman suffer silently and remain in the shadows rather than be seen and heard. Hollywood effectively incorporated this belief into their 2020 movie, "Promising Young Woman" which focuses on the web of complicity that hides sexual abuse, in order to protect the perpetrator's promising future.

The film highlights the disproportionate appropriation of a person's value based on their gender. Consideration is not given to the disintegration of a woman's promising future after she has been subjected to the trauma surrounding sexual harassment or assault, perhaps because of society's ever-insistent belief that men, not women, are destined to be leaders.

In order for anyone to dispassionately judge the merits of a sexual harassment accusation, all specifics of the event must be accurately recorded. However, a major problem in recounting the details of such an allegation is that it generally involves only two people, the alleged victim and the alleged perpetrator. There usually are no witnesses. Instead, it is a true example of "He said, She said." Perhaps, we can only really judge the veracity of an accusation if the incident occurs within the confines of a story in which the author controls the narrative.

To illustrate the above point, let me tell you a story about an incident in which I was involved. At first glance, my story might make some women angry, because it questions things that many feminists automatically assume are true. This is only one case of suspected abuse, but it underscores certain complexities underlying any accusation of sexual harassment. However, my tale needs to be told, and the determination of guilt or innocence will be in your, the reader's hands.

During my time as a Catholic elementary school assistant principal, I encountered many bizarre situations involving children, teachers and parents. Perhaps, one of the most emotional interactions involved a young male teacher and a thirteen-year-old girl in eighth grade. Michael, the teacher, was a 24-year-old married man with a baby, and was filled with the exuberance that comes with the first year of teaching, and unfortunately, sometimes fades with time.

As this was his first job, he rigorously followed all of the guidelines noted in numerous "How to" teaching books and his lesson plans were meticulous. He believed that development of a student's sterling character was just as important as a student's academic aptitude, and in his mind, these goals prompted him to become a strict disciplinarian, although his timid manner belied his aspirations.

Nancy, a young student in his class, was exhibiting many of the rebellious tendencies that girls experience upon entering their teenage years. She was acting out by not doing any work in school and had already tasted the sexual waters, with quite a few eager boys in her class.

Unfortunately, her home life was very unstable and basically consisted of uninvolved parents preoccupied with social interactions, who had no interest in their daughter's behavior. The young teacher viewed the girl as a personal challenge to his teaching skills and engaged in many confrontations with her over her failing grades and classroom misbehavior.

As an Assistant Principal, I often also acted as the school's dean of discipline and as such, got to deal up close and personal with wayward students, so Nancy and I spent many long afternoons getting to know each other in numerous detentions. Late one afternoon, the principal called me to come to her office. I wasn't surprised to see Nancy sitting in the room, as I had assumed it was only a matter of time before she would go too far in disregarding school regulations.

As tears flowed heavily down Nancy's face, the principal explained that Nancy claimed that Michael had sexually harassed her. Nancy asserted that she had been alone in the classroom with Michael, and he had remarked to her that she had beautiful breasts. The principal had ascertained that no one else had witnessed this event, but Nancy was adamant that it happened. I thought that this claim would result in the school initiating an investigation, but that's not how it went down.

The principal asked me to accompany her to Michael's classroom. We entered the room and she immediately repeated the accusation that Nancy had made. The principal told Michael that he was fired and to collect his personal items and leave. He started crying, and said he would never say something inappropriate to a student. He begged for a chance to clear his name, and then said that something like this would destroy his career forever.

He tried to explain what he said actually had taken place, the day he spoke to Nancy in his classroom. He said that he had told Nancy that she must repeat the year because of her failing grades, and that perhaps she was angry at him. As teenagers often had short fuses, her anger wasn't difficult to envision.

The school in question was part of the Catholic Diocese of Dallas school system. For decades, this diocese had dealt with allegations of sexual abuse of minors by priests. The principal vividly remembered the unpleasantness of being associated with a system that suffered for years with the reputation of being a hotbed of sex scandals. She was determined not to make any decisions that would result in a bad image for her school, and so the principal held fast to her decision that Michael be fired.

The above incident happened over 20 years ago, but it still bothers me, because of several unanswered questions. Was it an admission of guilt that Michael didn't pursue legal recourse, or did he just disappear because he was a naïve young man, ignorant of the legal avenues open to him? I also often wondered if Nancy's psychological development was damaged forever, regardless of what did, or didn't happen in that classroom.

Nancy's relationship with men might somehow be negatively affected if she were telling the truth about the harassment. If she fabricated the story, she would learn a different lesson. She would believe that she would best achieve her goals in life through manipulation and deceit.

The Journey of an "Invisible" Woman

If Michael was guilty, he got what he deserved, but if he was innocent his life was irrevocably changed. It's unlikely that he would get another job in his chosen profession and there would always be a seed of doubt about his innocence in the minds of those who loved him. For Michael, this certainly wasn't a case of "innocent until proven guilty."

After hearing this story, can you easily decide who is the guilty party? Unlike Michael's and Nancy's story, guilt is easier to discern when hearing harassment stories with serial predators like Harvey Weinstein and Matt Lauer.

My story, and others like it, involving everyday people may not be as scintillating as incidents when the perpetrators are famous people, but they still damage the very heart and soul of a woman, and sometimes even of a man. In any case, it is indisputable that sexual harassment defines a woman solely as a sexual being, stripping her of the unique qualities that illuminate her essence to the world and often making her hide behind a curtain of guilt.

A woman's destiny mustn't be controlled by arbitrary gender norms and bias. Whether Nancy was a victim or manipulative miscreant, one thing is indisputable. She has a right to have a place in the world. No woman deserves to become Invisible, not you, nor I, nor Nancy.

THE END

About The Author

Sandy Camillo

Sandy Camillo is an Italian-American native New Yorker who, at an early age, vowed never to become an "Invisible Woman." In her never-ending quest to remain visible, she explored various professions in her home state of New York and adopted states of Texas and Missouri, working as a teacher, school principal, paralegal, receivership specialist, realtor, court appointed special advocate, legal compliance and governance expert, before dedicating her pen to blogging and writing.

Her contributions as an educator began as a teacher in the most destitute area of New York's inner-city, before she rose to prominence as the principal of an elementary and middle school in Texas, tasked with applying evidence-based principles to meaningfully impact the emotional and intellectual development of diverse students.

Her determination to radically resist the societal encodings of male hegemony that subdued women in her mother's generation and spurred the dynamism of the baby-boomer movements of the 60s and 70s, led her to success in several other professions, including some known to be cut out just for men. Sandy has always practiced walking the walk, not just talking the talk. Throughout her life, she has dedicated herself to promoting equity for women through advocacy.

She served as a Director, Secretary and Governance Consultant of the National Board of the American Association of University Women (AAUW), a top-ranked women's advocacy nonprofit dedicated to empowering women, and travelled across the U.S to speak to AAUW stakeholders about women's issues.

During her spare time, Sandy is happiest hanging out at the beach with her family. When she gets home all sunburned, her dog Sophie and cat Chloe are there to greet her. She is an avid reader and a micro-blogger, focusing on women's issues and aging, with approximately 1,500 followers on Twitter. Ms. Camillo holds a Bachelor's and Master's degree in Education, a postgraduate Certification in Administration, a Court-Appointed Special Advocate Certification and real estate licenses from New York and Texas.

Her educational background has prepared her to assume leadership roles in her various careers. Just as she started contemplating whether her next profession would be as an astronaut or racecar driver, a light bulb in her head went on. It shone on the harsh reality that, regardless of her career choice, barriers existed that threatened the attainment of her professional and personal goals, simply because she is a woman.

In her book, *The Journey of an "Invisible" Woman*, she shares stories of the intimate struggles that she, her friends and other women throughout history have experienced in combatting gender bias. She invites you to journey with her, beginning with her rebellion against playing in the doll corner in kindergarten, to the discovery that her knight on the white horse actually had a black heart. Then continue your journey with her as she realizes that the fight to remain visible becomes even more difficult as a woman ages.

Many women discover, as they age, that their light is fading in the world and they are expected to be satisfied sealing envelopes as a volunteer for a nonprofit organization or babysitting a precious grand-baby, in lieu of running a board meeting. A young woman reading these words might be thinking that these scenarios can't happen to her, but unless she plans on dying at a young age, she will get older, and the specter of becoming an invisible woman may become very real for her.

And for those brave men who are secure in their own skin and are debating whether this book is for them, the answer is yes, because this is your chance to finally understand how women think.

Sources

Abraham, A. (2020, December). "Gender-reveal parties need to end with 2020 –here's why". www.vogue.in.

Aggarwal, N., Patel, H., Mahta, L, et al (2018, February). "Sex differences in ischemic heart disease. Circ Cardiovasc Qual Outcomes", 11(2).

Akoye, K. (2013, October). "Widow sexual cleansing ritual continues in Tanzania". Thomas Reuters Foundation.

American Association of University Women, Nutley Branch Presentation, Nutley New Jersey, October 2, 1996.

American Bar (2020, January). "Broken Rungs on the Career Ladder". www.americanbar.org.

American Society of Plastic Surgeons. (2019). "Plastic Surgery Statistics Report." www.plasticsurgery.org.

Army, I., & Gittleman, S. (2018, February). "Female service in the IDF: The challenge of an 'Integrated' Army. lawfareblog.com.

Askins, J. (2019, July). "Where are all the women in surgery?" www.aamc.org.

Bailey, A. (2019, August). "Taylor Swift and other stars rally around Bebe Rexha after a music executive told her 29 was 'too old' to be sexy." Elle Magazine. Elle.com.

Bank of America. (2008). "Bank of America buys Merrill lynch creating unique financial services firm." http://investor.bankofamerica.com/news-releases/news-release details bank-america-buys-merrill-lynch-creating unique-financial.

Barnes, P. (2019, July). "Age discrimination is a women's issue that women's groups tend to ignore."Forbes, Forbes.com.

Bornstein, M.H. (1985). "How infant and mother jointly contribute to developing cognitive competence in the child." National Academy of Sciences.

Bornstein, M.H. (1992) "Functional analysis of maternal speech to infants." Developmental Psychology.

Boston College (2021, April). "A gender gap in negotiation emerges between boys and girls as early as eight." www.sciencedaily.com.

Bryner, J. & Pappas, S. (2011, June). "The animal kingdom's most devoted dads." www.livescience.com.

Calaprice, A. (2010). "The ultimate quotable Einstein." www.quoteinvestigator.com.

Campbell, J. W. (2010). "Getting it wrong: Ten of the greatest misreported stories in American journalism" University of California Press: Berkley.

Cash, M. (2020, October). "WNBA legend Sue Bird says call for equality with the NBA are not about equal pay." www.insider.com.

Catholic Straight Answers. (2021). "How old was St. Joseph when Jesus was born?" www.catholicstraightanswers.com.

Chen, G. (2020, February). "Why single –sex schools are growing in popularity." www.publicschoolreview.

Cherry, K. (April, 2021). "What is self-esteem?" www.verywellmind.

Cleary, K. (2019, June). "The notebook." www.hypable.com.

Cleaver, Eldridge (1960). "Eldridge Cleaver Quotes." [Online Posting] Double Quotes https:// www.doublequotes.org/ quotes/eldridge-cleaver- 2-5242/.

CNBC (2018). "NYSE appoints Stacey Cunningham as its first female president." https://www.cnbc.com/ 2018/05/22/ nyse-appoints-stacey-cunningham-as-first female-president.html.

Cornell, B. (2014, April). *Betty Cornell's Teen-Age Popularity Guide*,eBook. Dutton Books.

Das, A. (2020, February). "U.S. women's soccer team sets price for ending lawsuit: $67 million." The New York Times.

Dawson, A. (2019, January). "What the death of a parent can teach us, if we're willing to learn." www.latimes.com.

Dixon-Fyle, S. & Dolan, K. (May,2013). "Diversity wins: How inclusion matters." www.mckinsey.com

Donavan, L. & O'Neil, H. (2018, October). "These Kenyan widows are fighting against sexual cleansing." The World. Pri.org.

Doward, J. & Fraser, T. (2019, September). "Hollywood's gender pay gap revealed: male stars earn $1 million more per film than women." The Guardian.

Ducharme, J. (2018). "Why some people have aviophobia, or fear of flying." Time.Com https://time.com/ 5330978/fear-of-flying-aviophobia/.

Eady, D. D, & Wright, D. L. (2011). "Accuracy and inaccuracy in teachers' perceptions of young children's cognitive abilities." American Educational Research Journal, 48, 268-302.

Ehrman, B. D. (2011). "The apocryphal gospels: Texts and translations Oxford University Press, history of Joseph the Carpenter, 5th century."

Enjuris (2021, March). "Where do women go to law school in the US?" www.newswire.com.

Epstein, R. H. (2010). "Get me out: A history of childbirth from the garden of Eden to the sperm bank." New York: W.W. Norton & Company, Inc.

Esposito, L. (2014, July). "How to overcome extreme fear of doctors." Health News. health.usnews.com.

Fabian, R. (2017, August). "Why mental health is a feminist issue." Talk Space. www.talkspace.

Facebook (2020, September). "How to maximize results from anti-aging skin care products."

Facebook, AAD. Fels, A. (2014, April). "Do women lack ambition?" Harvard Business Review.

Firestone, S. (1970). *The dialectic of sex.* New York William Morrow and Company.

Fluker, D. (2019). "How this 24-year-old former NYSE equity trader made history."

Forbes, https:// www.forbes.com/sites/dominiquefluker/ 2019/01/28/ laurensimmons/#24d3edd0543b.

Forbes, E. L. (2012, April). "The Complexities when Women Use Beauty as a Career Tactic."

Gay, R. (2018). "Fifty years ago, protestors took on the miss America pageant and electrified the feminist movement."

Smithsonian Magazine. Retrieved from https://
www.smithsonianmag.com/history/fifty-yearsago-
protestors-took-on-miss-america pageant-electrified-
feminist-movement-180967504/ on August 6, 2020.

Gee, A. (January,2015). "Who first said the pen is mightier than
the sword?" BBC.Com.

Gibbens, S. (2018, May). "Is maternal instinct only for moms:
Here's the science?" National Geographic.

Glynn, S. J. (2012, August). "Fact sheet: Child care." Center for
American Progress.

Govender, V. & Penn-Kekana, L. (2007, June). "Gender bias
and discrimination: a review of health care interpersonal
interactions." World Health Organization. Retrieved on
March 23 from https:// www.who.int/social_determinants/
resourcesgenderbiases_and_discrimination_wgkn_2007.p
df.

Greenfieldboyce, N. (2008). "Pageant protest sparked bra-
burning myth." National Public Radio. Retrieved from
https://www.npr.org/templates/story/story.php?
storyId=94240375 on August 6, 2020.

Grose, J. (2014, November). "It's not your kids holding your
career back. It's your husband." www.Slate.com.

Gross, J. (2014) *Handbook of emotion regulation*, New York,
Guilford.

Guenard, R. (2015, January). "Hair dye: A History." The
Atlantic, theatlantic.com.

Halford, M. (September,2009). "Was Holly Golightly really a
prostitute?" The New Yorker.

Heller, K. (2018). "The bra burning feminist trope started at
Miss America, except that's not what really happened." The
Washington Post, Retrieved from https://
www.washingtonpost.com/news/retropolis/ wp/
2018/09/07/the-bra-burning-feminist-trope-startedat-
miss-america-except-thats-not-what-really happened/ on
August 6, 2020.

Hill, K. (2012, February). "How Target figured out a teen girl
was pregnant before her father did." www.forbes.com.

Hinnant, J. B, O'Brien, M, & Ghazarian, S. R. (2009). "The
longitudinal relations of teacher expectations to

achievement in the early school years", Journal of Educational Psychology, 101, 662-670.

Hobbs, J. (2019, August). "When did Millennials start taking style tips from senior citizens?" Vogue Magazine. vogue.co.uk.

Holland, K. (2018, June). "How to identify and manage phubbing." Healthline. www.healthline.com.

Hopp, D. (2019, October). "From 1500 BC to 2015 AD: The extraordinary history of hair color." Byrdie. Birdie.com.

Huhtanen, H. (2017, November). "Gender bias in sexual assault response and investigation." www.endviolence.com.

Jackson, A. E. (2018, September). "6 Real –Life examples of Age Discrimination." www.glassdoor.com.

Jain, R. (2018, May). "The History Behind Sati, A Banned Funeral Custom in India. The Culture Trip." www.theculturetrip.com.

Jamal, L. (2020, March). "A push to get more women on corporate boards gains momentum." www.npr.org.

Johnson, S. (1998). *Who moved my cheese?* NY: G.P. Putnam's Sons.

Jussim, L.& Eccles. J. (1992). "Teacher expectations ll." Journal of Personality and Social Psychology, 63, 947-961.

Karraker, A. & Latham, K (2016, September). "In sickness and in health? Physical Illness as a risk factor for marital dissolution in later life." Journal of Health and Social Behavior. 56(3), 420-435.

Kettler, S. (June,2020). "How Sonny and Cher went from tv's power couple to bitter execs." Retrieved Fromhttps:// www.biography.com/news/sonny-cher-relationship, June 1, 2020.

Kim, J. (November,2016). "Do men really get over breakups faster than women?" Psychology Today. https:// www.psychologytoday.com/us/blog/valley-girlbrain/ 201611/ do-men-really-get-over-breakups-fasterwomen.

Lamb, V. M. (2011). "The 1950's and the 1960's and the American woman: The transition from the "housewife" to the feminist." https:// dumas.ccsd.cnrs.fr/ dumas-00680821/document.

Lauro, P. W. (2021, March). "The Media Business: Advertising; After years of selling products, Clairol now hopes to sell its image." The New York Times.

Legge, J. (2013, September). "Attractive people-particularly women-more likely to get a job than unattractive, says study." Independent, www.independent.co.uk.

Leonhardt, M. (2020, January). "60% of woman say they've never negotiated their salary-and many quit their job instead." www.cnbc.com.

Lisa Miller, L. (2014, June). "Why are we grossed out: Women with armpit hair?" The Cut, www.the cut.com.

Logan, E. (December,2016). "Breakfast at Tiffany's, problems no one ever talks about." Glamour. Retrieved from https://www.glamour.com/story/ breakfast-at-tiffanys-problems.

Mamo, H. (2020, March). "How Paulina Porizkova felt after learning she was cut from Ric Ocasek's will." www.billboard.com.

Manders, K. (2020, April). "The renegades." The New York Times, www.nytimes.com.

Marcus, R., & Harper, C. (September,2015). "How do norms change?" www.odi.org.

Marshall, K. (2014). "Charivari 3 disgusting ways independent women were tortured and shamed in Shakespeare's England." The Week.com.

McFadden & Whitehead, "DJ Goldfingers." Jerry Allen Cohen, Gene McFadden, John Whitehead, Sony/ATV Music Publishing LLC. Warner Chappell Music,www.lyrics.com.

McLeod, L. (2020). "Lev Vygotsky's Sociocultural Theory." Simply Psychology. www.simplypsychology.com.

Mervosh, S. & Ambrose, S. (2017, October). "Raped, fondled, flashed: what female patients say happened to them at Timberlawn psych hospital." Dallas News. https://www.dallasnews.com. /news/investigations/ 2017/10/26/raped-fondled-flashed-what-female-patients-say-happened-to-them-at-timberlawn- psych-hospital/.

Mikelionis, L. (2019, January). "French author, 50 mocked after saying he's 'incapable' of loving women over the age of 50." Fox News. www.foxnews.com.

Miller, L. (July,2013). "Diagnosing Anthony Wiener; Sick or just plain stupid?" New York Magazine.

Min, A. (July, 2019). "The past, present and future of women in stem." www.edventures.com.

Moeller, P. (2010). "10 Reasons seniors continue to work: Accelerated by the great recession, the concept of retirement is changing." US News and World Report. https://money.usnews.com/money/blogs/the-best-life/ 2010/10/07/10-reasons-seniors-continue-to-work.

Morello, K. B. (1986). *The invisible bar: The woman lawyer in America, 1638 to the present.* NY: Random House.

Morris, C. (August,2015). "Women hurt more by breakups but recover more fully." Binghamton University. https:// binghamton.edu/communications-and-marketing/ media-public-relations/pr-archives/ index.html?id=2315.

Museum of the City of New York (2014). "Revolutionary sisters; Victoria Woodhull and Tennessee Claflin." Posted by Susannah Broyles in Digital Project, Photography Collection, Portrait Archive, Print Collection and tagged Cornelius Vanderbilt, "Scandal, Suffrage, Tennessee "Tennie" Claflin, Victoria Clafin Woodhull, Women's rights." https://blog.mcny.org/ 2014/06/24/revolutionary-sisters-victoria-woodhull-and-tennessee-claflin/.

Neumark, D., Burn, I., & Button, P. (2016). "Experimental age discrimination evidence and the Heckman critique." American Economic Review, 106 (5): 303-08.

Neumark, D., Burn, I., Button, P. (2017, November). "Is it harder for Older Workers to find Jobs? New and Improved Evidence from a Field Experiment." National Bureau of Economic Research.

O'Dea, S. (2020). Smartphone ownership in the U.S 2011-2019. Statista.com.

O'Shea, S. (2016, August). "Fires of hell: Medieval fear and loathing of red hair." Interesly.https://www.interesly.com/ red-hair-fear-loathing-medieval-times/.

Odette, F. (2013, November). "Ableism: A form of violence against women." Learning Network,www.learningnetwork.com.

Olson, B. & Bayles K. (1984). "Mother-infant interaction and the development of individual differences in children's cognitive competence." Developmental Psychology.

Orsborn, C. (2014, January). "Worst ads of 2014 for boomer." Huffington Post, www.huffpost.com.

Owens, M. (2019, May). "TimeLine: The investigation into the catholic diocese of Dallas sex abuse scandal."www.wfaa.com.

Pak, E. (September 4, 2018). "When women became nuns to get a good education." www.history.com.

Paschall, K. (2019, September). "Early Childhood." Childtrends.org.

Pawlowski, A. (2019, March). "The invisible woman, the challenge at the doctor's office every woman needs to know about." www.today.com.

PayScale. (2020). "The State of the Gender pay gap 2020: Pay equity analysis can show if your organization pays women less than men for equal work." https:// www.payscale.com/ data/gender-pay-gap.

Payscale.com. (2020). "The state of gender pay gap in 2020-How to advocate for pay equity analysis", retrieved August 10,2020 from https:// www.payscale.com. /data/gender-pay-gap.

Penfold-Mounce, R. (2019, November). "How gender inequality lasts into death." British Broadcasting Company, www.bbc.com.

Petersen, M. (2017, July). "Lobbying for Equal Rights on the 18 Hole and Beyond." The New York Times.

Preidt, R. (2019, November). "Stereotypes about girls and math don't add up, scans show." www.consumer.healthday.com.

Quotes, (2016, May). "Scarlett O'Hara quotes." www.quotes.net.

Rich, A. (1976). "Of woman born." Journal of Constitutional Law.

Roderick, L. (2017). "Unilever: more than half of women believe men should lead high stakes projects." www. marketingweek.com.

Russell, R. (2009, October). "6 Women with unusual careers." www.sheknows.com.

Saad, L. (2018, June). "Trimesters still key to U.S. Abortion Views", Gallup.

Safe Cosmetics. (2013, July). "International Laws, EU Cosmetic Regulation" www.safecosmetics.org

Schreiber, S. (2004, November). "When a parent dies." www.oprah.com.

Schuder, K. (2020, June). "Practices from history you'll never believe were real." Babygaga, History.com, https://www.babygaga.com/weird-pregnancy-practiceshistory/.

Scutts, J. (2016). "The woman who kicked down wall street's doors." Time. https://time.com. /4297571/ muriel-siebert-wall-street-history/.

Serena, K. (February,2018). "The scold's bridle: How men in the middle ages dealt with gossiping wives." Allthatsinteresting.com.

Serico, C. (2015, February). "What does your hair say about you? The message your style is sending." Today, www.today.com.

Shewfelt, R. (2020, March). "Paulina Porizkov shares poem that 'perfectly describes' the end of her marriage to Ric Ocasek." www.ca.style.yahoo.com.

Shields, J. (2018, March). "Age discrimination: Older applicants vs. young pretty People." Jobscan, www.jobscan.com.

Skulason, B., Hauksdottir, A., & Helgason, A. R. (2014, March). "Death talk: Gender differences in talking about one's own impending death." BMC Palliative Care.

Steely, D. (1976). "Haitian divorce." Songfacts.com.

Stempel, J. (2013). "Bank of America, Merrill in 39 million gender bias settlement." https:// www.reuters.com/article/us-bankofamerica-bias-settlement/ bank-of-america-merrill-in-39-million-genderbias-settlement-idUSBRE98512720130906.

Stephens, S. (2019, August). "Women in neurosurgery." Cedars–sinai.org.

The Lancelet. (2019, March). "Cardiology's problem: Women." www.thelancet.com.

Thompson, E. (2002). "Corporal punishment by parents and associated child behaviors and experiences: A meta-analytic and theoretical review." Psychological Bulletin, American Psychological Association, Inc. 128 (4), 539–579.

Titcher, A. (2016). "Ultimate Guide: How to personalize marketing for millennials." 2016blog.idomoo.com.

Titelman, G. Y. (1996). *Dictionary of popular proverbs and sayings*. New York: Random House.

Trautner, H. M. (2008). "Entwicklung der Geschlechtsidentität [Development of gender identity]."In R. Oerter & L. Montada (Eds.), Entwicklungspsychologie (pp. 625– 651). Weinheim: Beltz. [Google Scholar].

Trend. (2019, October). "Catalyst gendered ageism. Trend Brief."

UK Essays. (2018, November). "History of men controlling Women." https://www.ukessays.com. /essays/english-literature/ history-of-men-controlling-women-englishliterature-essay.php.

Verde, T. (2017, November). "The protoevangelium of james-150ad century", Greek document. Politico Magazine.

Vincent, T. (2017, November). "The Law is a jealous mistress." www.michbar.org.

Ward, M. (2020, November). "There are now more women CEO's of Fortune 500 companies than ever before-but the numbers are still depressingly low. www.businessinsider.com.

Waxman, S. (January,1998). "Tears and smiles for Sonny Bono." The Washington Post. Retrieved from https://www.washingtonpost.com/archive/lifestyle/ 1998/01/10/tears-and-smiles-for-sonny-bono/ 0acd8213-cd18-47d6-9aa4-1b1363a231bb/ on July 10, 2020.

Werber, C. (2019, March). "Wealthy millennial women are more likely to defer to their husbands on investing." https://qz.com/work/1573457/wealthy-millennial-womenare-deferring-to-their-husbands-on-financial-planning/.

Wood, K. C., Smith, H., Grossniklaus, D. (2001). "Piaget's stages of cognitive development." In M. Orey (Ed.), Emerging perspectives on learning, teaching, and technology. http://projects.coe.uga.edu/epltt/.

Wright-Mendoza, J. (2016, May). "I don't got you babe: The end of Sonny and Cher." www.blankonblank.org.

Youn, S. (2018, September). "Do Facebook ads discriminate against women?" ACLU files compliant saying yes. www.abcnews.go.com.

Young, M. (2021, March). "6 women with disabilities who made history." www.sheknows.com.

Zillman, C. (2019). "The fortune 500 has more female CEOs than ever before." Fortune. https://fortune.com/2019/05/16/fortune-500-female-ceos/.

Penmore Press
Challenging, Intriguing, Adventurous, Historical and Imaginative

www.penmorepress.com